SPECTRE DEEP 6

VOLUME 1
Deep Sixed

Jennifer Brody   Jules Rivera

TURNER
PUBLISHING COMPANY

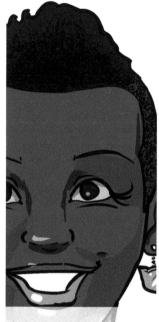

WRITER: Jennifer Brody
ARTIST: Jules Rivera

Color Assistants: Fable Siegel | Brian Wolf

Turner Publishing Company
4507 Charlotte Ave| Suite 100 | Nashville, Tennessee 32709

www.turnerpublishing.com

Library of Congress Cataloging-in-Publication Data Available Upon Request

Names: Brody, Jennifer. Rivera, Jules.
Title: Spectre Deep 6 by Jennifer Brody and Jules Rivera Other Titles:

Description: Nashville ,TN: Turning Publishing Company [2020] Series: Spectre Deep 6; Book 1 | Summary: "" -- Provided by publisher.

Identifiers: ISBN 9781684424139 (paperback)
Subjects: COMICS & GRAPHIC NOVELS / Science Fiction
Clasffification: CGN004070
LC Record Available at http://lccn.loc.gov/...

Printed in the United States of America
15 14 13 12 11 10 9 8 7 6 5 4 3 2 1

CONTENTS

PROLOGUE
I've Died Twice

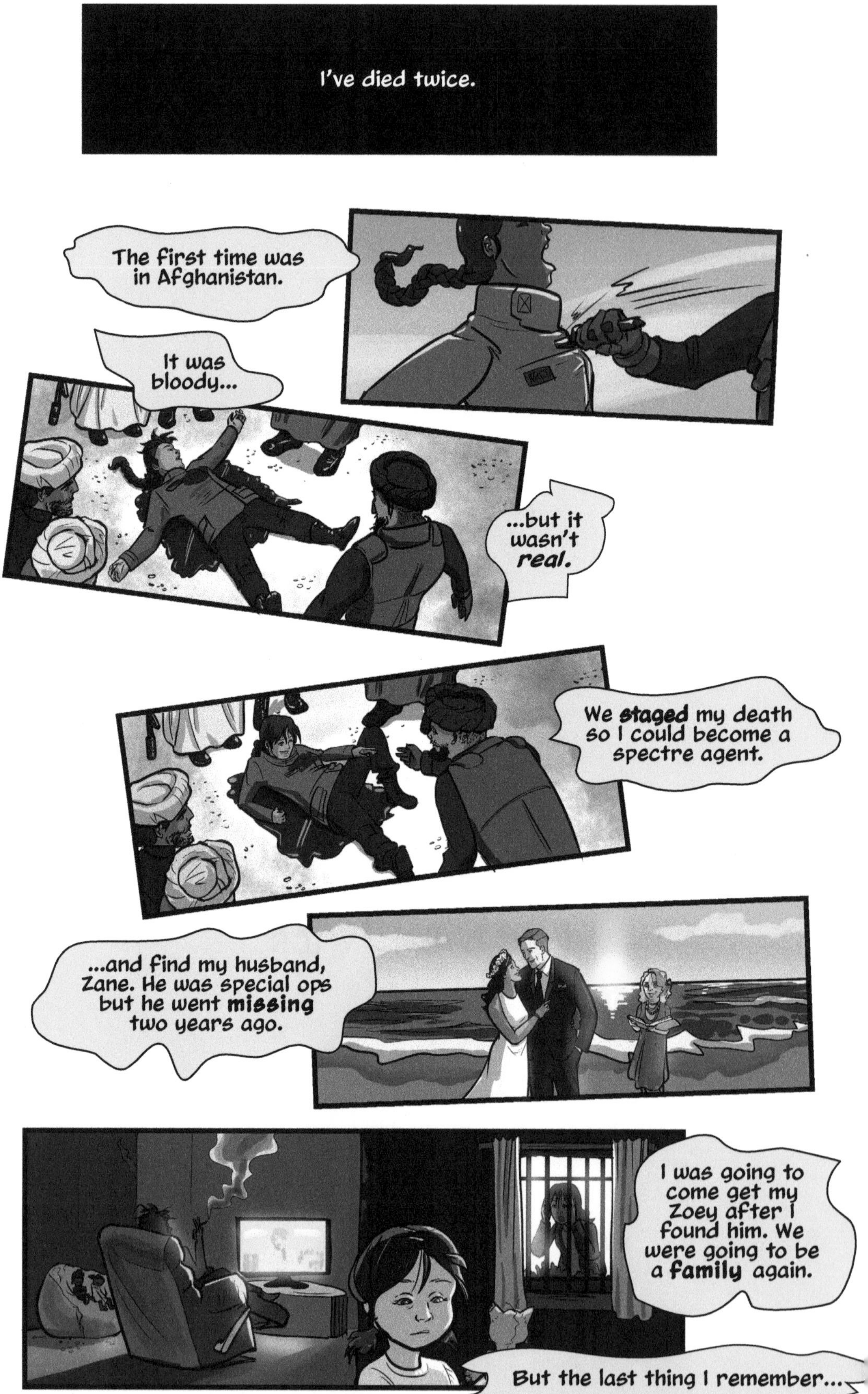
I've died twice.
The first time was in Afghanistan.
It was bloody...
...but it wasn't ***real.***
We **staged** my death so I could become a spectre agent.
...and find my husband, Zane. He was special ops but he went **missing** two years ago.
I was going to come get my Zoey after I found him. We were going to be a **family** again.
But the last thing I remember...

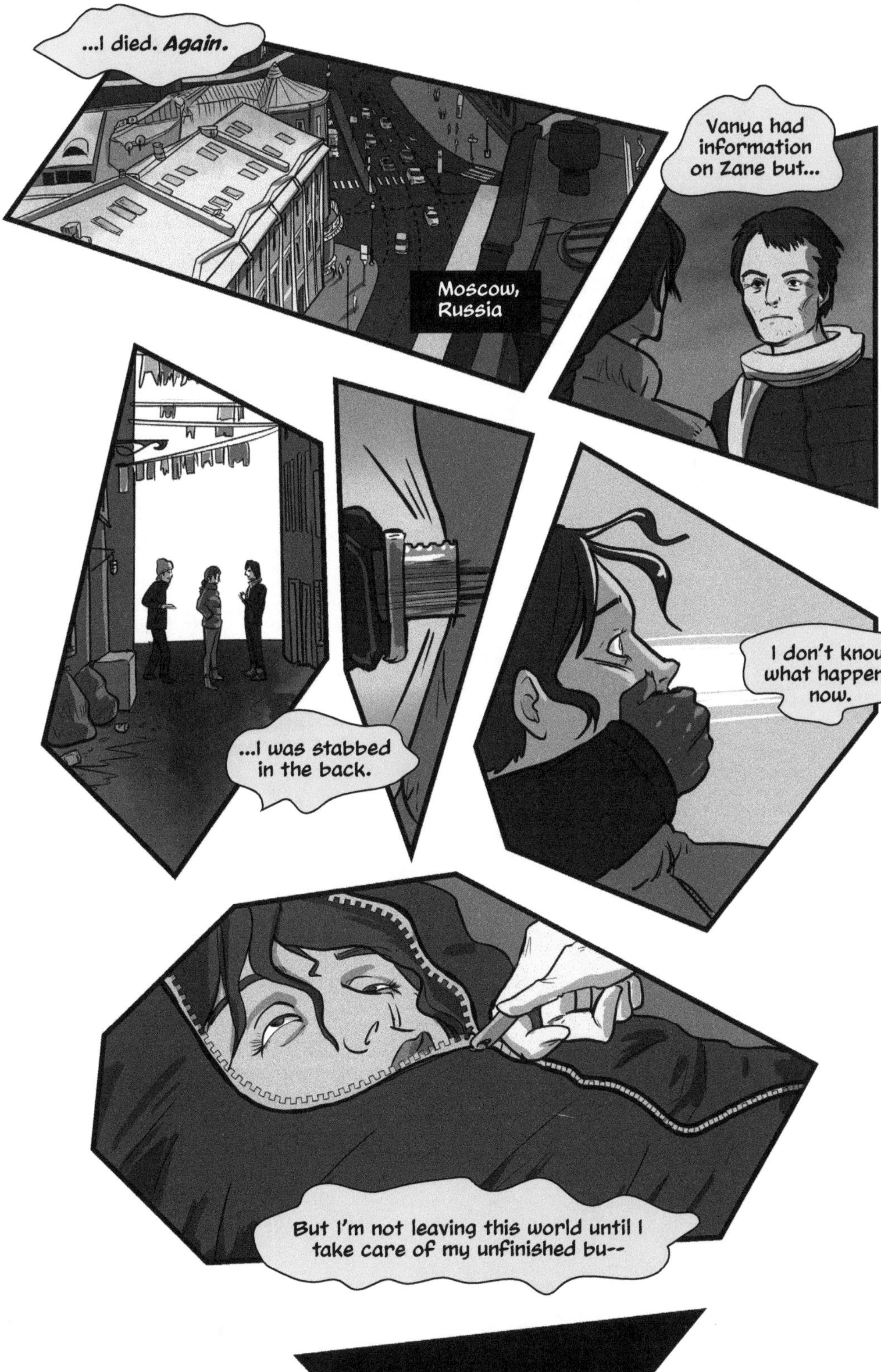
...I died. Again.
Moscow, Russia
Vanya had information on Zane but...
...I was stabbed in the back.
I don't know what happens now.
But I'm not leaving this world until I take care of my unfinished bu--

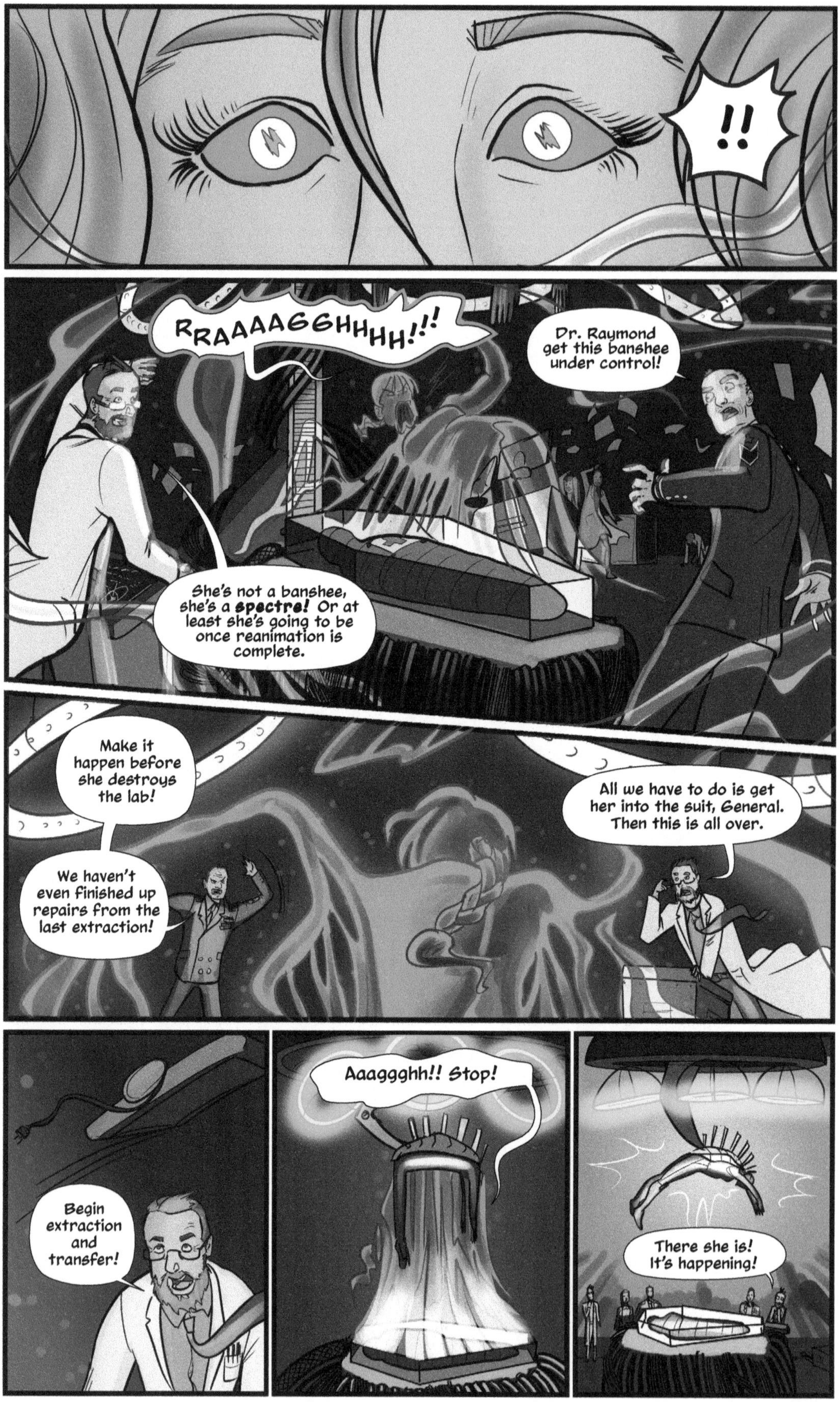
!!
RRAAAAGGHHHHH!!!
Dr. Raymond get this banshee under control!
She's not a banshee, she's a spectre! Or at least she's going to be once reanimation is complete.
Make it happen before she destroys the lab!
We haven't even finished up repairs from the last extraction!
All we have to do is get her into the suit, General. Then this is all over.
Begin extraction and transfer!
Aaaggghh!! Stop!
There she is! It's happening!

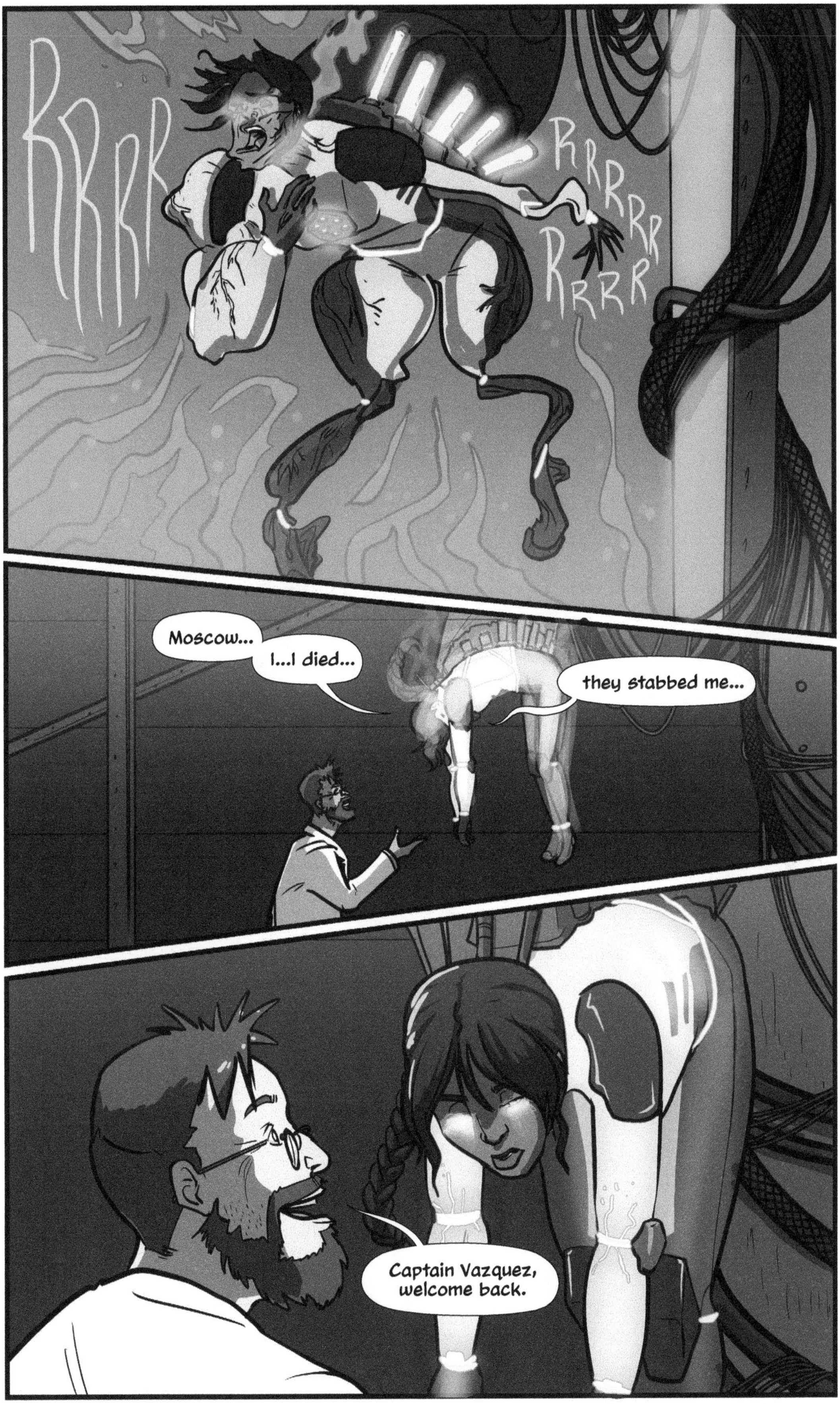
RRRRR
RRRRRR
RRRRR
Moscow...
I...I died...
they stabbed me...
Captain Vazquez, welcome back.

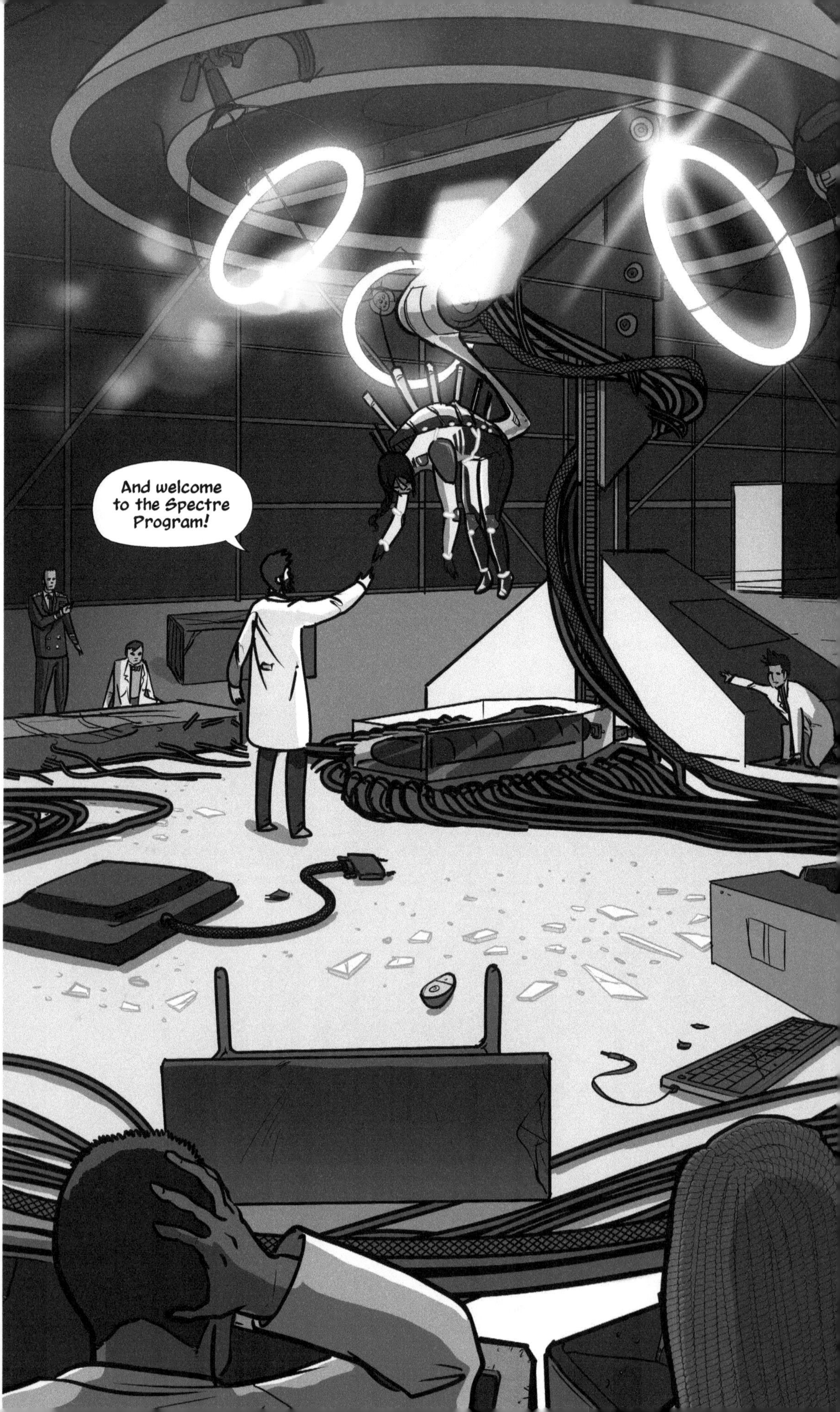
And welcome to the Spectre Program!

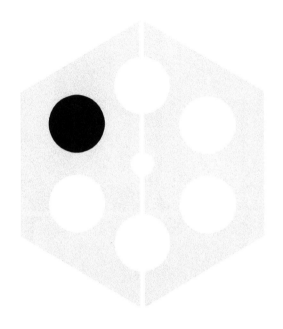

CHAPTER 1
The Package

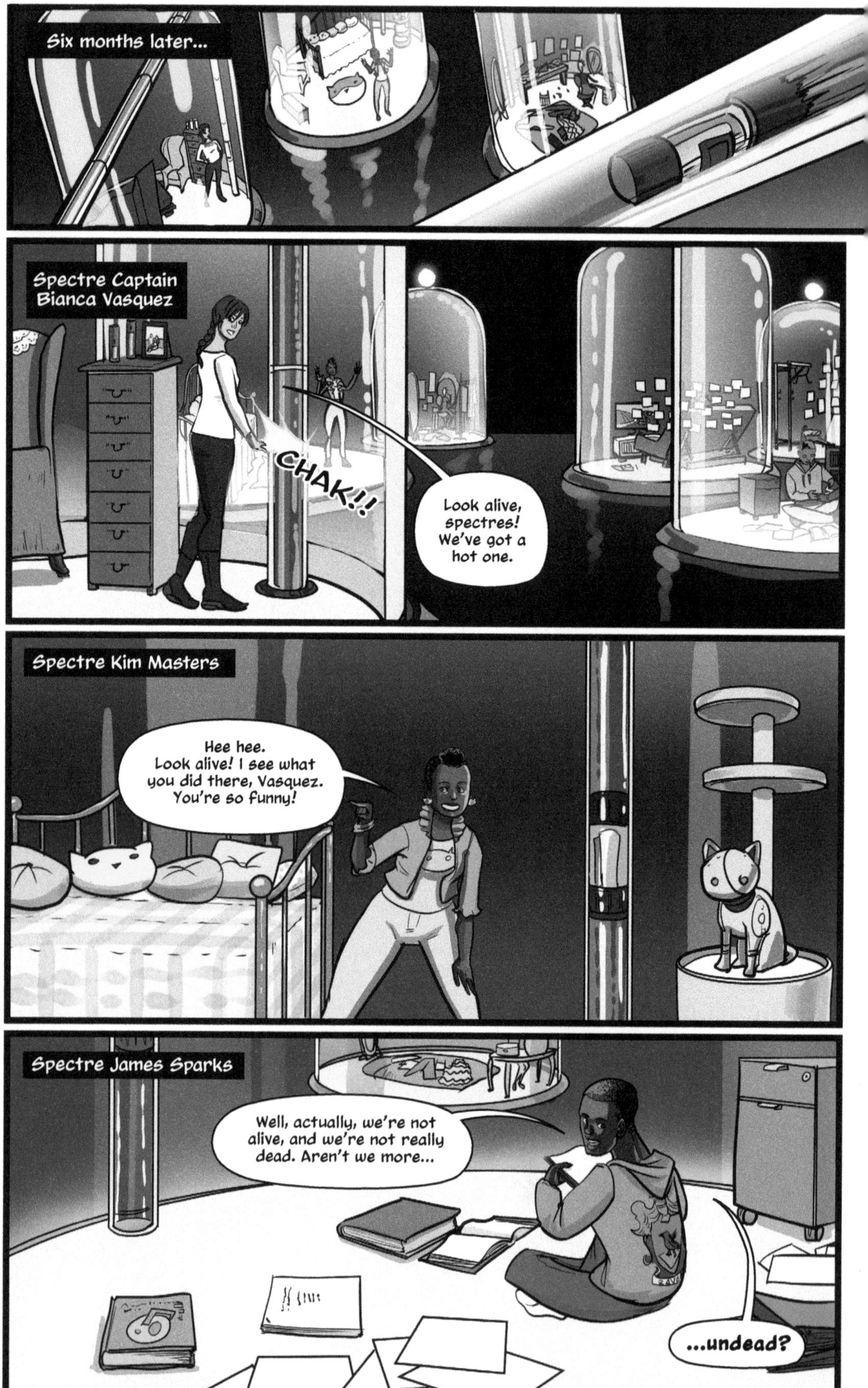

Six months later...
Spectre Captain Bianca Vasquez
CHAK!!
Look alive, spectres! We've got a hot one.
Spectre Kim Masters
Hee hee. Look alive! I see what you did there, Vasquez. You're so funny!
Spectre James Sparks
Well, actually, we're not alive, and we're not really dead. Aren't we more...
...undead?

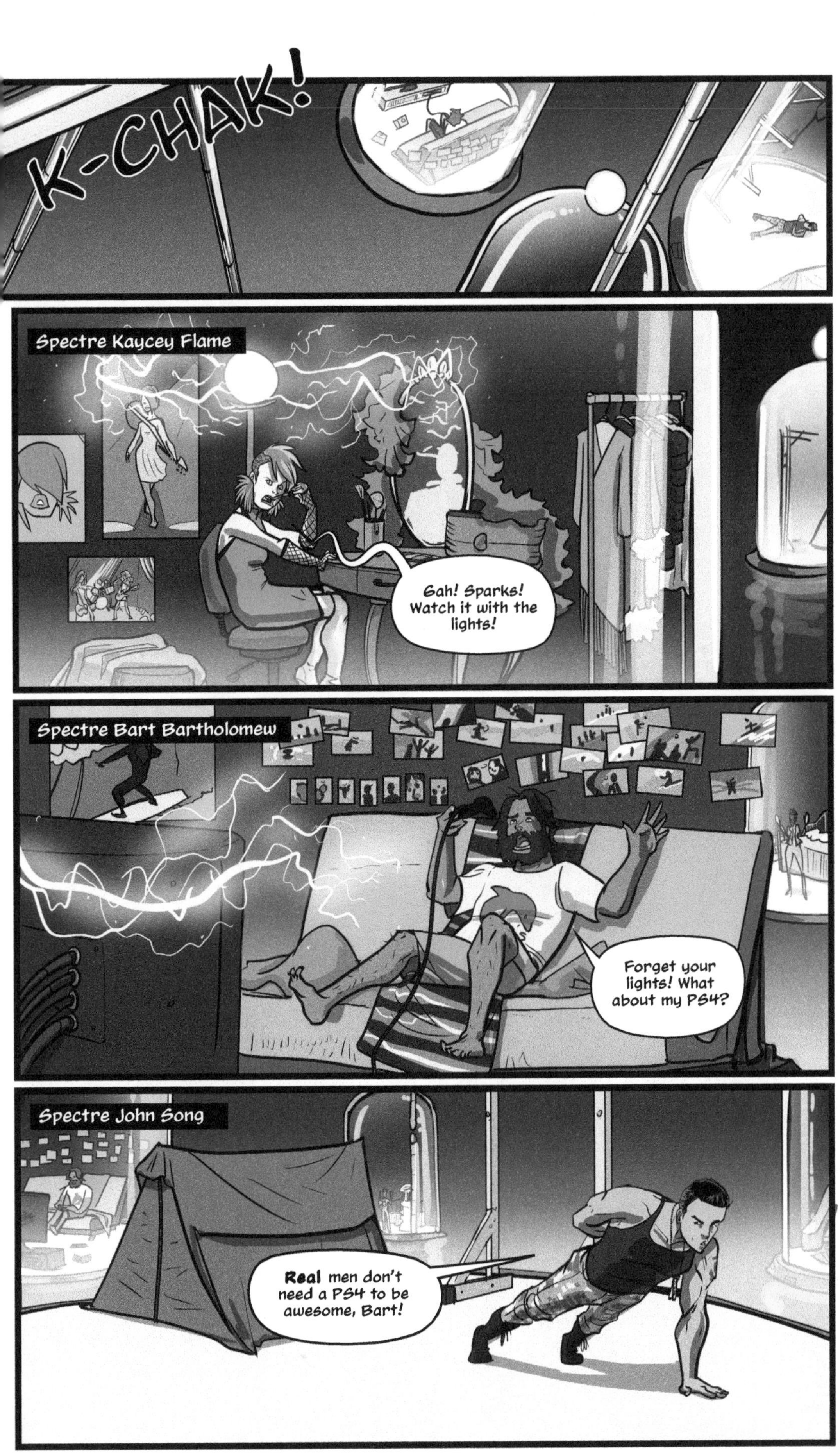
K-CHAK!
Spectre Kaycey Flame
Gah! Sparks! Watch it with the lights!
Spectre Bart Bartholomew
Forget your lights! What about my PS4?
Spectre John Song
Real men don't need a PS4 to be awesome, Bart!

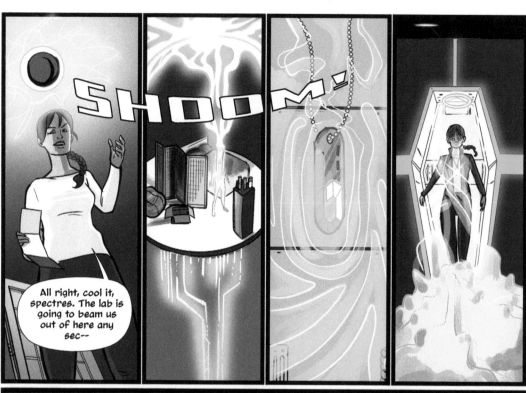

All right, cool it, spectres. The lab is going to beam us out of here any sec--

Good morning Spectres, rise and shine! We've got your next assignment fresh from the big boys upstairs. The General himself is coming to brief us.

Ooh! Must be good! Do I get to put on my murder face?

I don't know, Bart. It's not that scary. You're almost caspering.

Am not! John, what do you think? Am I caspering? You always tell the truth.

When I killed myself, I expected to *stay dead*.

Wow, *too much* truth, John.

Sparks!

Spectres, the General is here. Let's try to keep it formal.

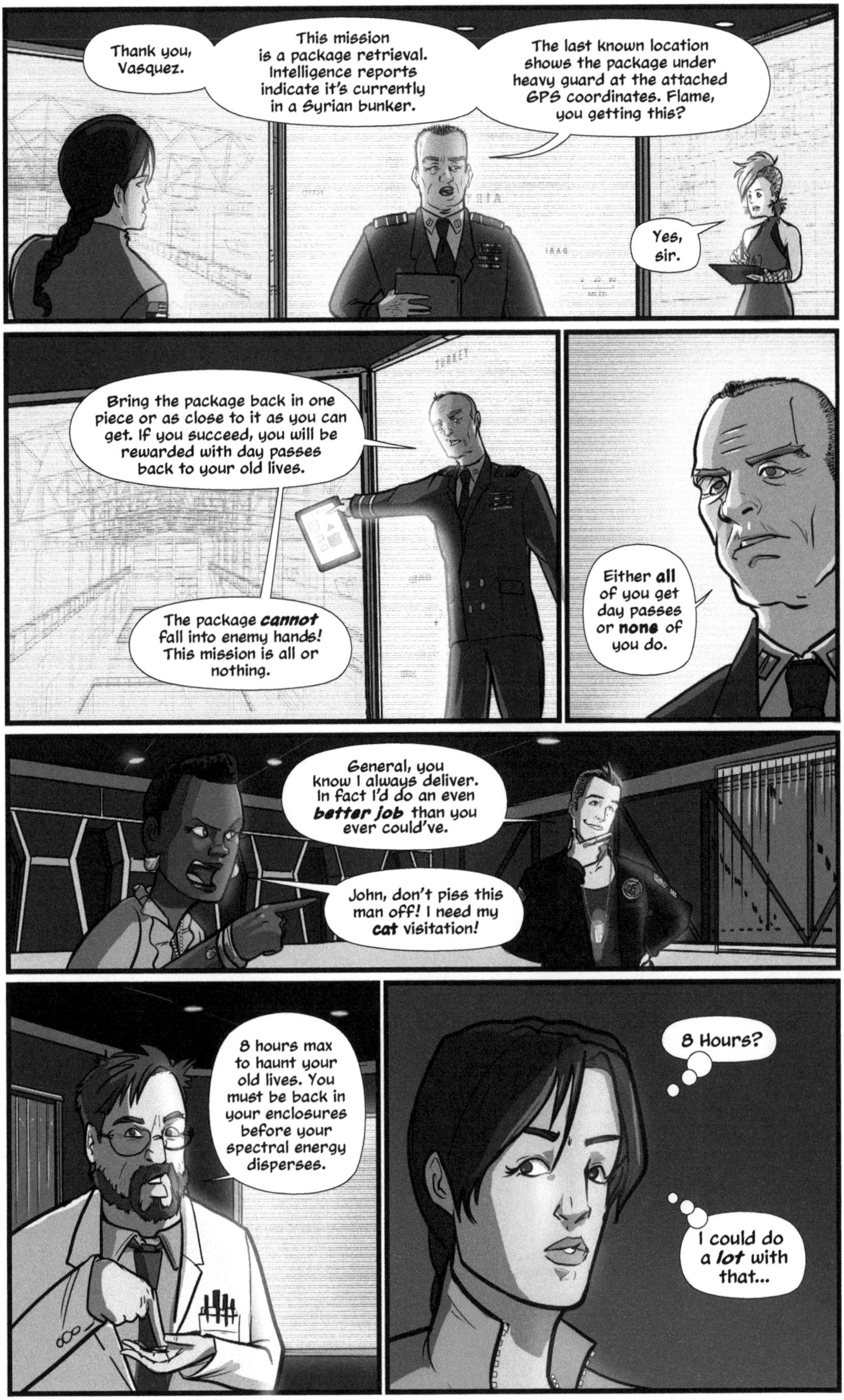
Thank you, Vasquez.
This mission is a package retrieval. Intelligence reports indicate it's currently in a Syrian bunker.
The last known location shows the package under heavy guard at the attached GPS coordinates. Flame, you getting this?
Yes, sir.
Bring the package back in one piece or as close to it as you can get. If you succeed, you will be rewarded with day passes back to your old lives.
The package ***cannot*** fall into enemy hands! This mission is all or nothing.
Either **all** of you get day passes or **none** of you do.
General, you know I always deliver. In fact I'd do an even ***better job*** than you ever could've.
John, don't piss this man off! I need my **cat** visitation!
8 hours max to haunt your old lives. You must be back in your enclosures before your spectral energy disperses.
8 Hours?
I could do a ***lot*** with that...

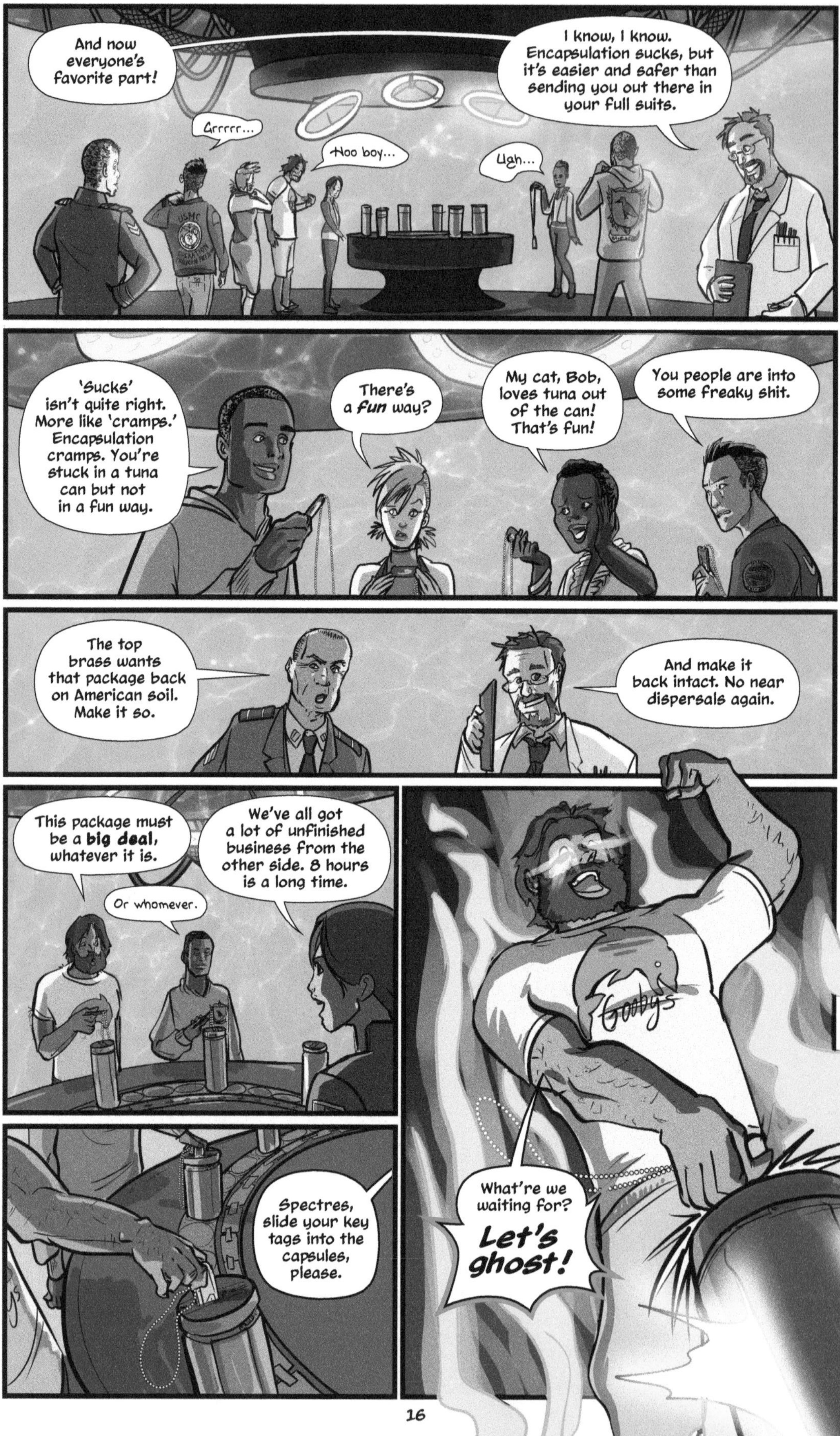

And now everyone's favorite part!
Grrrrr...
Hoo boy...
Ugh...
I know, I know. Encapsulation sucks, but it's easier and safer than sending you out there in your full suits.
'Sucks' isn't quite right. More like 'cramps.' Encapsulation cramps. You're stuck in a tuna can but not in a fun way.
There's a **fun** way?
My cat, Bob, loves tuna out of the can! That's fun!
You people are into some freaky shit.
The top brass wants that package back on American soil. Make it so.
And make it back intact. No near dispersals again.
This package must be a **big deal**, whatever it is.
Or whomever.
We've all got a lot of unfinished business from the other side. 8 hours is a long time.
Spectres, slide your key tags into the capsules, please.
What're we waiting for? **Let's ghost!**

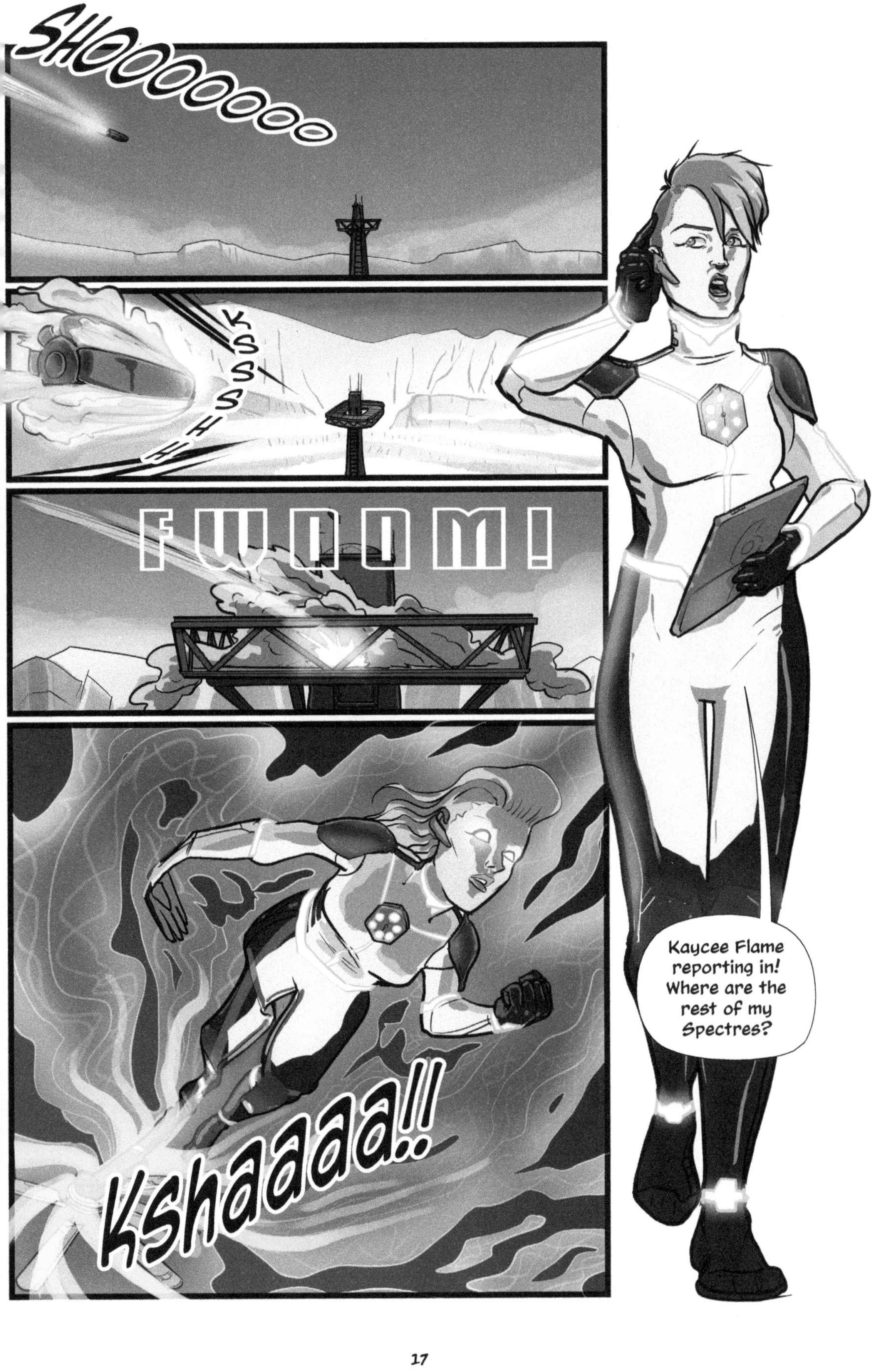
SHOOOOOOOO
KSSSHH
FWOOM!
Kshaaaaa!!
Kaycee Flame reporting in! Where are the rest of my Spectres?

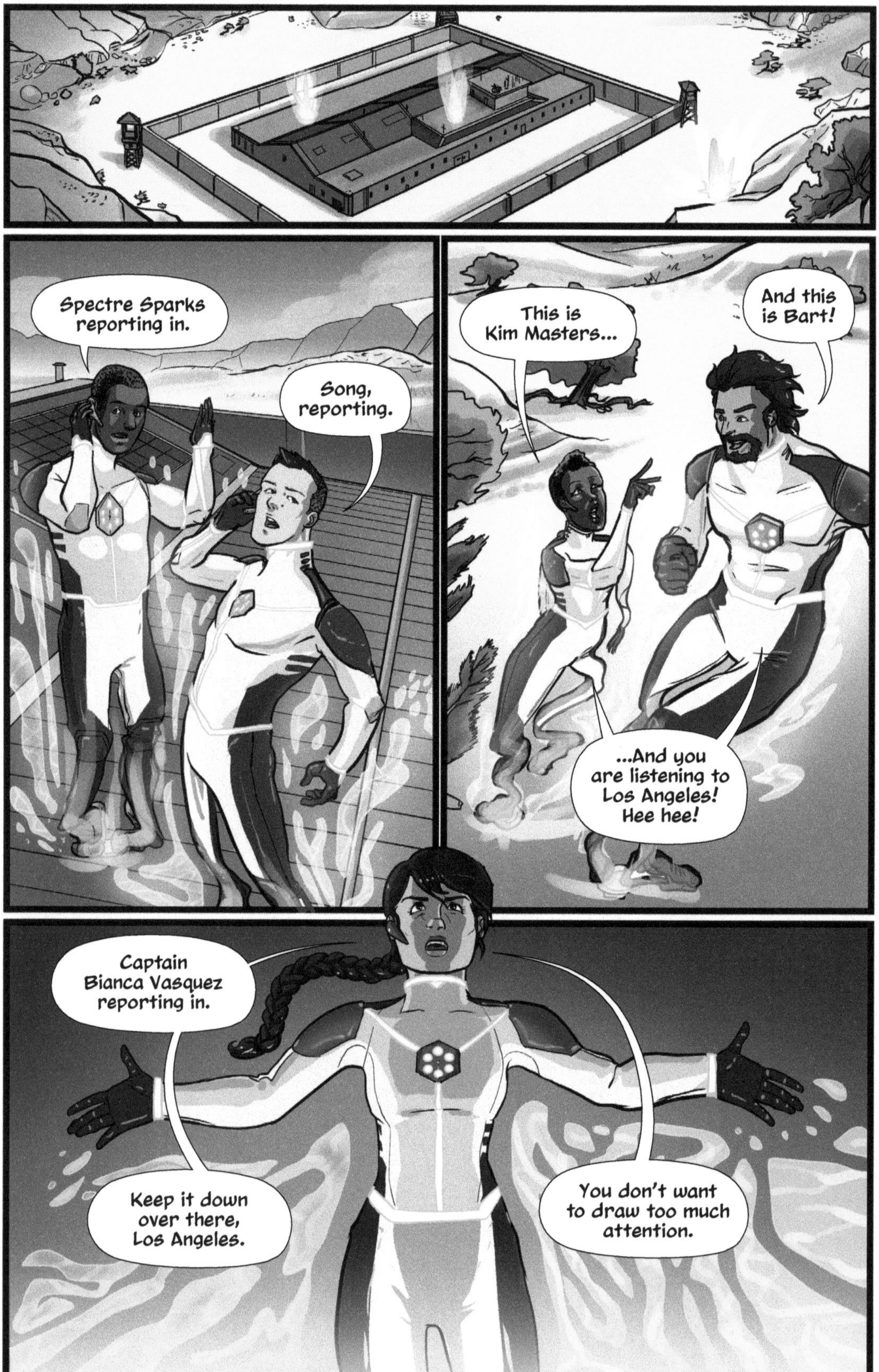
Spectre Sparks reporting in.
Song, reporting.
This is Kim Masters...
And this is Bart!
...And you are listening to Los Angeles! Hee hee!
Captain Bianca Vasquez reporting in.
Keep it down over there, Los Angeles.
You don't want to draw too much attention.

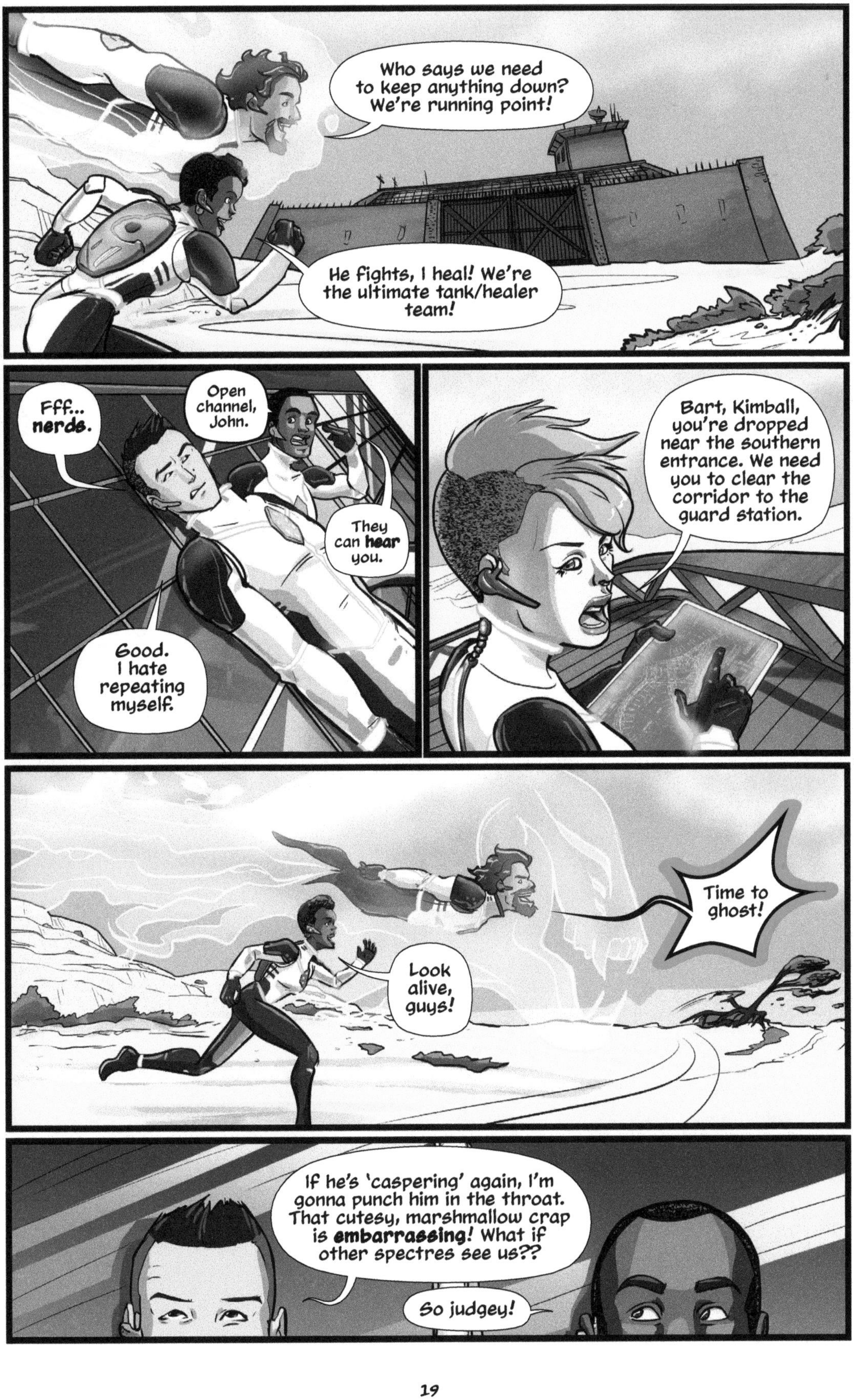

Who says we need to keep anything down? We're running point!
He fights, I heal! We're the ultimate tank/healer team!
Fff... **nerds**.
Open channel, John.
They can **hear** you.
Good. I hate repeating myself.
Bart, Kimball, you're dropped near the southern entrance. We need you to clear the corridor to the guard station.
Look alive, guys!
Time to ghost!
If he's 'caspering' again, I'm gonna punch him in the throat. That cutesy, marshmallow crap is **embarrassing**! What if other spectres see us??
So judgey!

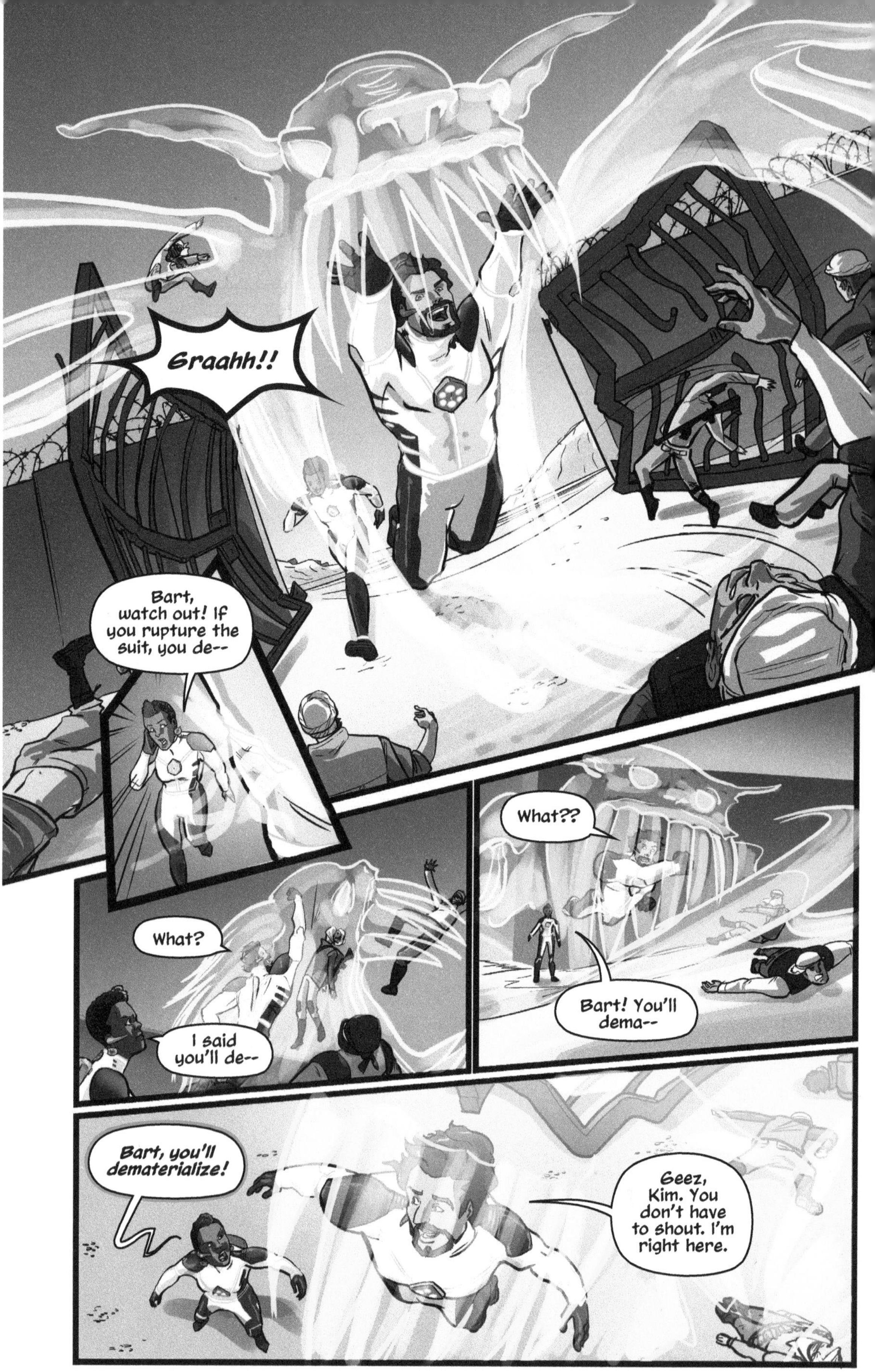

Graahh!!
Bart, watch out! If you rupture the suit, you de--
What?
I said you'll de--
What??
Bart! You'll dema--
Bart, you'll dematerialize!
Geez, Kim. You don't have to shout. I'm right here.

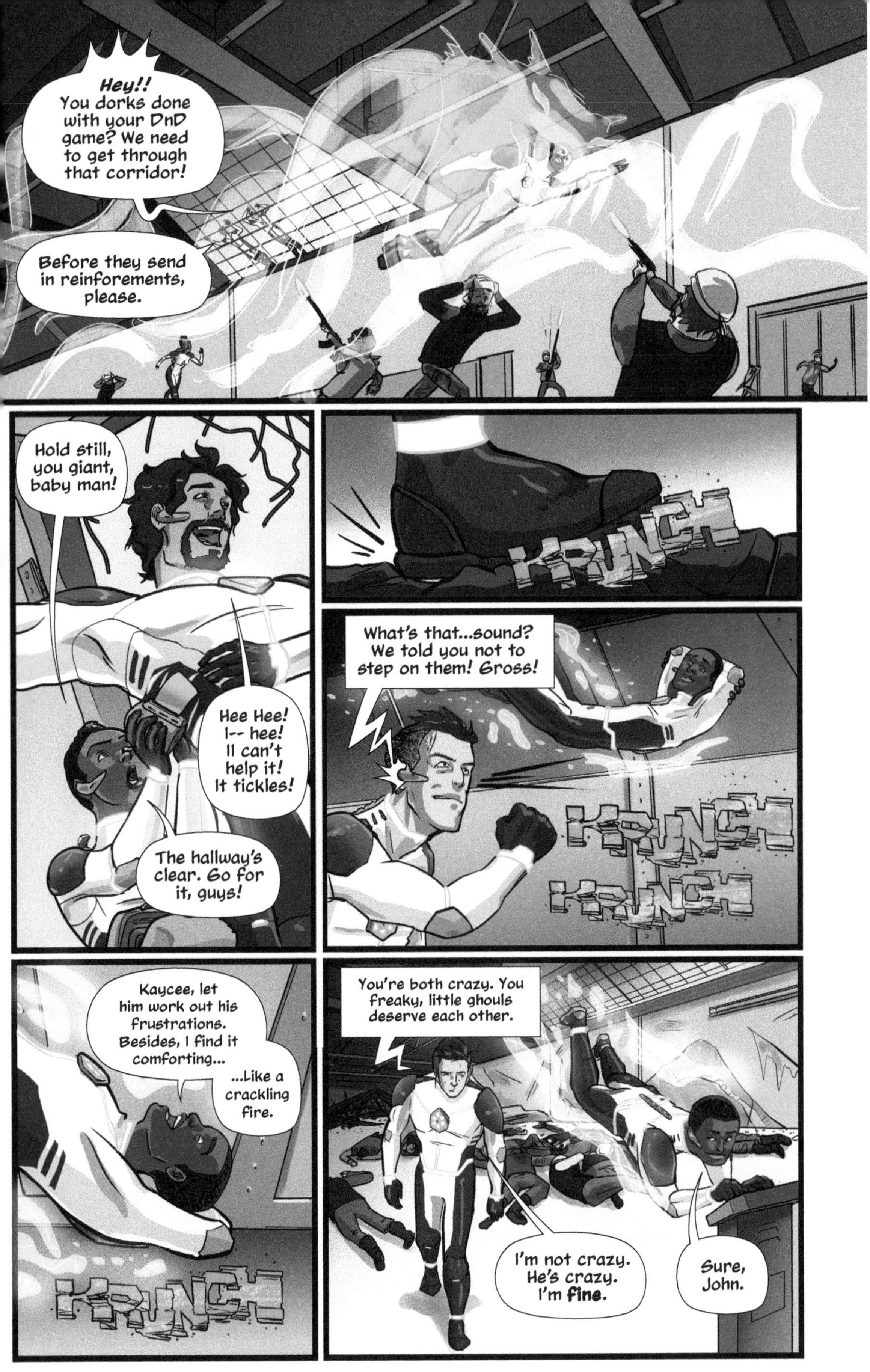

Hey!! You dorks done with your DnD game? We need to get through that corridor!
Before they send in reinforements, please.
Hold still, you giant, baby man!
Hee Hee! I-- hee! Il can't help it! It tickles!
The hallway's clear. Go for it, guys!
KRUNCH
What's that...sound? We told you not to step on them! Gross!
KRUNCH
KRUNCH
Kaycee, let him work out his frustrations. Besides, I find it comforting...
...Like a crackling fire.
KRUNCH
You're both crazy. You freaky, little ghouls deserve each other.
I'm not crazy. He's crazy. I'm **fine**.
Sure, John.

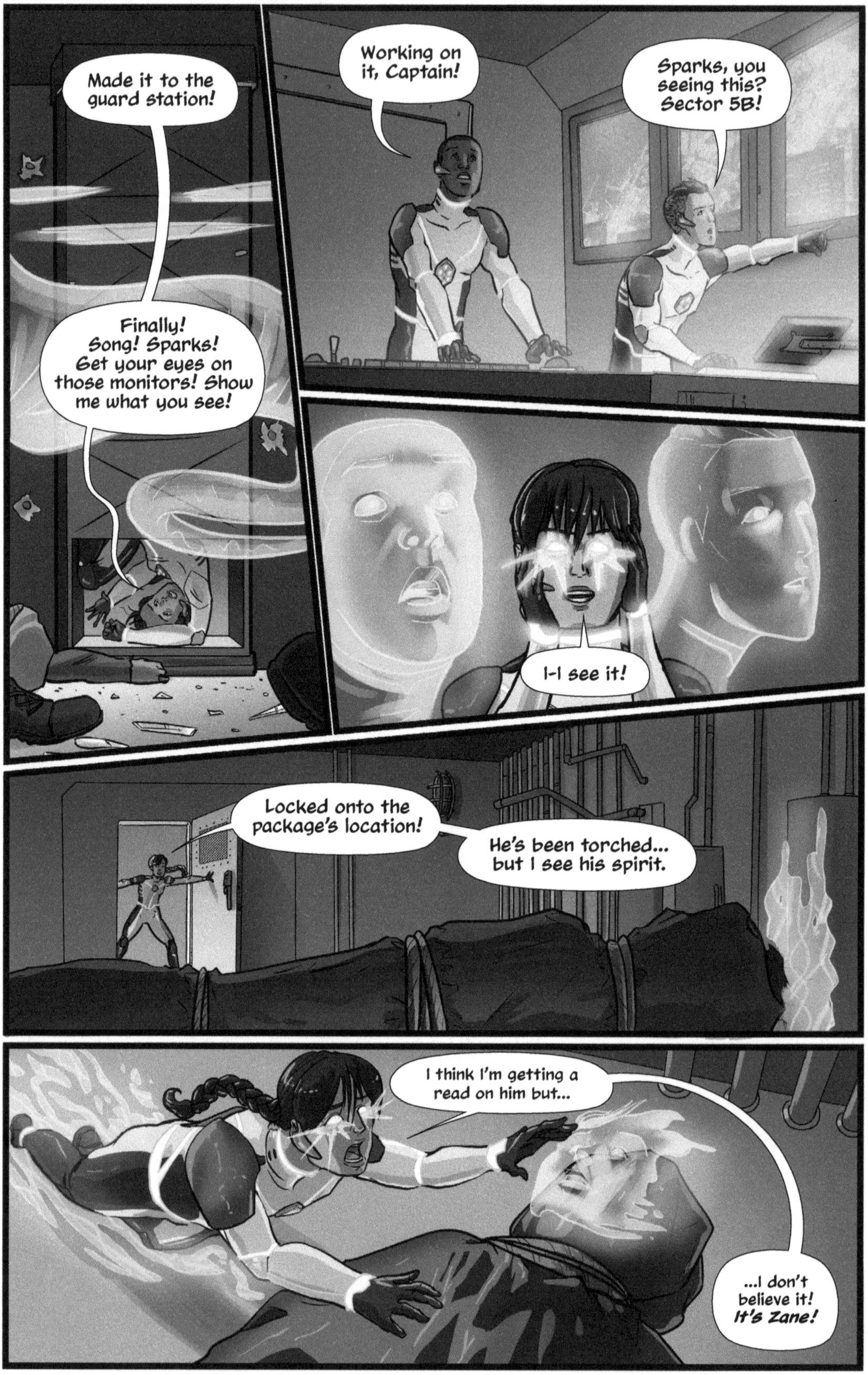
Made it to the guard station!
Finally! Song! Sparks! Get your eyes on those monitors! Show me what you see!
Working on it, Captain!
Sparks, you seeing this? Sector 5B!
I-I see it!
Locked onto the package's location!
He's been torched... but I see his spirit.
I think I'm getting a read on him but...
...I don't believe it! *It's Zane!*

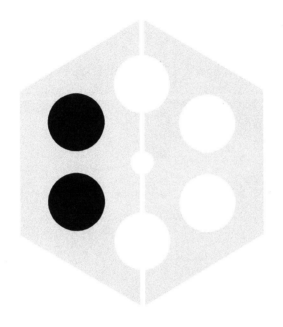

CHAPTER 2
Reanimation

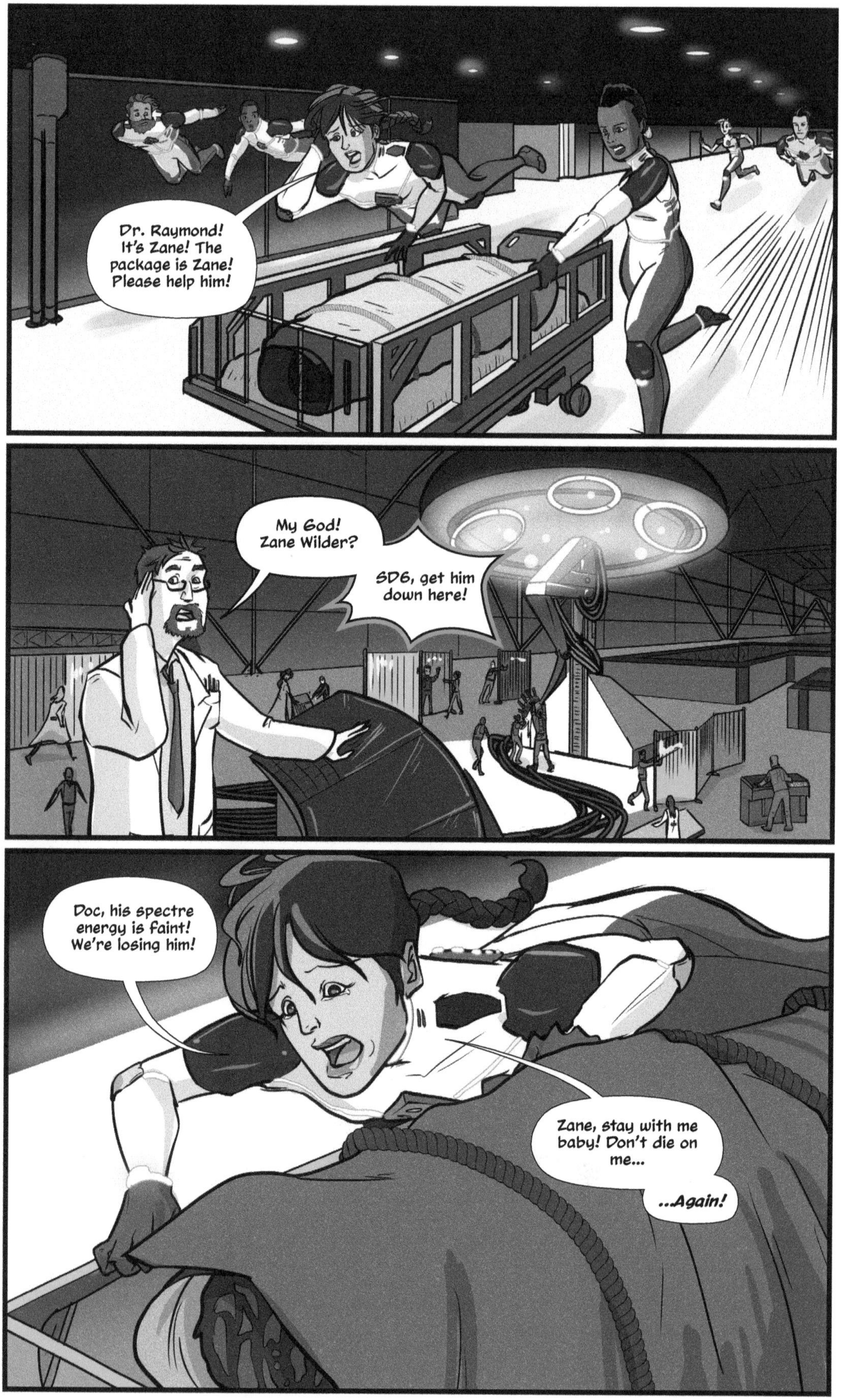

Dr. Raymond! It's Zane! The package is Zane! Please help him!
My God! Zane Wilder?
SD6, get him down here!
Doc, his spectre energy is faint! We're losing him!
Zane, stay with me baby! Don't die on me...
...Again!

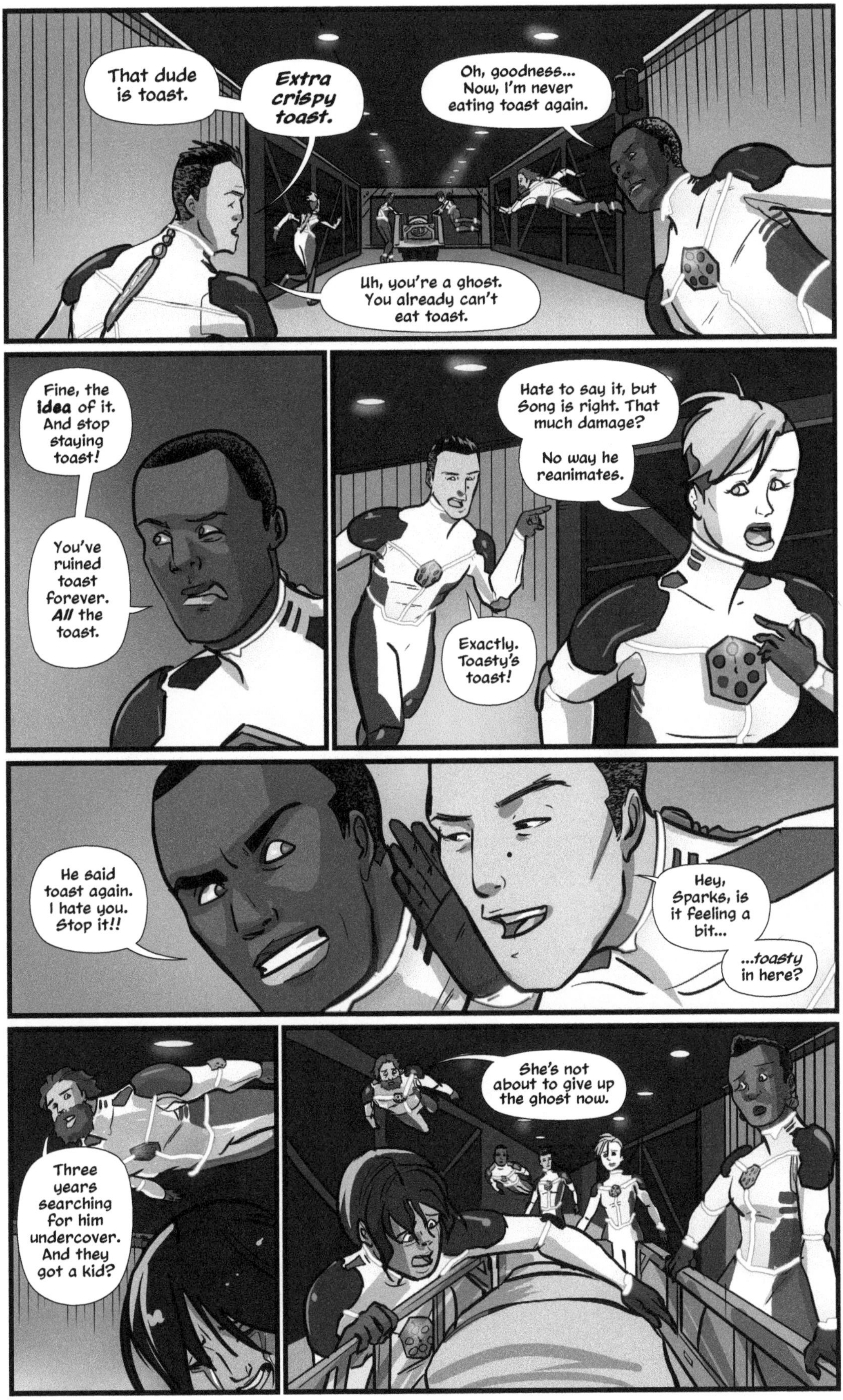
That dude is toast.
Extra crispy toast.
Oh, goodness... Now, I'm never eating toast again.
Uh, you're a ghost. You already can't eat toast.
Fine, the idea of it. And stop staying toast!
You've ruined toast forever. All the toast.
Hate to say it, but Song is right. That much damage?
No way he reanimates.
Exactly. Toasty's toast!
He said toast again. I hate you. Stop it!!
Hey, Sparks, is it feeling a bit...
...toasty in here?
Three years searching for him undercover. And they got a kid?
She's not about to give up the ghost now.

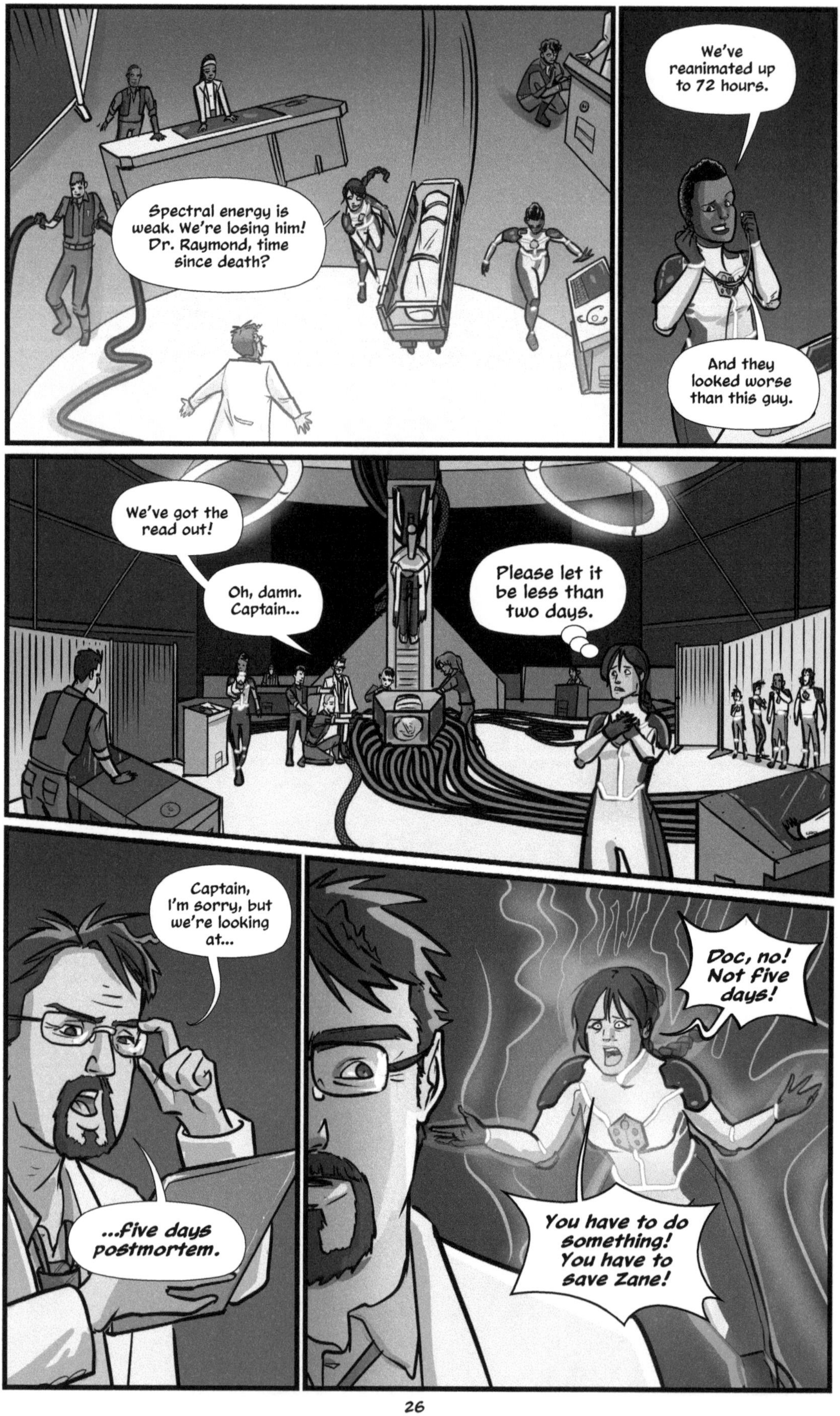
Spectral energy is weak. We're losing him! Dr. Raymond, time since death?
We've reanimated up to 72 hours.
And they looked worse than this guy.
We've got the read out!
Oh, damn. Captain...
Please let it be less than two days.
Captain, I'm sorry, but we're looking at...
...five days postmortem.
Doc, no! Not five days!
You have to do something! You have to save Zane!

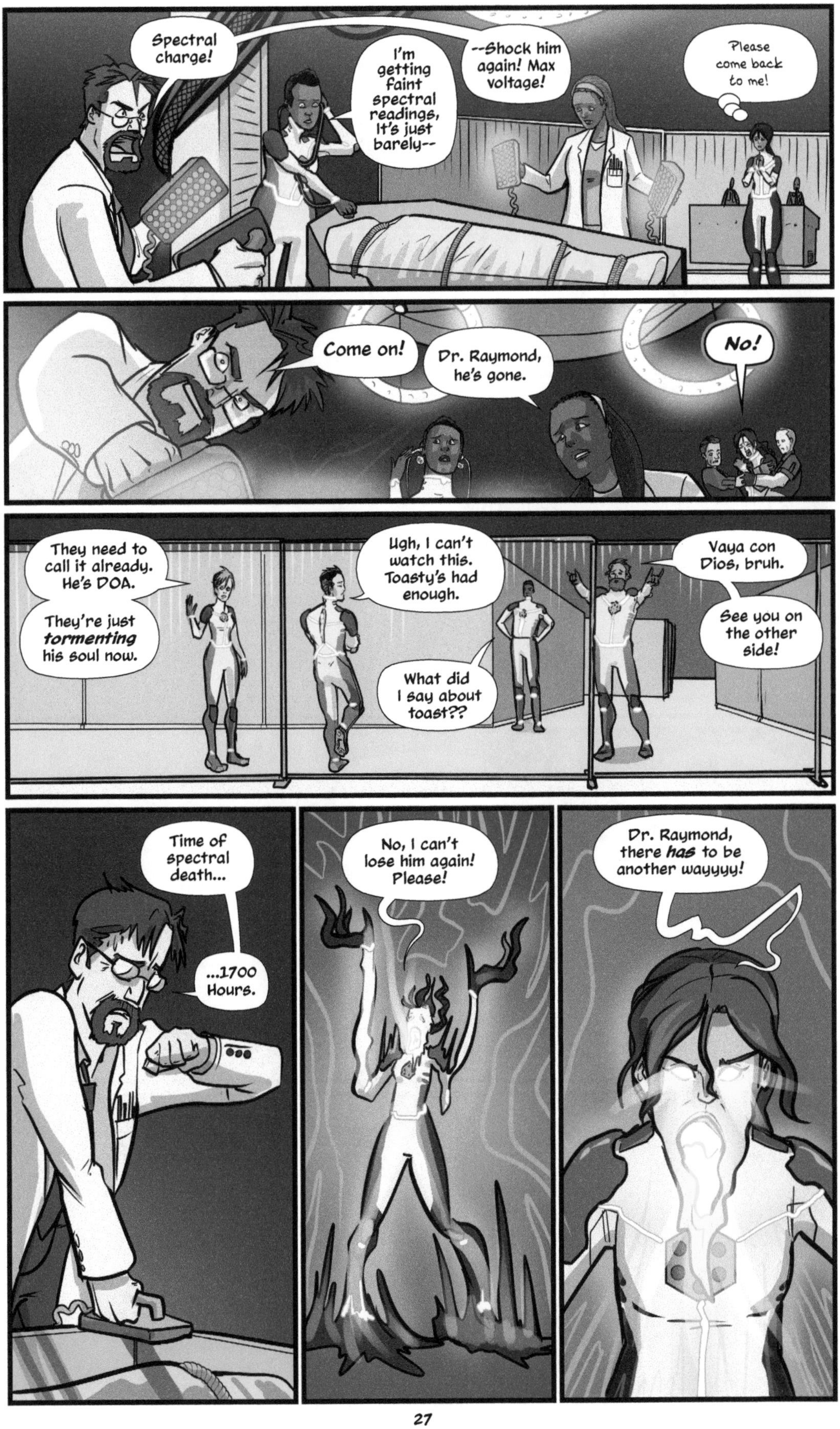
Spectral charge!
I'm getting faint spectral readings, It's just barely--
--Shock him again! Max voltage!
Please come back to me!
Come on!
Dr. Raymond, he's gone.
No!
They need to call it already. He's DOA.
They're just ***tormenting*** his soul now.
Ugh, I can't watch this. Toasty's had enough.
What did I say about toast??
Vaya con Dios, bruh.
See you on the other side!
Time of spectral death...
...1700 Hours.
No, I can't lose him again! Please!
Dr. Raymond, there ***has*** to be another wayyyy!

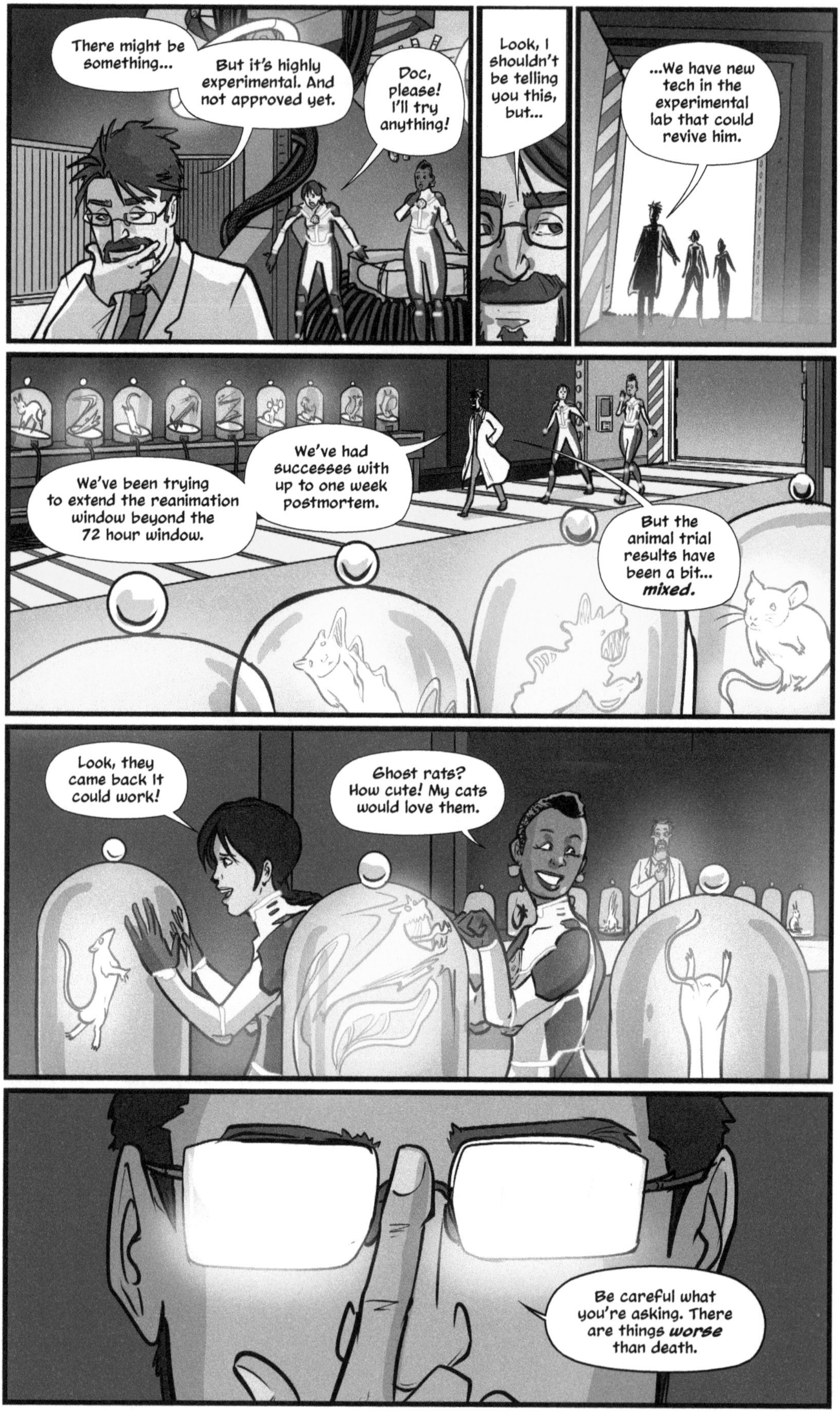
There might be something...
But it's highly experimental. And not approved yet.
Doc, please! I'll try anything!
Look, I shouldn't be telling you this, but...
...We have new tech in the experimental lab that could revive him.
We've been trying to extend the reanimation window beyond the 72 hour window.
We've had successes with up to one week postmortem.
But the animal trial results have been a bit... ***mixed.***
Look, they came back It could work!
Ghost rats? How cute! My cats would love them.
Be careful what you're asking. There are things ***worse*** than death.

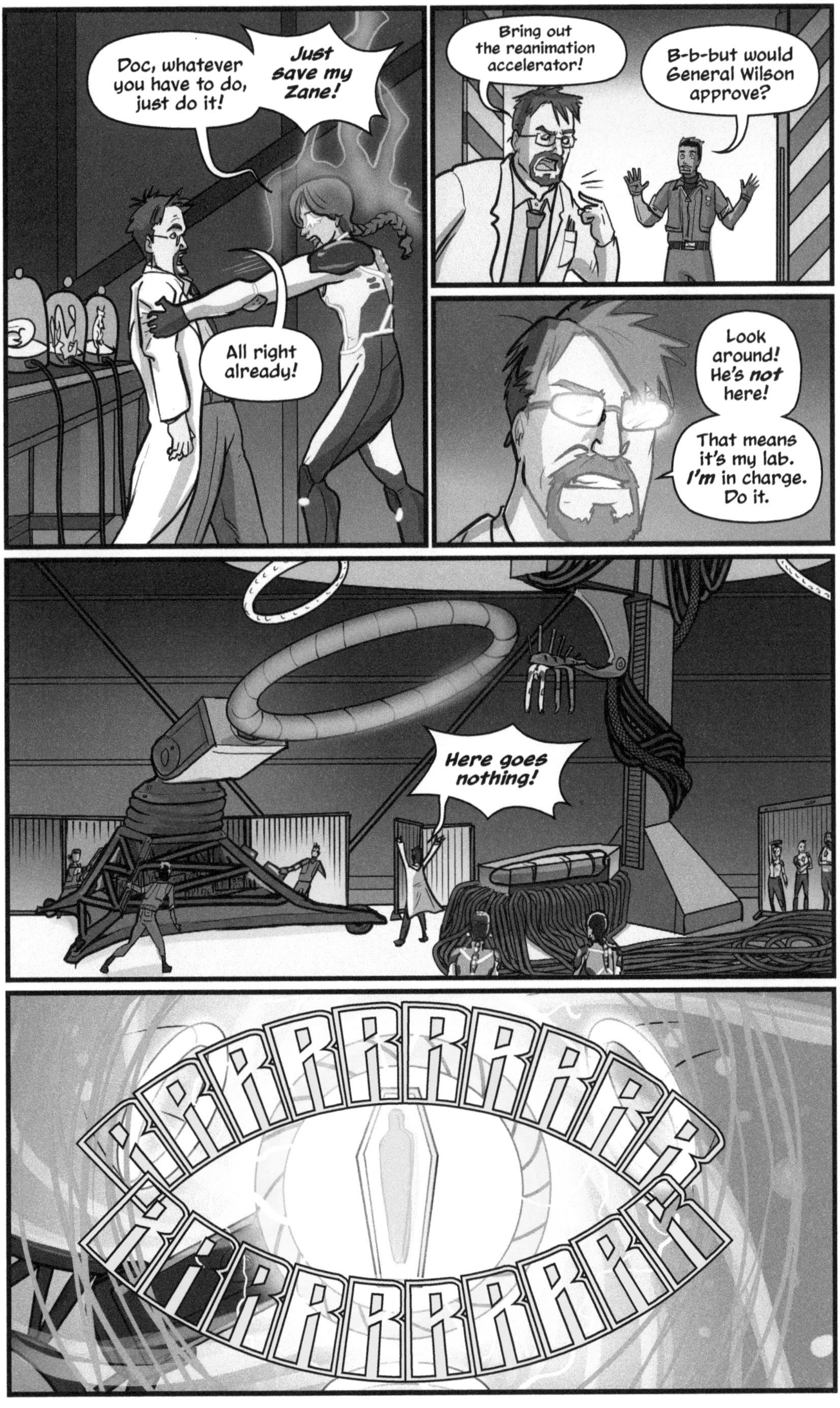
Doc, whatever you have to do, just do it!
Just save my Zane!
All right already!
Bring out the reanimation accelerator!
B-b-but would General Wilson approve?
Look around! He's *not* here!
That means it's my lab. *I'm* in charge. Do it.
Here goes nothing!
RRRRRRRRRR
RRRRRRRRRR

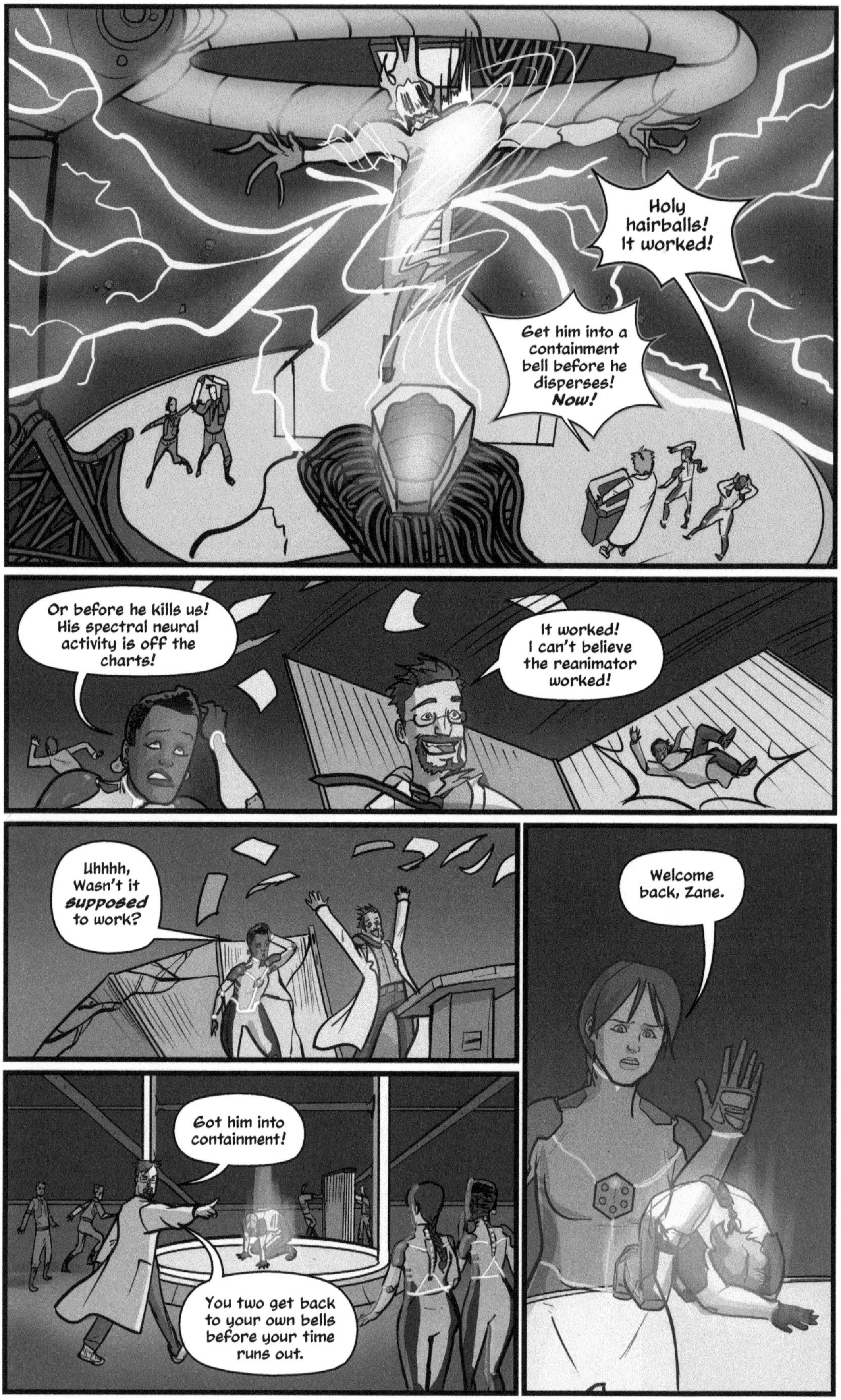
Holy hairballs! It worked!
Get him into a containment bell before he disperses! ***Now!***
Or before he kills us! His spectral neural activity is off the charts!
It worked! I can't believe the reanimator worked!
Uhhhh, Wasn't it ***supposed*** to work?
Got him into containment!
You two get back to your own bells before your time runs out.
Welcome back, Zane.

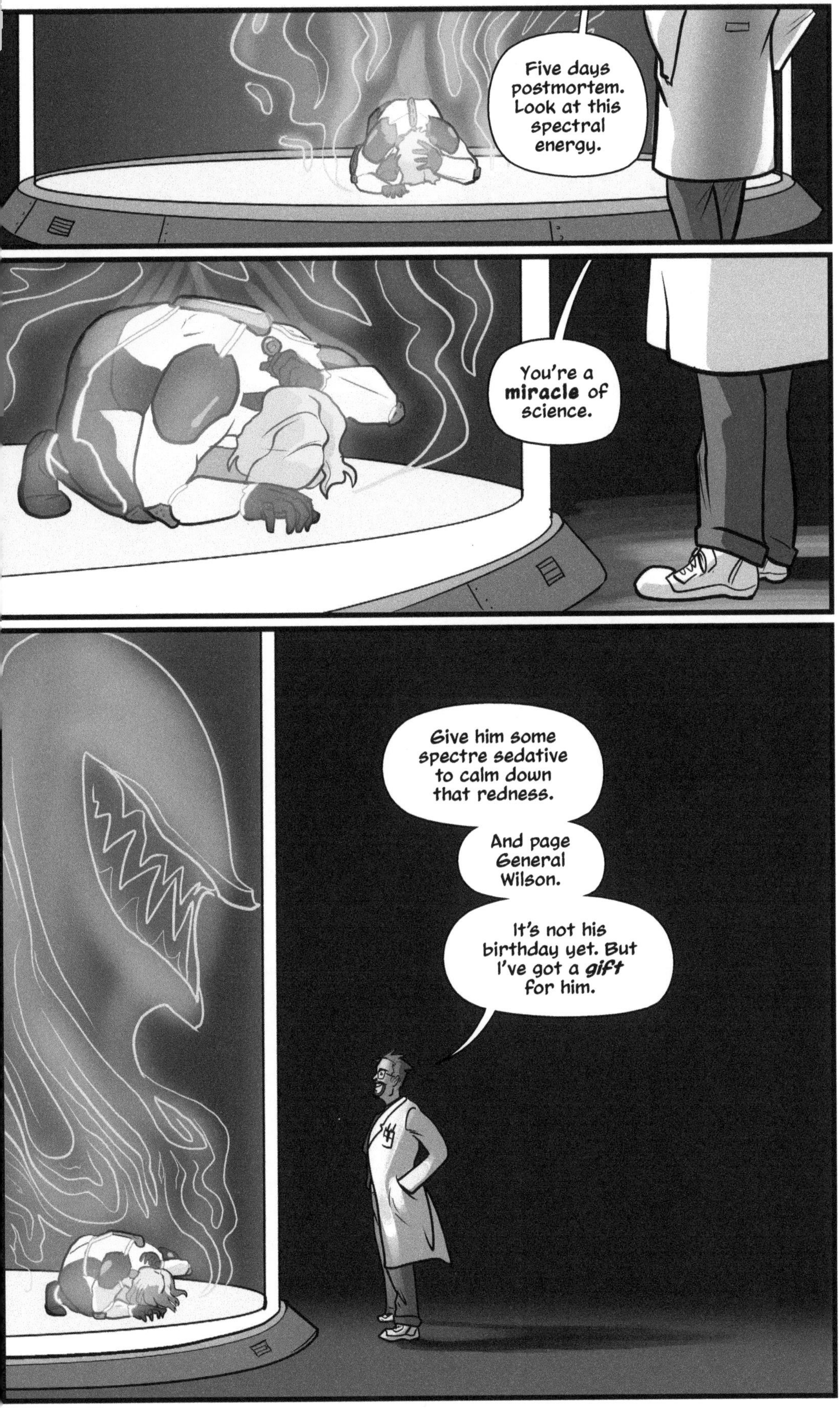
Five days postmortem. Look at this spectral energy.
You're a **miracle** of science.
Give him some spectre sedative to calm down that redness.
And page General Wilson.
It's not his birthday yet. But I've got a *gift* for him.

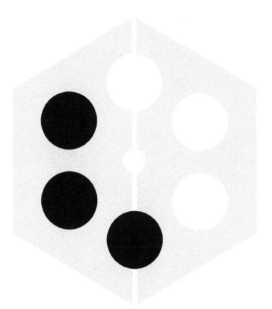

CHAPTER 3
Everybody Haunts

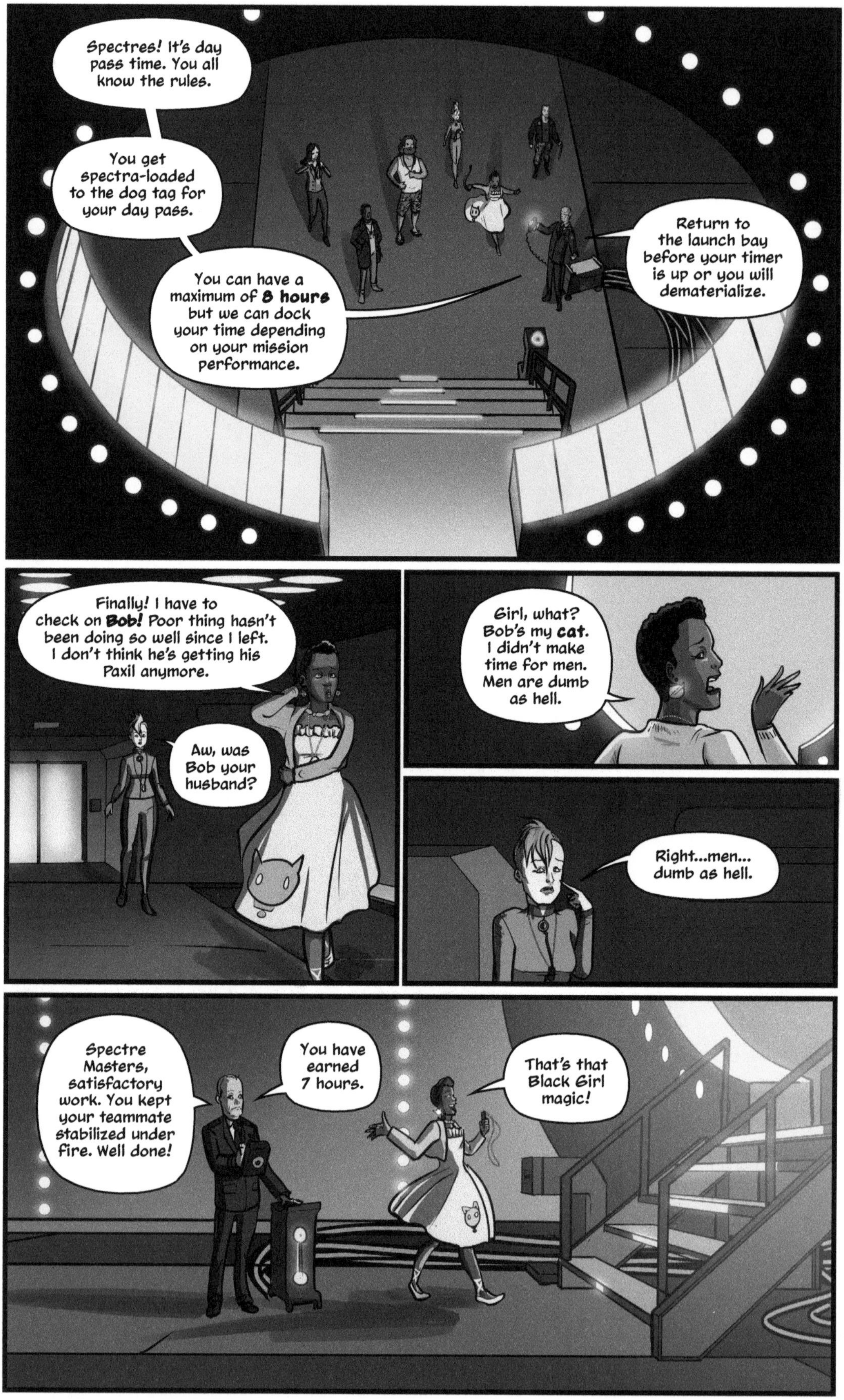

Spectres! It's day pass time. You all know the rules.
You get spectra-loaded to the dog tag for your day pass.
You can have a maximum of **8 hours** but we can dock your time depending on your mission performance.
Return to the launch bay before your timer is up or you will dematerialize.
Finally! I have to check on **Bob!** Poor thing hasn't been doing so well since I left. I don't think he's getting his Paxil anymore.
Aw, was Bob your husband?
Girl, what? Bob's my **cat**. I didn't make time for men. Men are dumb as hell.
Right...men... dumb as hell.
Spectre Masters, satisfactory work. You kept your teammate stabilized under fire. Well done!
You have earned 7 hours.
That's that Black Girl magic!

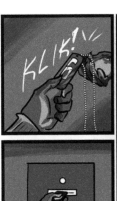

See ya later, alligator!

Spectre Flame. Great team coordination and extraction. Well done! 7 hours.

bip!

Thank you, General.

Bart, satisfactory work...

Yes!

...but the team felt you were *caspering* again. Time docked. 6 Hours.

Aw, man... gnarly.

What did I tell you about caspering?? Do **not** make me look bad out there!

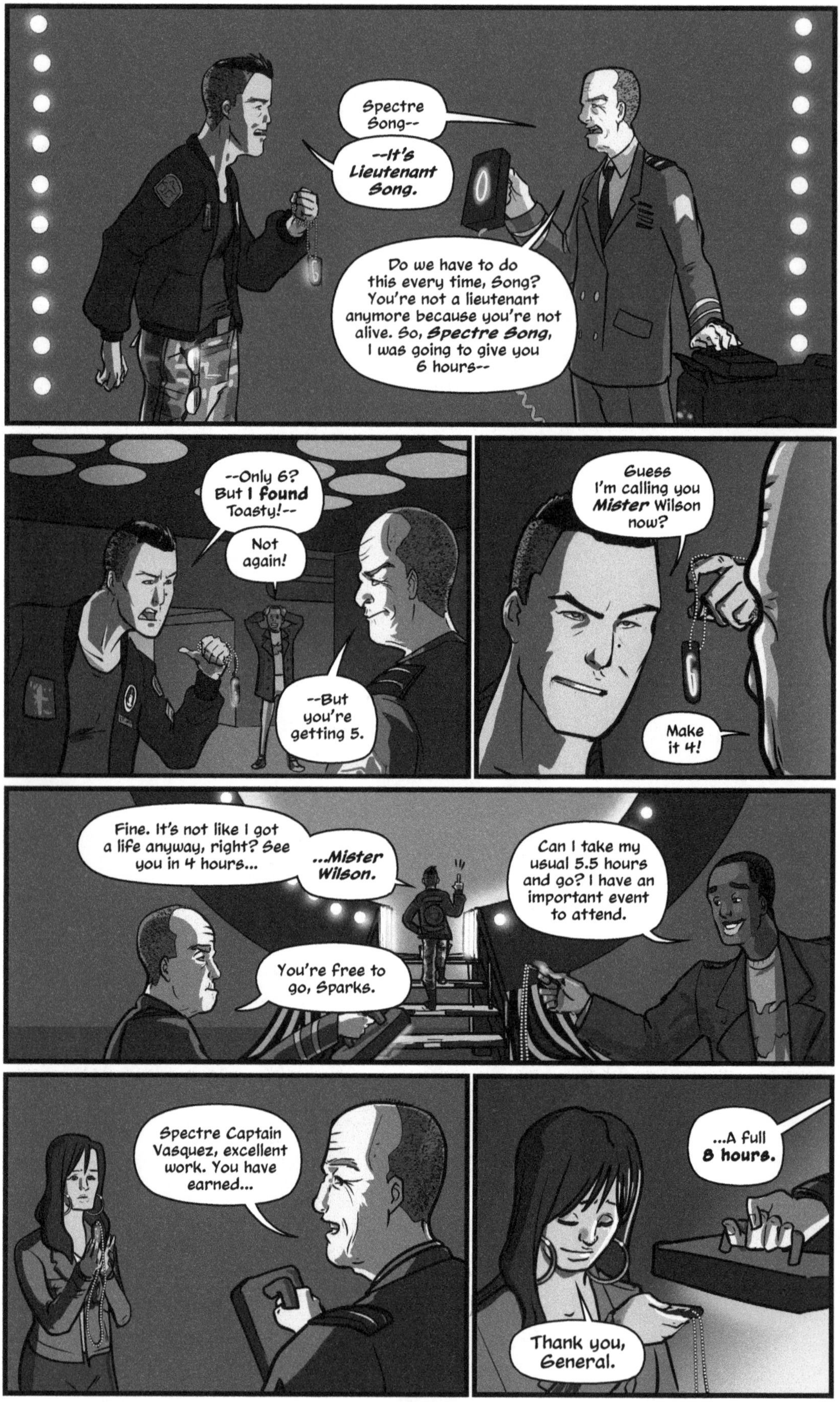
Spectre Song--
--It's Lieutenant Song.
Do we have to do this every time, Song? You're not a lieutenant anymore because you're not alive. So, Spectre Song, I was going to give you 6 hours--
--Only 6? But I found Toasty!--
Not again!
--But you're getting 5.
Guess I'm calling you Mister Wilson now?
Make it 4!
Fine. It's not like I got a life anyway, right? See you in 4 hours...
...Mister Wilson.
Can I take my usual 5.5 hours and go? I have an important event to attend.
You're free to go, Sparks.
Spectre Captain Vasquez, excellent work. You have earned...
...A full 8 hours.
Thank you, General.

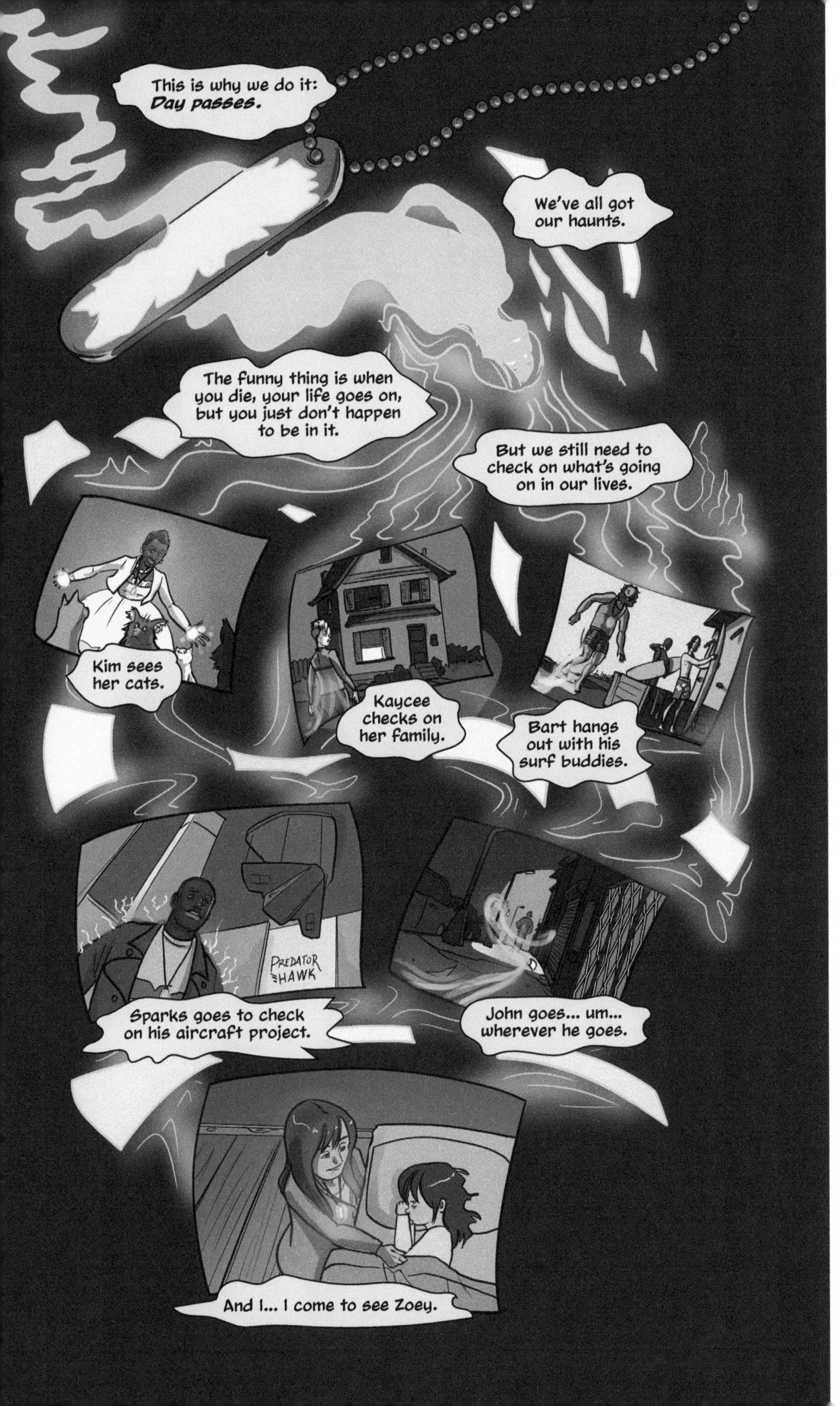
This is why we do it: *Day passes.*
We've all got our haunts.
The funny thing is when you die, your life goes on, but you just don't happen to be in it.
But we still need to check on what's going on in our lives.
Kim sees her cats.
Kaycee checks on her family.
Bart hangs out with his surf buddies.
PREDATOR HAWK
Sparks goes to check on his aircraft project.
John goes... um... wherever he goes.
And I... I come to see Zoey.

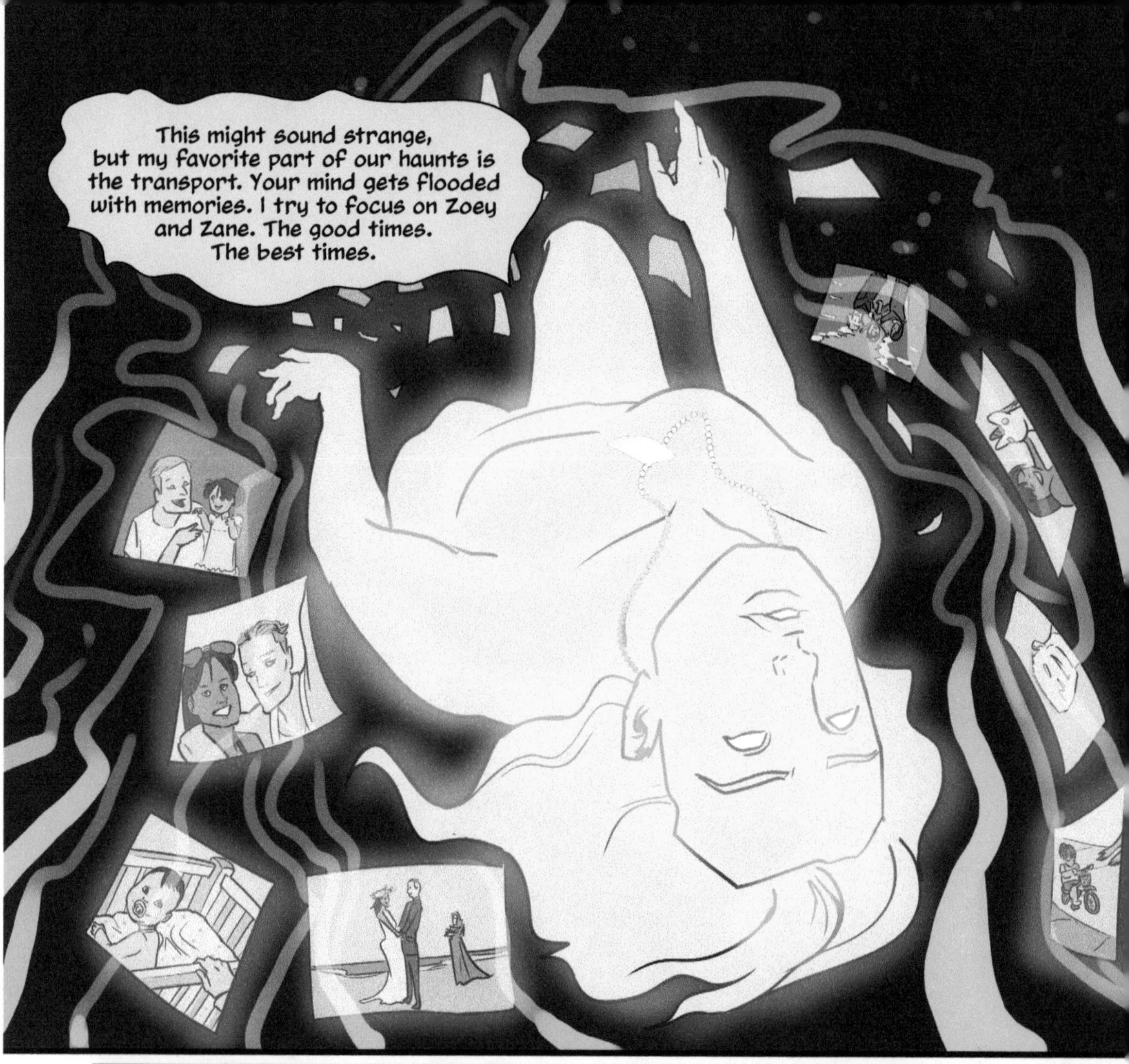
This might sound strange, but my favorite part of our haunts is the transport. Your mind gets flooded with memories. I try to focus on Zoey and Zane. The good times. The best times.

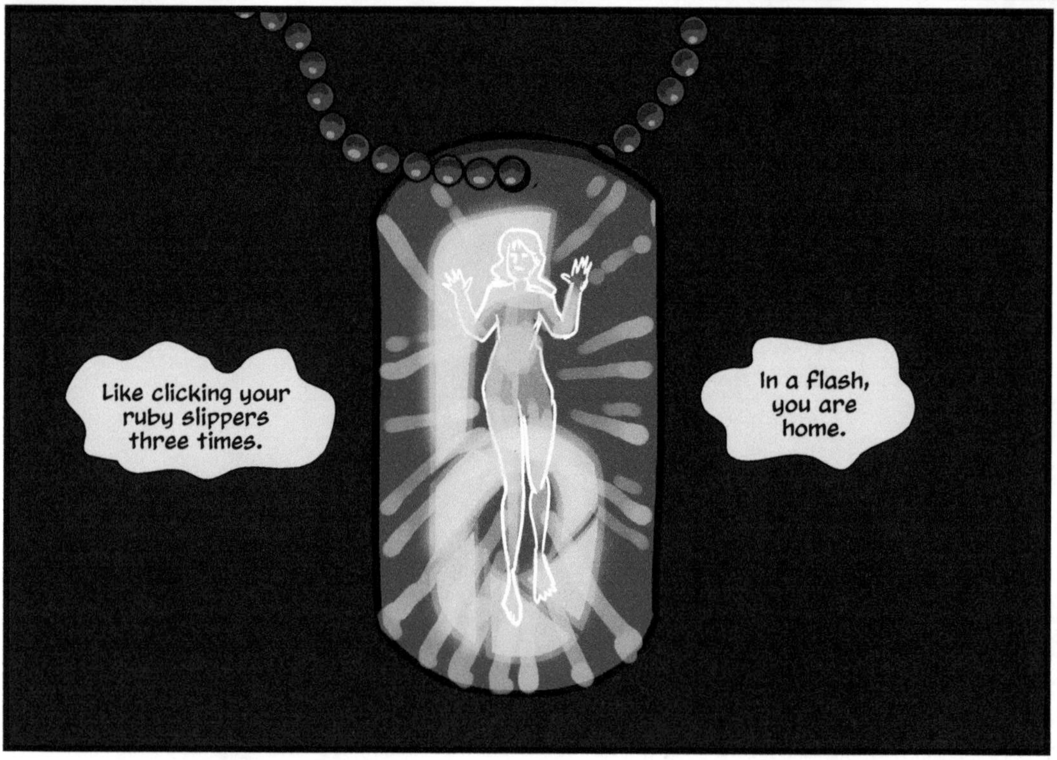
Like clicking your ruby slippers three times.
In a flash, you are home.

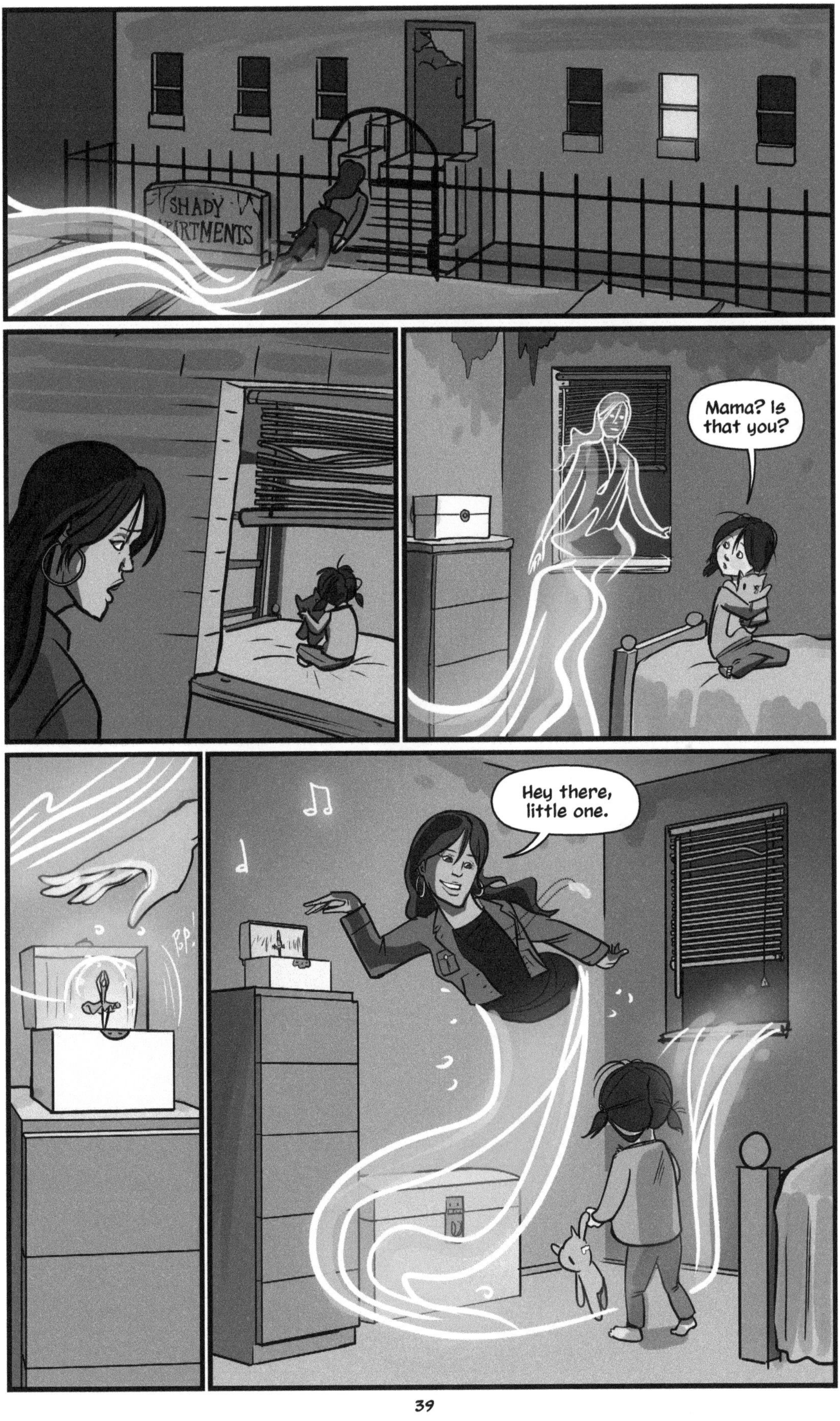
SHADY APARTMENTS
Mama? Is that you?
BP!
Hey there, little one.

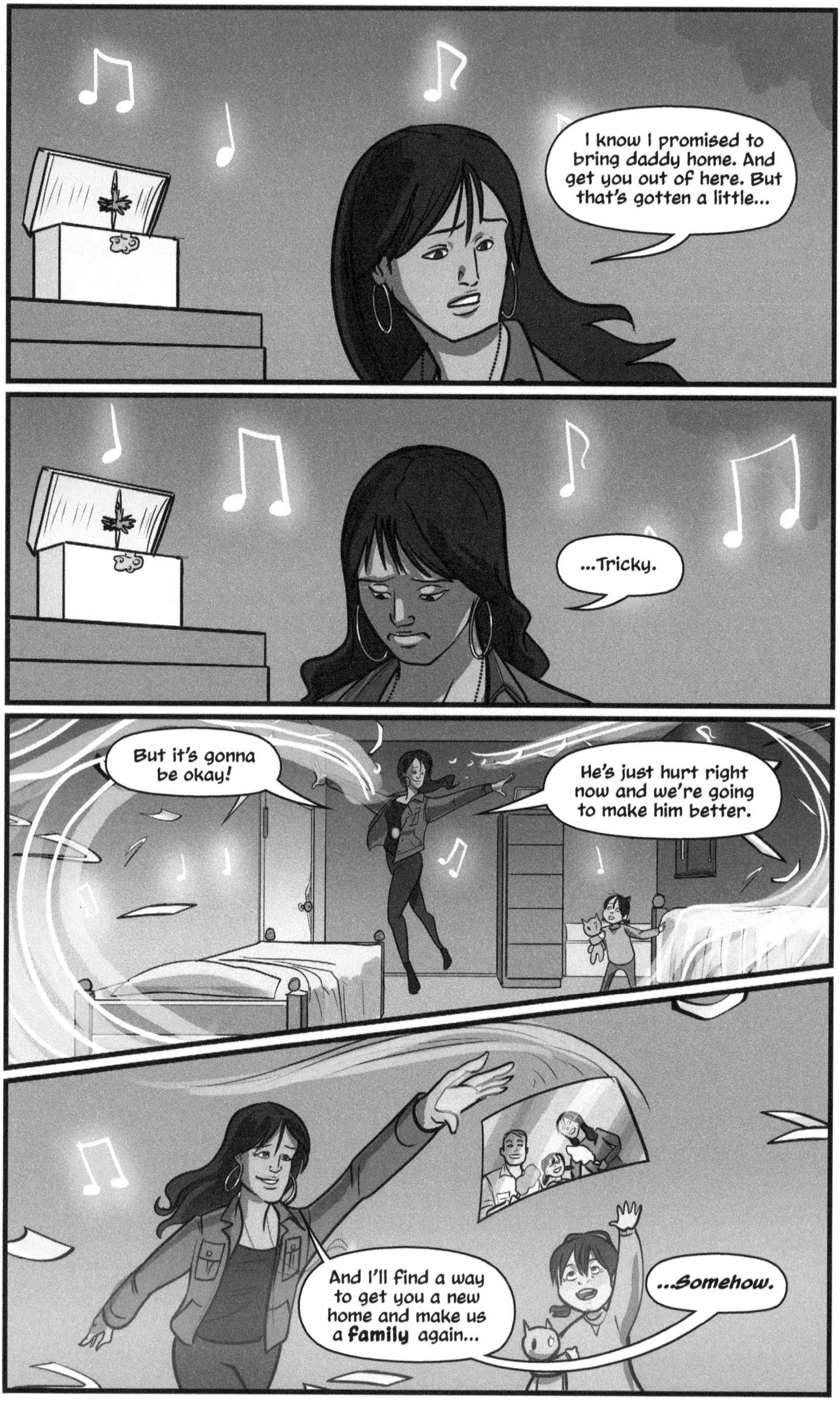
I know I promised to bring daddy home. And get you out of here. But that's gotten a little...
...Tricky.
But it's gonna be okay!
He's just hurt right now and we're going to make him better.
And I'll find a way to get you a new home and make us a **family** again...
...Somehow.

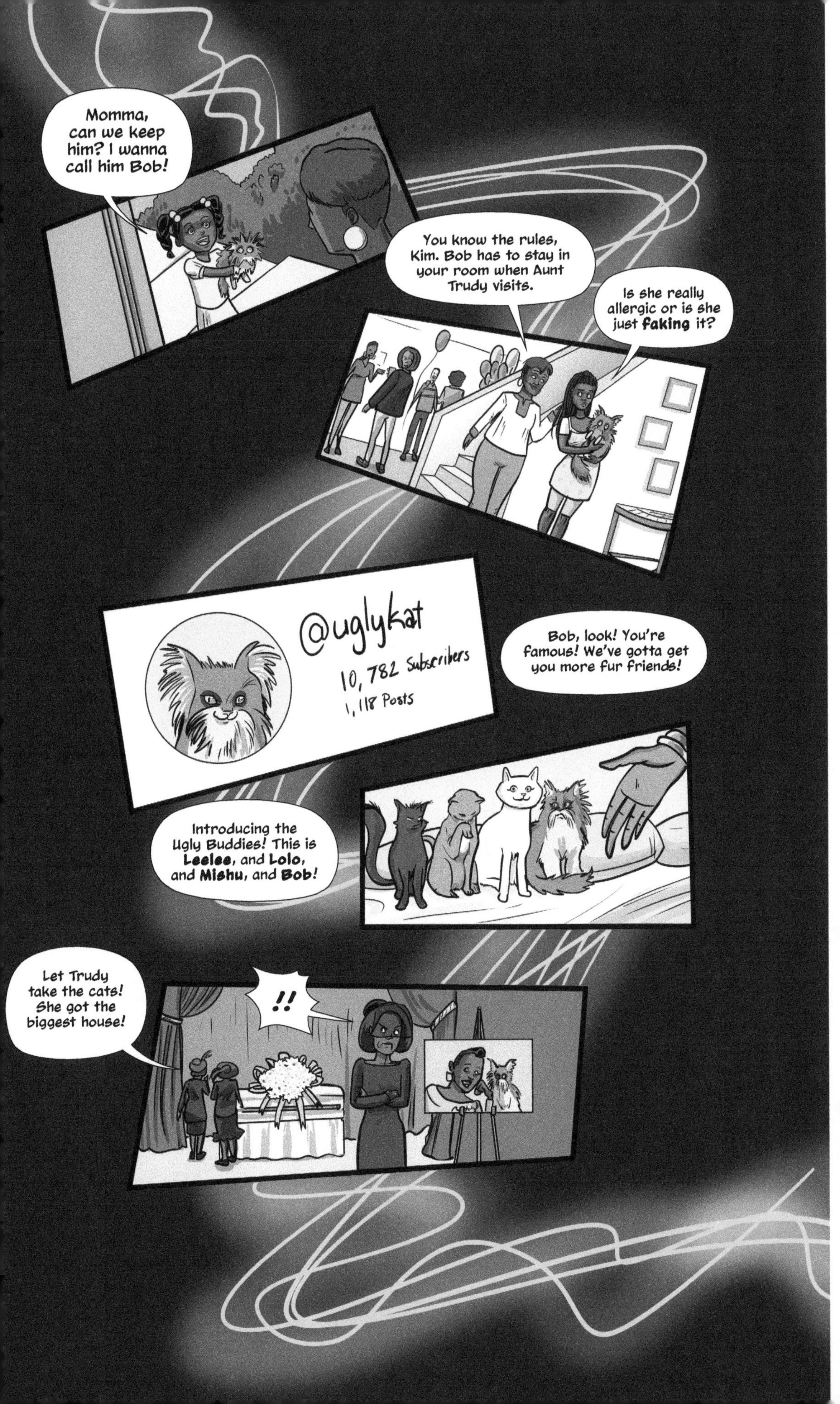

Momma, can we keep him? I wanna call him Bob!
You know the rules, Kim. Bob has to stay in your room when Aunt Trudy visits.
Is she really allergic or is she just **faking** it?
@uglykat
10,782 Subscribers
1,118 Posts
Bob, look! You're famous! We've gotta get you more fur friends!
Introducing the Ugly Buddies! This is **Leelee**, and **Lolo**, and **Mishu**, and **Bob**!
Let Trudy take the cats! She got the biggest house!
!!

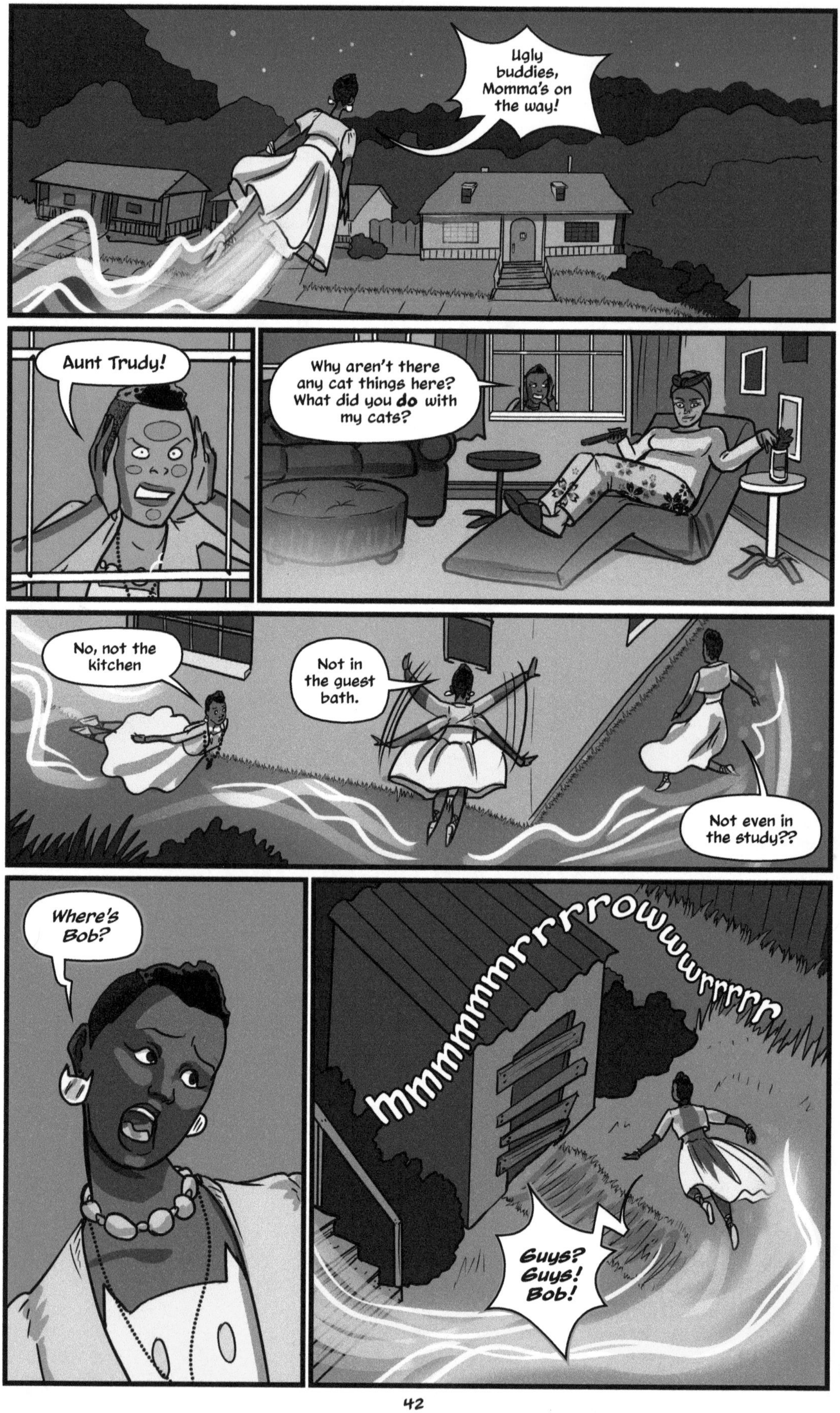
Ugly buddies, Momma's on the way!
Aunt Trudy!
Why aren't there any cat things here? What did you **do** with my cats?
No, not the kitchen
Not in the guest bath.
Not even in the study??
Where's Bob?
mmmmmrrrrrowwwwrrrrr
Guys? Guys! Bob!

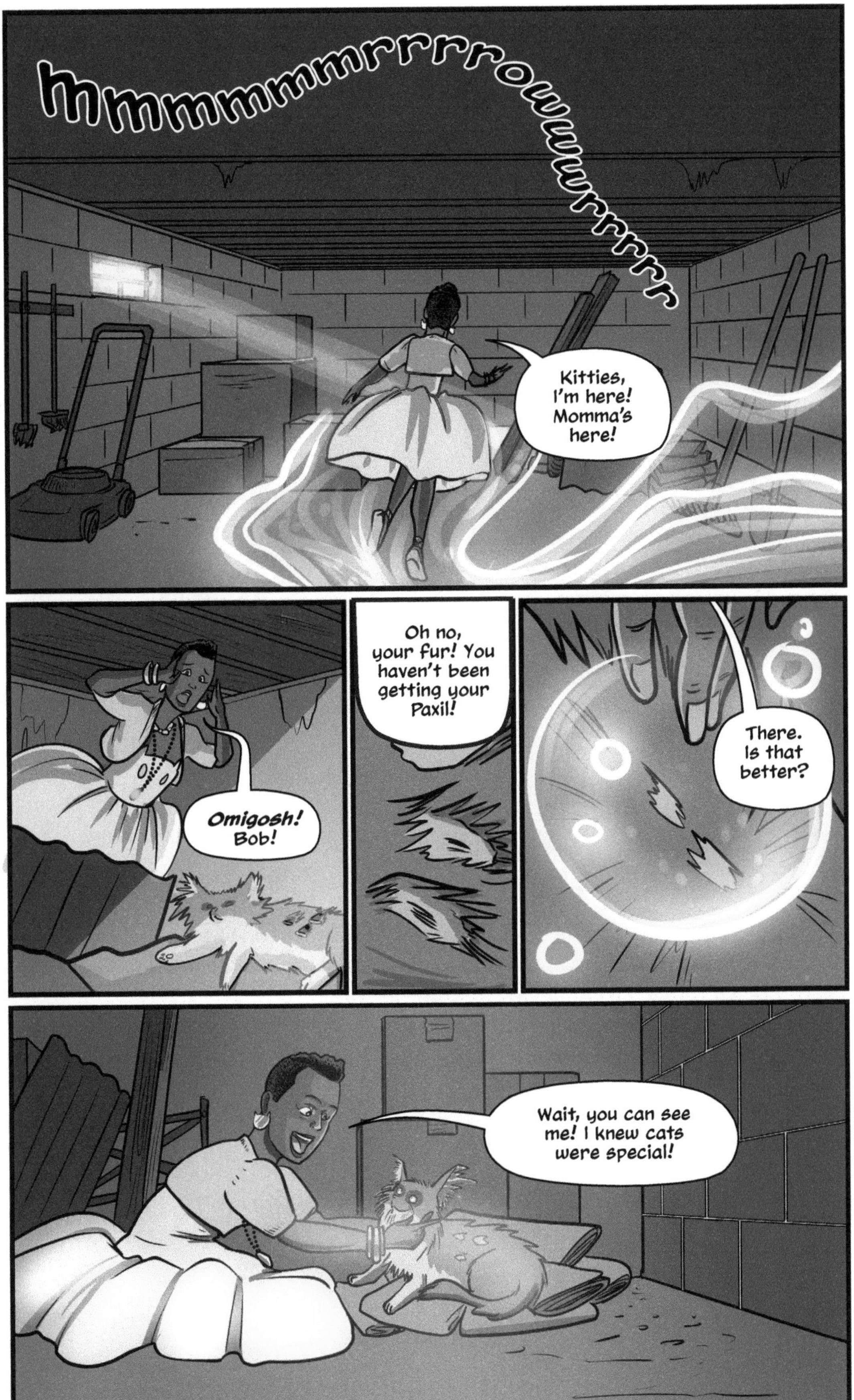
Mmmmmmrrrrowwurrrrr
Kitties, I'm here! Momma's here!
Omigosh! Bob!
Oh no, your fur! You haven't been getting your Paxil!
There. Is that better?
Wait, you can see me! I knew cats were special!

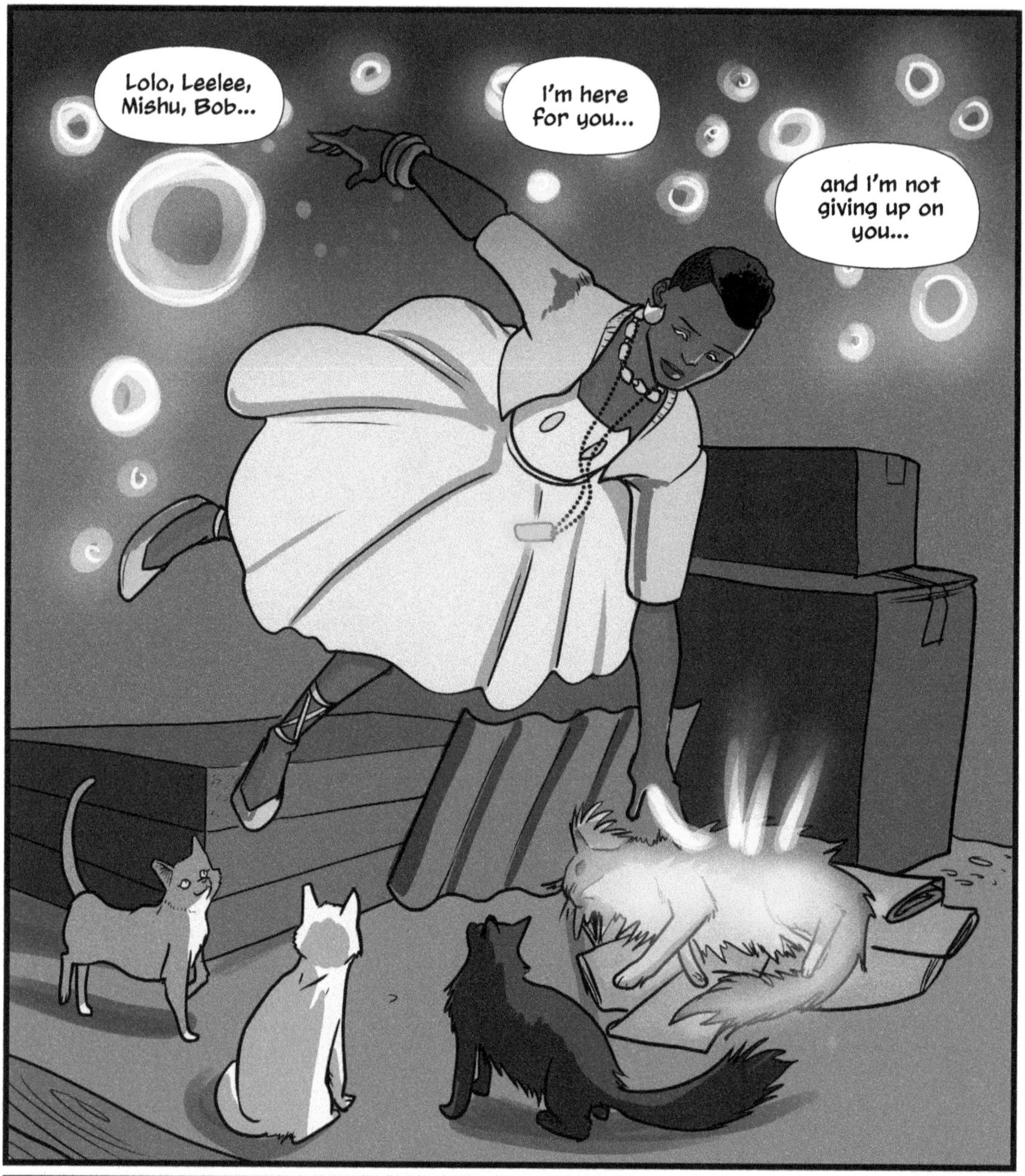
Lolo, Leelee, Mishu, Bob...
I'm here for you...
and I'm not giving up on you...

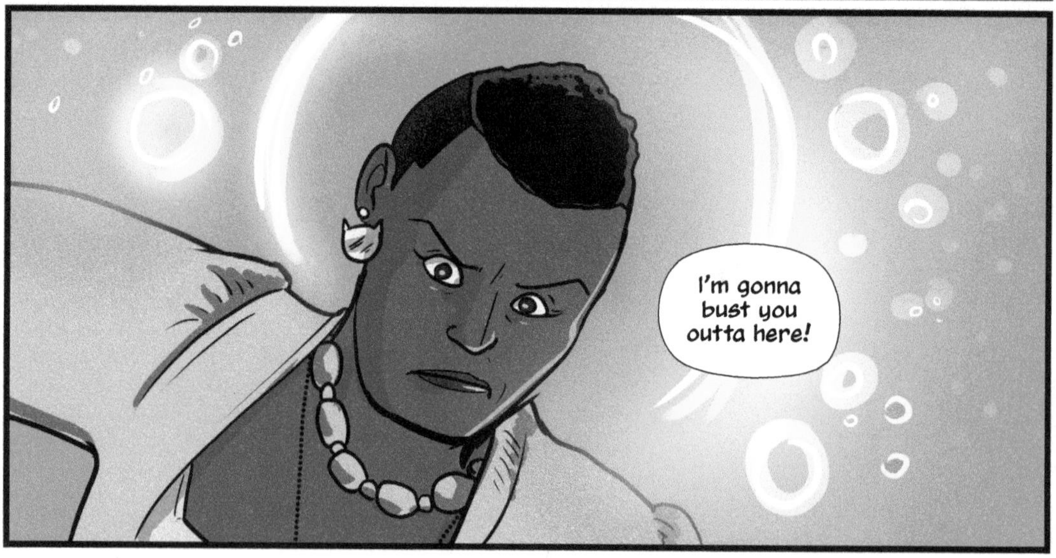
I'm gonna bust you outta here!

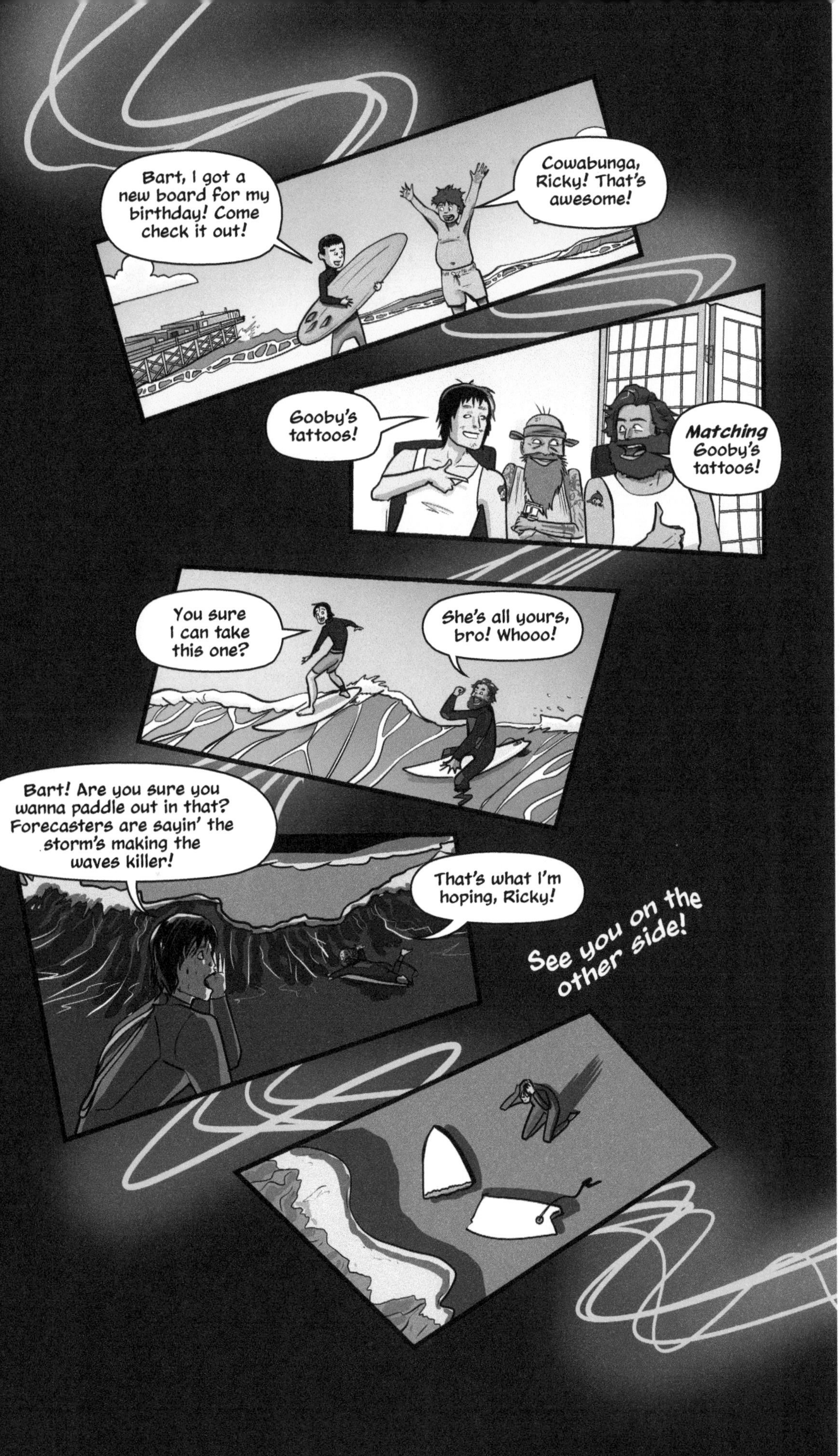
Bart, I got a new board for my birthday! Come check it out!
Cowabunga, Ricky! That's awesome!
Gooby's tattoos!
Matching Gooby's tattoos!
You sure I can take this one?
She's all yours, bro! Whooo!
Bart! Are you sure you wanna paddle out in that? Forecasters are sayin' the storm's making the waves killer!
That's what I'm hoping, Ricky!
See you on the other side!

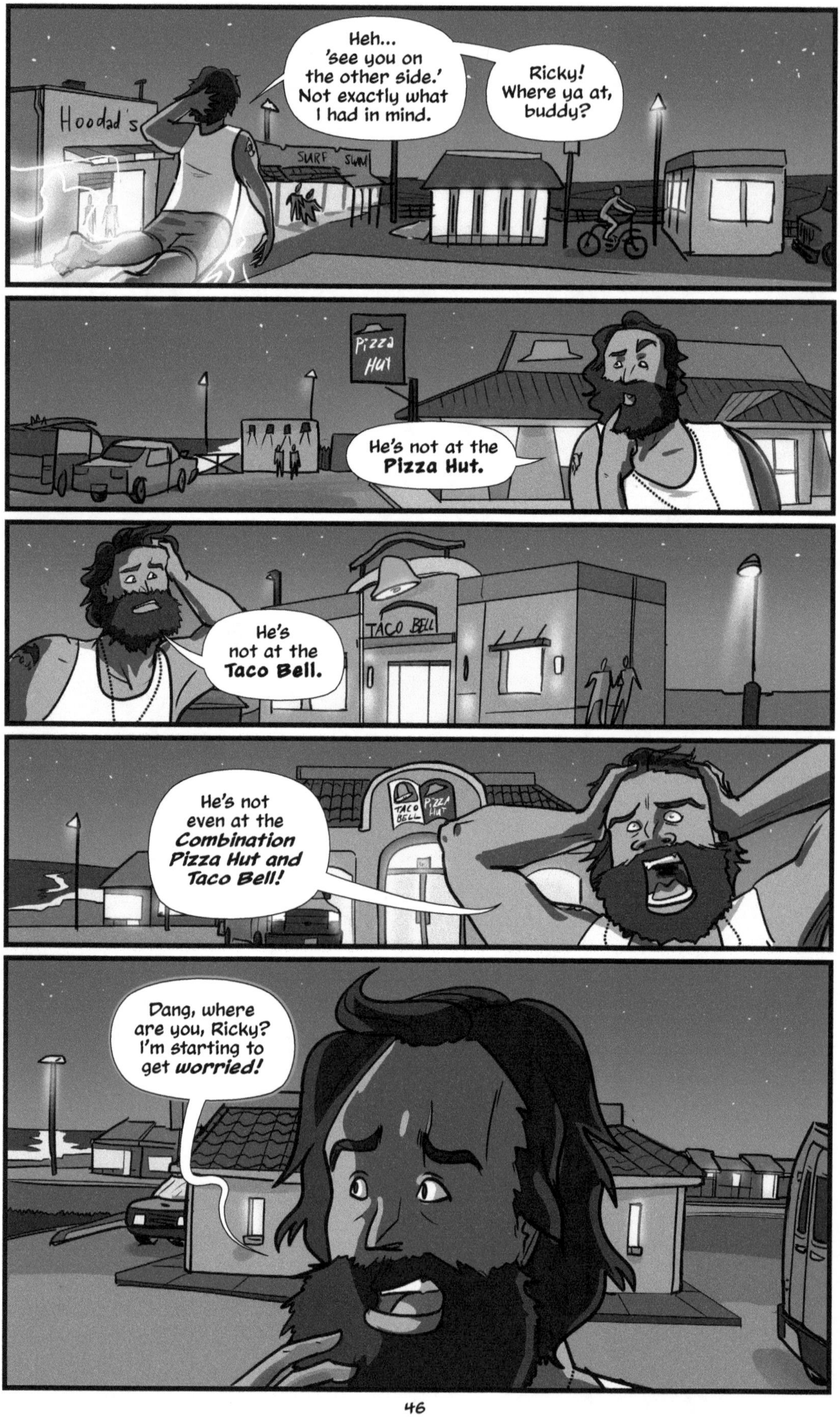
Hoodad's
SURF SWIM
Heh... 'see you on the other side.' Not exactly what I had in mind.
Ricky! Where ya at, buddy?
PIZZA HUT
He's not at the **Pizza Hut.**
TACO BELL
He's not at the **Taco Bell.**
TACO BELL PIZZA HUT
He's not even at the ***Combination Pizza Hut and Taco Bell!***
Dang, where are you, Ricky? I'm starting to get ***worried!***

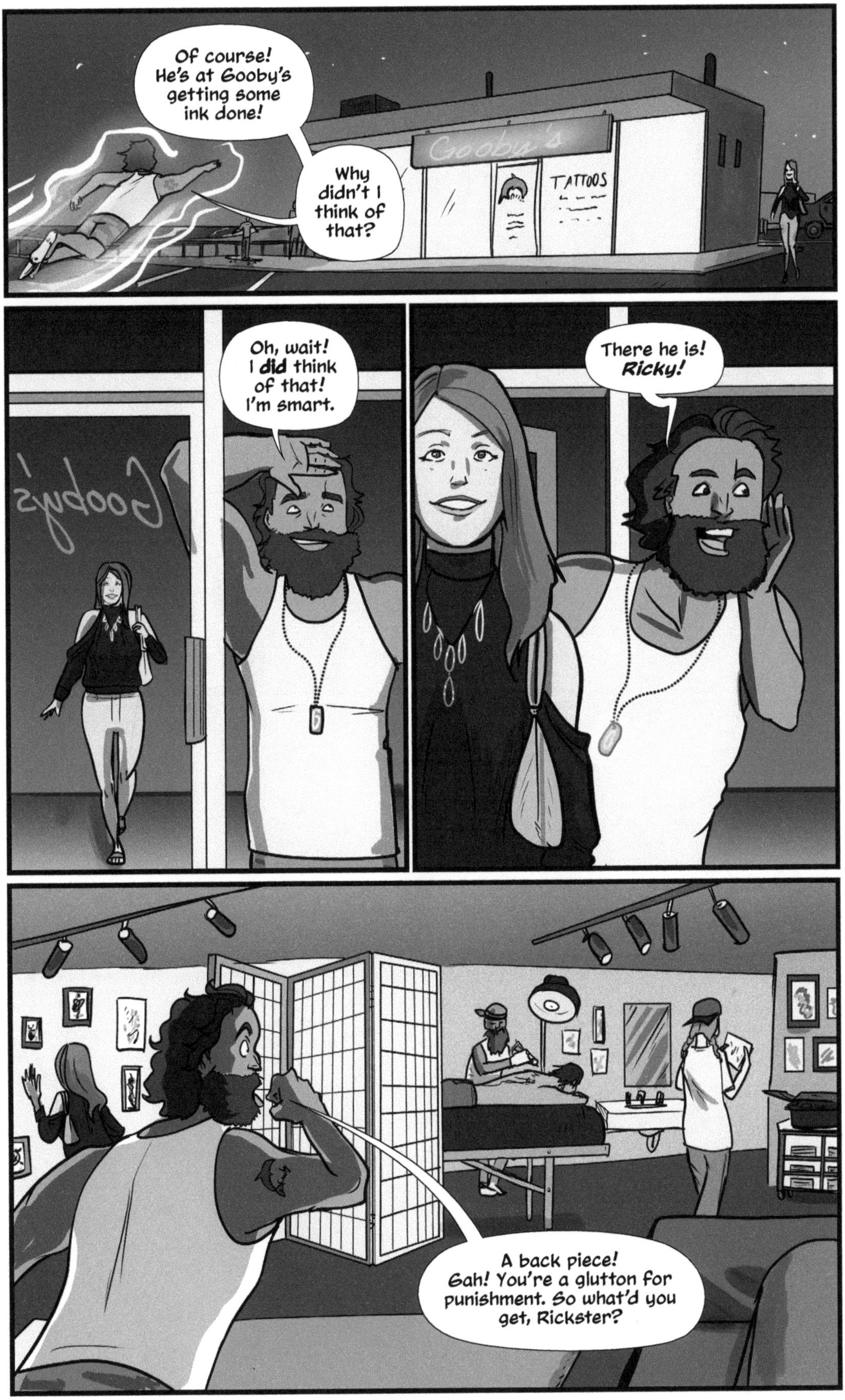
Of course! He's at Gooby's getting some ink done!
Why didn't I think of that?
Gooby's
TATTOOS
Oh, wait! I **did** think of that! I'm smart.
Gooby's
There he is! ***Ricky!***
A back piece! Gah! You're a glutton for punishment. So what'd you get, Rickster?

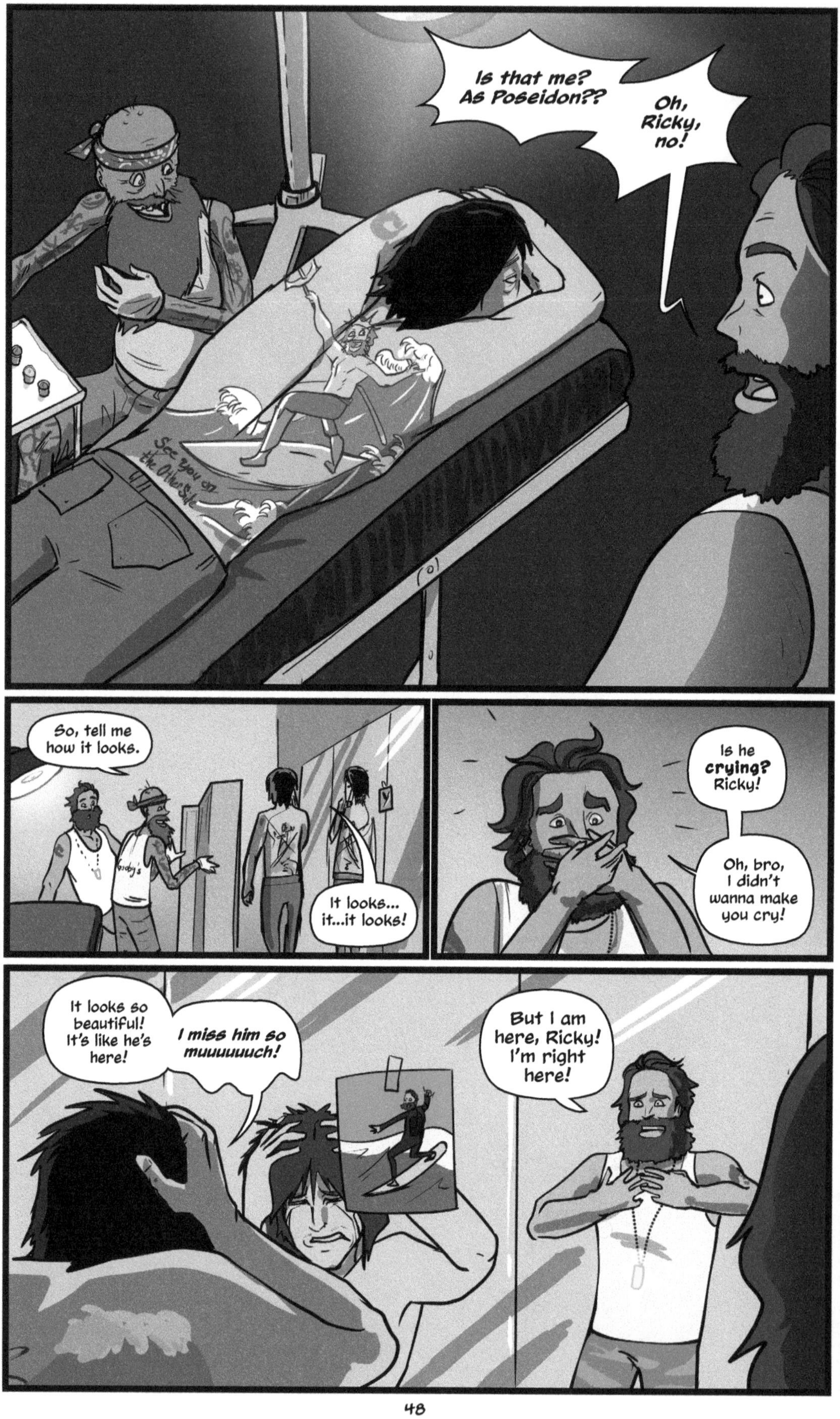
Is that me? As Poseidon??
Oh, Ricky, no!
See you on the Other Side
So, tell me how it looks.
It looks... it...it looks!
Is he crying? Ricky!
Oh, bro, I didn't wanna make you cry!
It looks so beautiful! It's like he's here!
I miss him so muuuuuuch!
But I am here, Ricky! I'm right here!

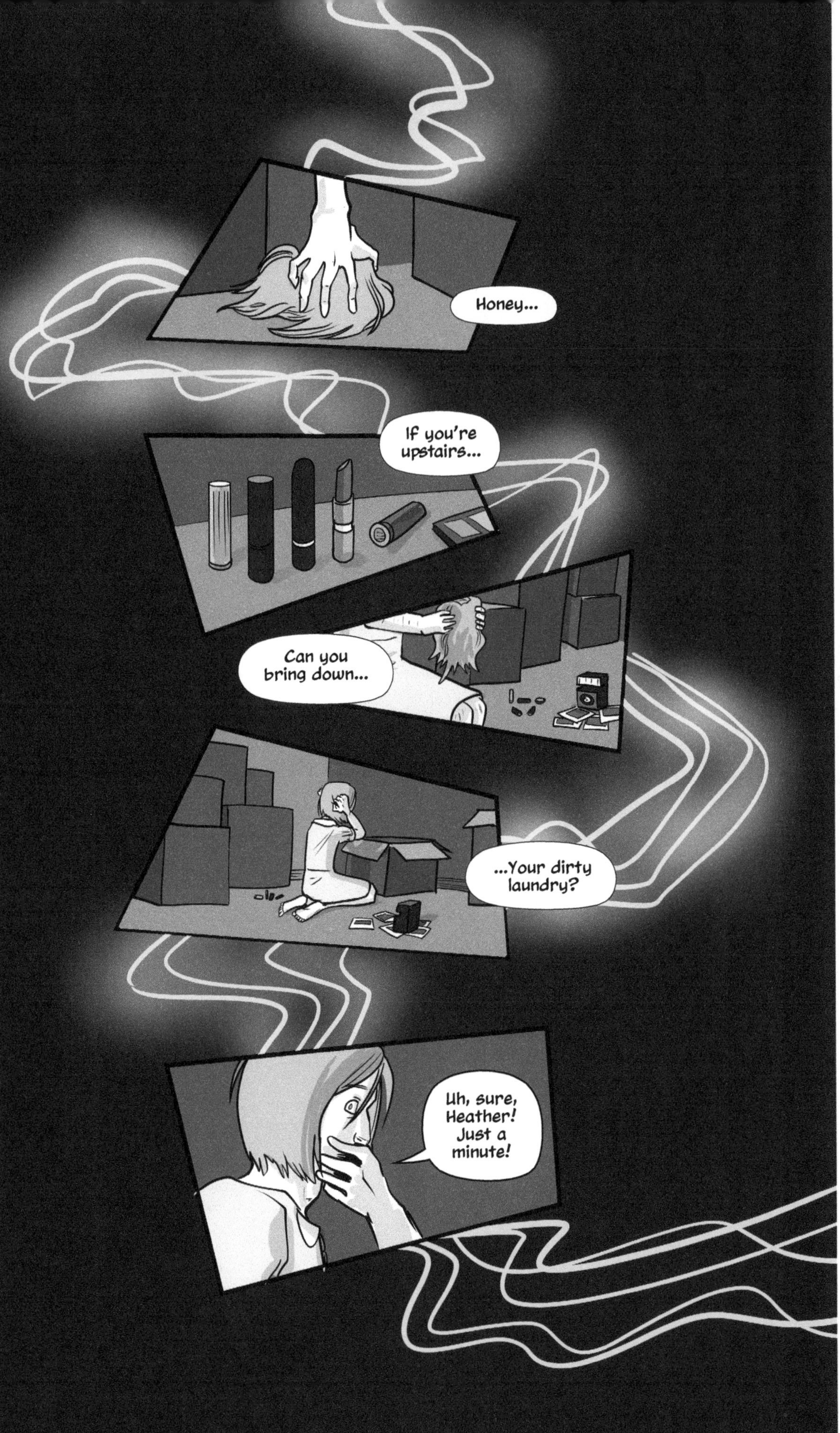
Honey...
If you're upstairs...
Can you bring down...
...Your dirty laundry?
Uh, sure, Heather! Just a minute!

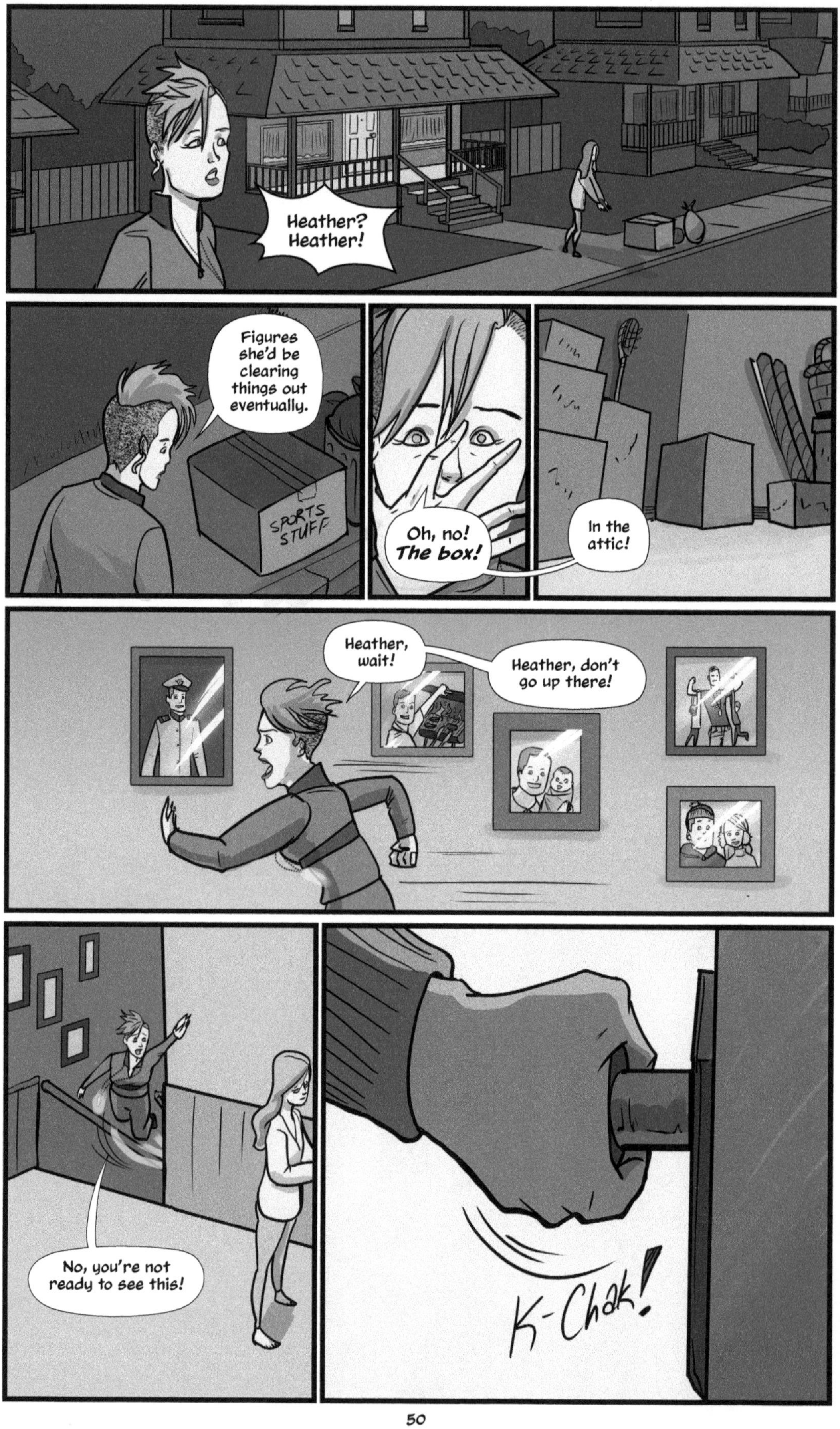

Heather? Heather!
Figures she'd be clearing things out eventually.
SPORTS STUFF
Oh, no! *The box!*
In the attic!
Heather, wait!
Heather, don't go up there!
No, you're not ready to see this!
K-Chak!

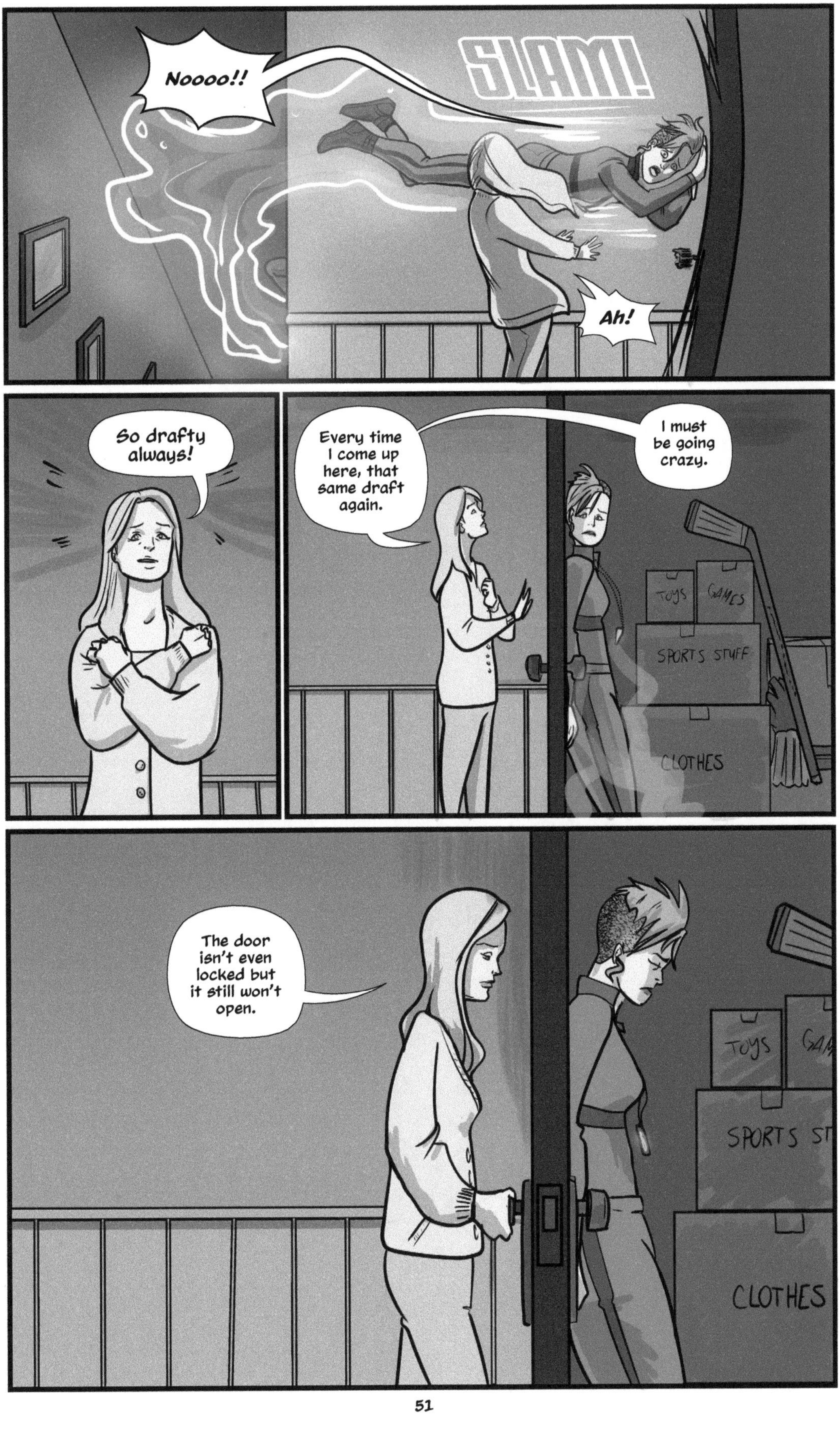
Noooo!!
SLAM!
Ah!
So drafty always!
Every time I come up here, that same draft again.
I must be going crazy.
TOYS
GAMES
SPORTS STUFF
CLOTHES
The door isn't even locked but it still won't open.
TOYS
CLOTHES

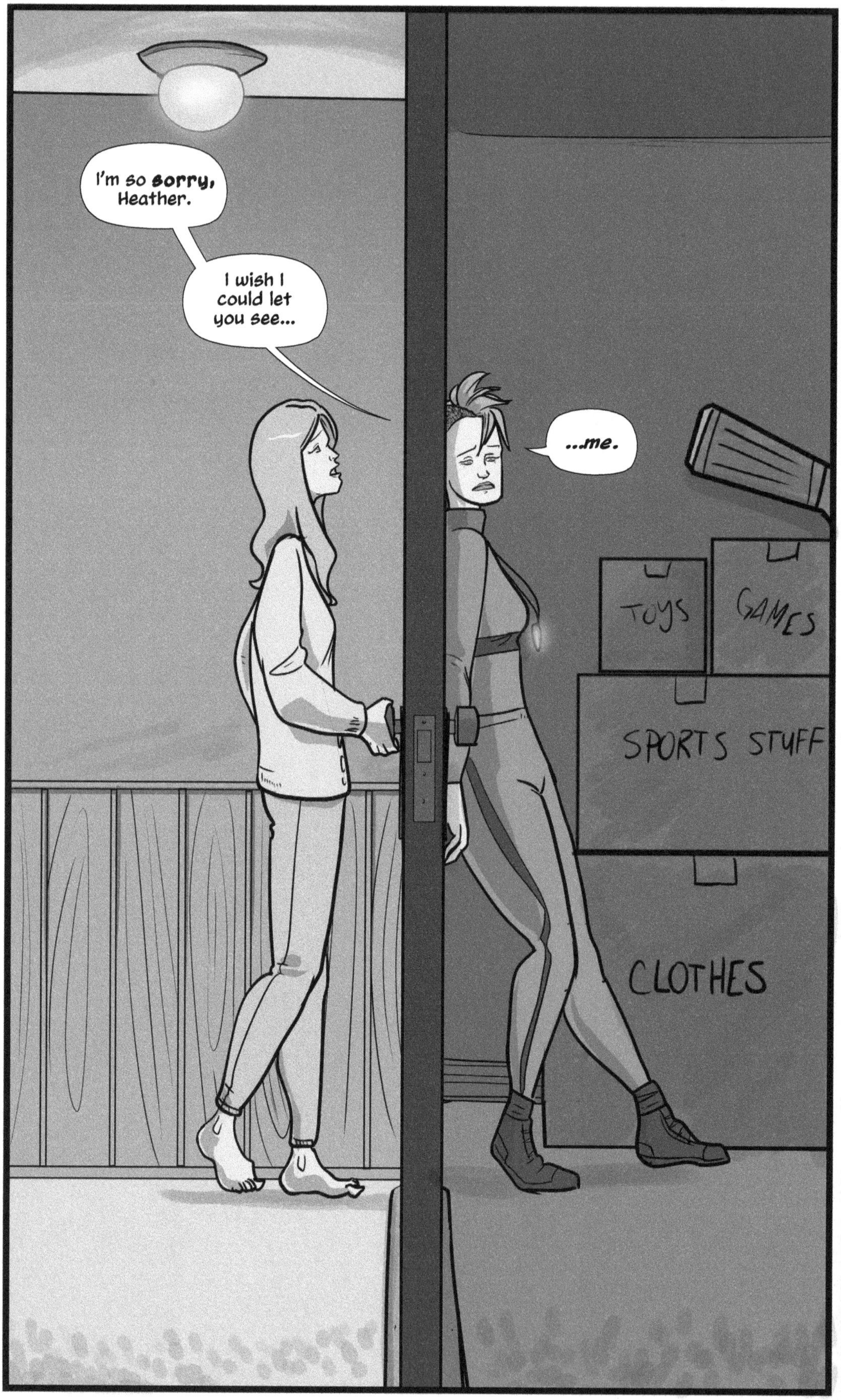
I'm so **sorry,** Heather.
I wish I could let you see...
...me.
TOYS
GAMES
SPORTS STUFF
CLOTHES

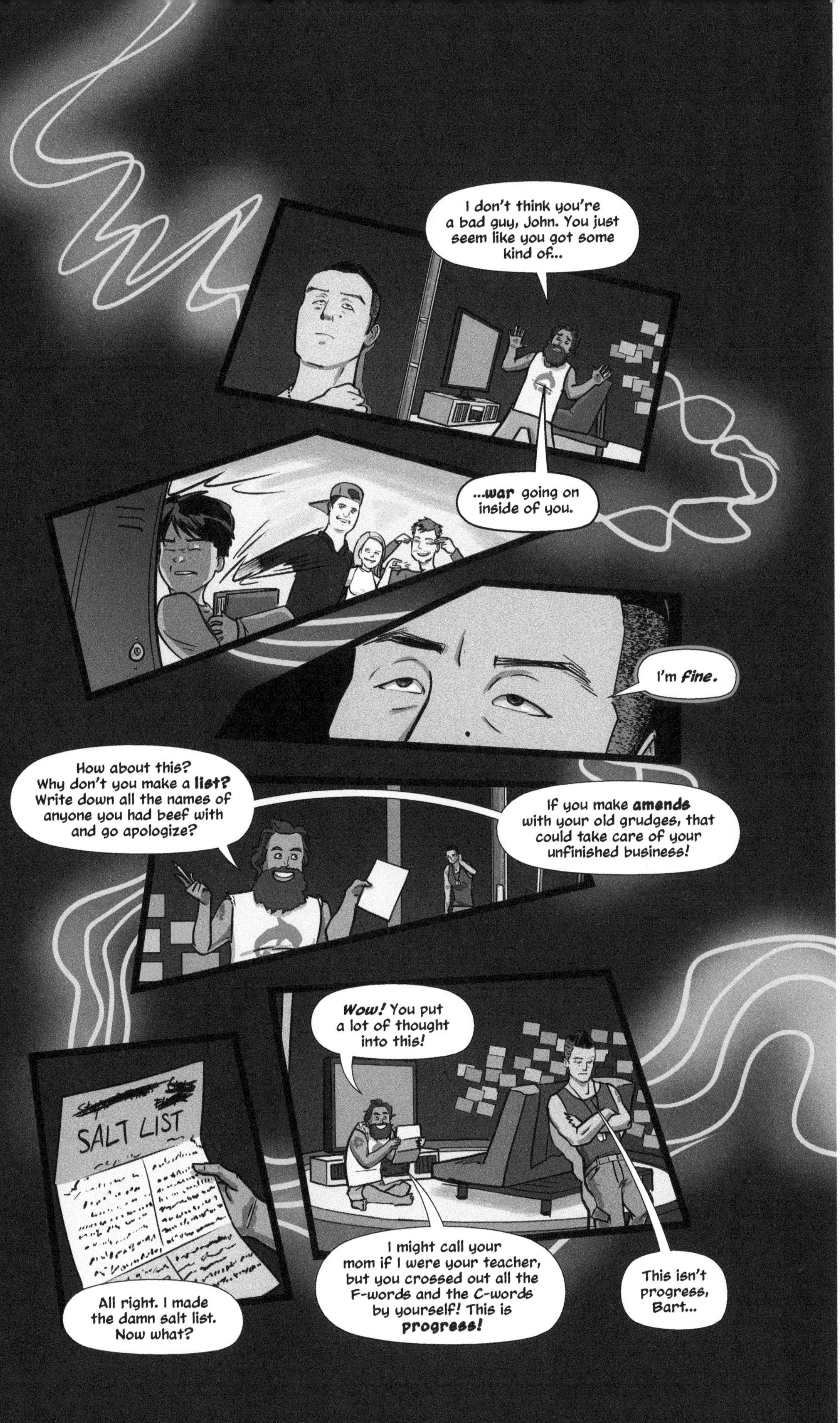

I don't think you're a bad guy, John. You just seem like you got some kind of...
...war going on inside of you.
I'm fine.
How about this? Why don't you make a list? Write down all the names of anyone you had beef with and go apologize?
If you make amends with your old grudges, that could take care of your unfinished business!
SALT LIST
All right. I made the damn salt list. Now what?
Wow! You put a lot of thought into this!
I might call your mom if I were your teacher, but you crossed out all the F-words and the C-words by yourself! This is progress!
This isn't progress, Bart...

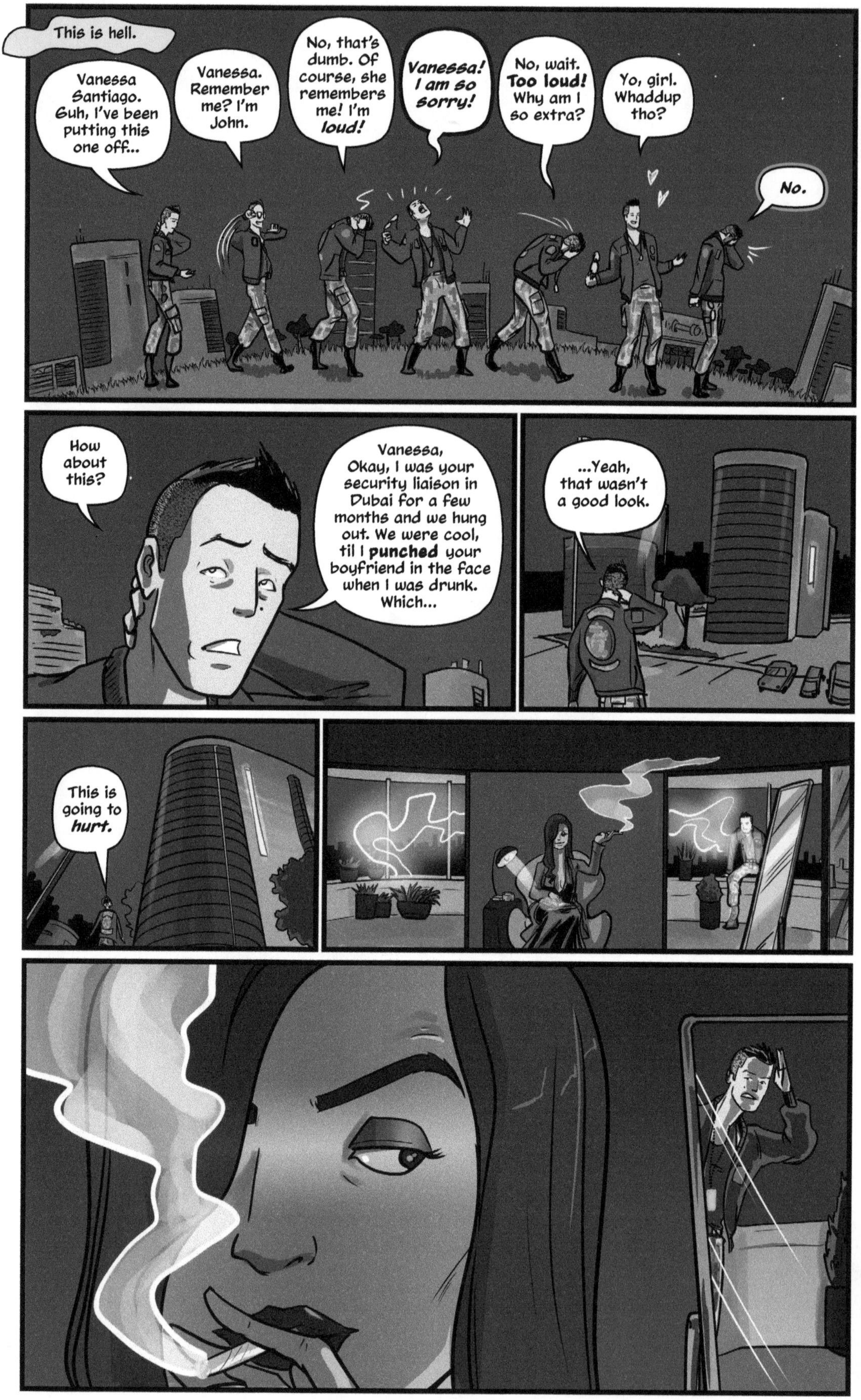
This is hell.
Vanessa Santiago. Guh, I've been putting this one off...
Vanessa. Remember me? I'm John.
No, that's dumb. Of course, she remembers me! I'm *loud!*
Vanessa! I am so sorry!
No, wait. **Too loud!** Why am I so extra?
Yo, girl. Whaddup tho?
No.
How about this?
Vanessa, Okay, I was your security liaison in Dubai for a few months and we hung out. We were cool, til I **punched** your boyfriend in the face when I was drunk. Which...
...Yeah, that wasn't a good look.
This is going to *hurt.*

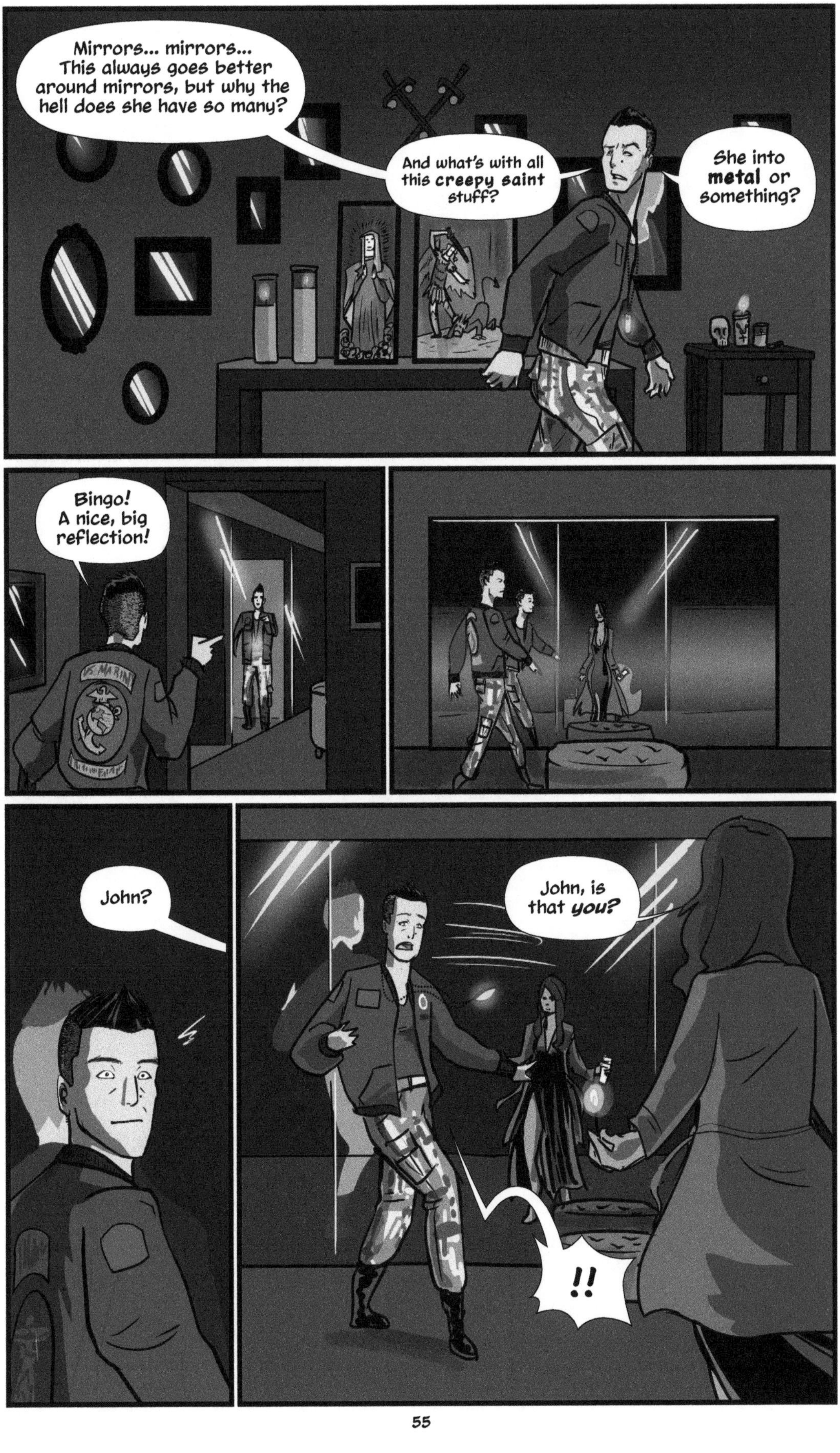

Mirrors... mirrors... This always goes better around mirrors, but why the hell does she have so many?
And what's with all this **creepy saint** stuff?
She into **metal** or something?
Bingo! A nice, big reflection!
John?
John, is that *you?*
!!

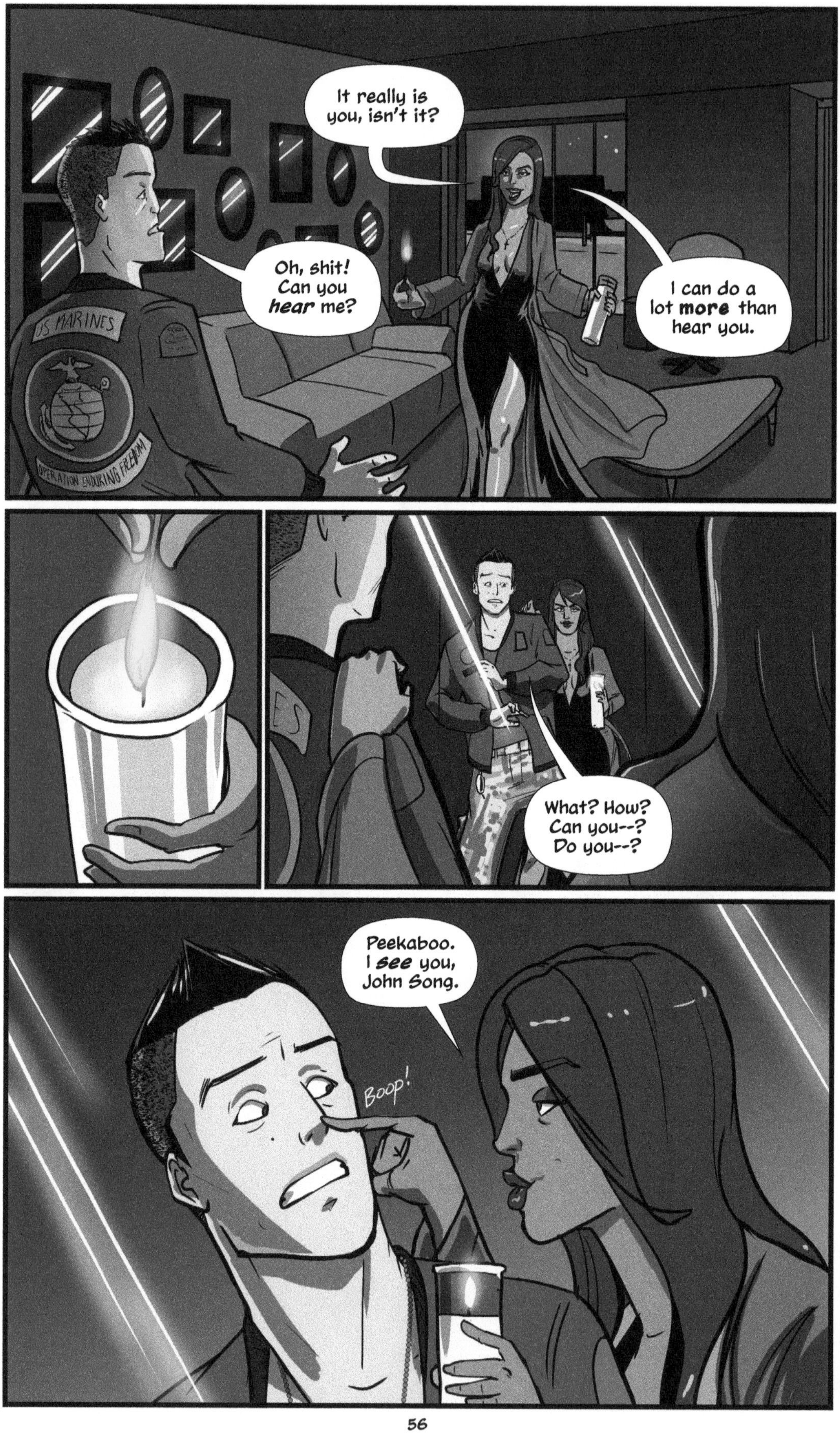
It really is you, isn't it?
Oh, shit! Can you *hear* me?
I can do a lot **more** than hear you.
US MARINES
OPERATION ENDURING FREEDOM
What? How? Can you--? Do you--?
Peekaboo. I *see* you, John Song.
Boop!

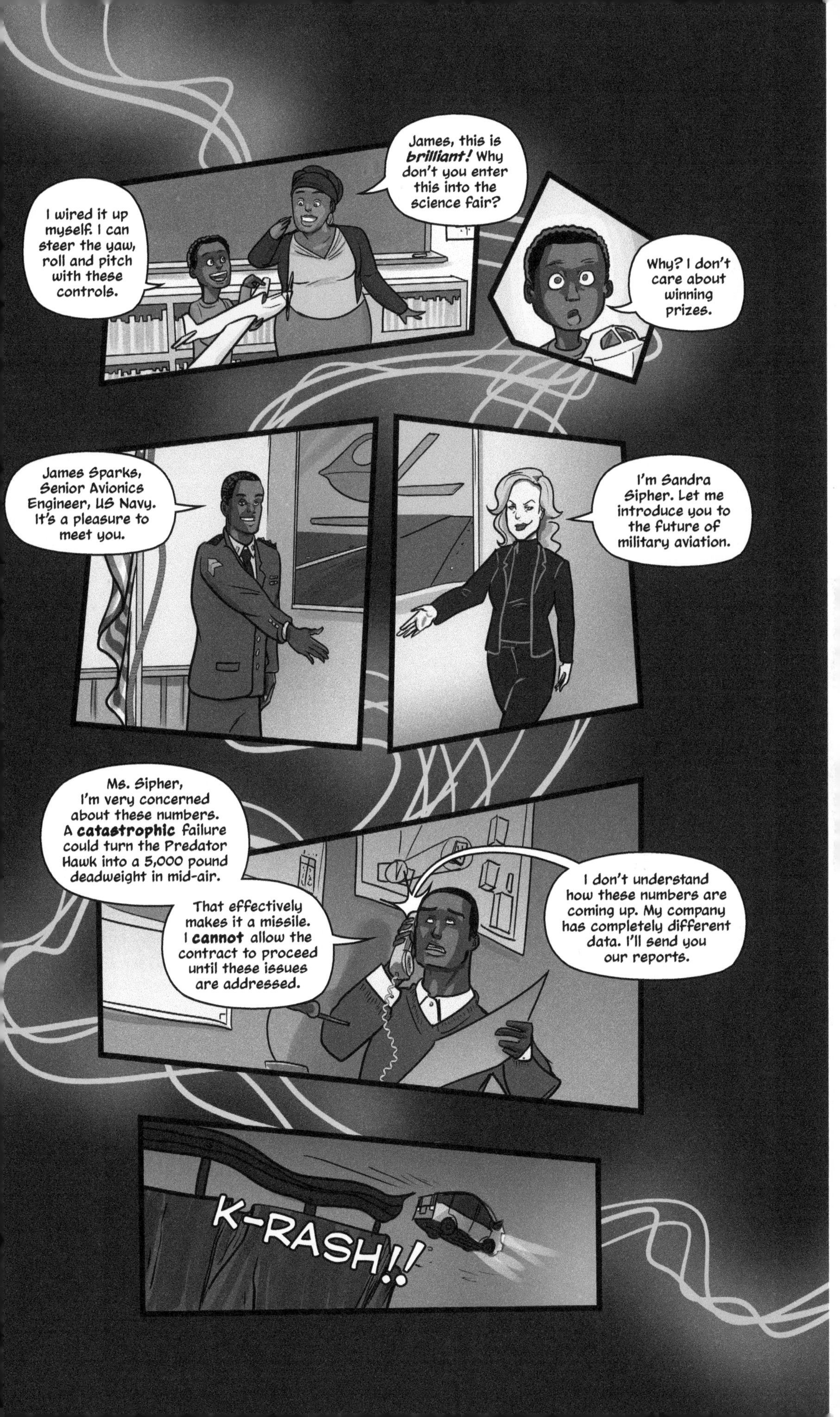
I wired it up myself. I can steer the yaw, roll and pitch with these controls.
James, this is **brilliant!** Why don't you enter this into the science fair?
Why? I don't care about winning prizes.
James Sparks, Senior Avionics Engineer, US Navy. It's a pleasure to meet you.
I'm Sandra Sipher. Let me introduce you to the future of military aviation.
Ms. Sipher, I'm very concerned about these numbers. A **catastrophic** failure could turn the Predator Hawk into a 5,000 pound deadweight in mid-air.
That effectively makes it a missile. I **cannot** allow the contract to proceed until these issues are addressed.
I don't understand how these numbers are coming up. My company has completely different data. I'll send you our reports.
K-RASH!!

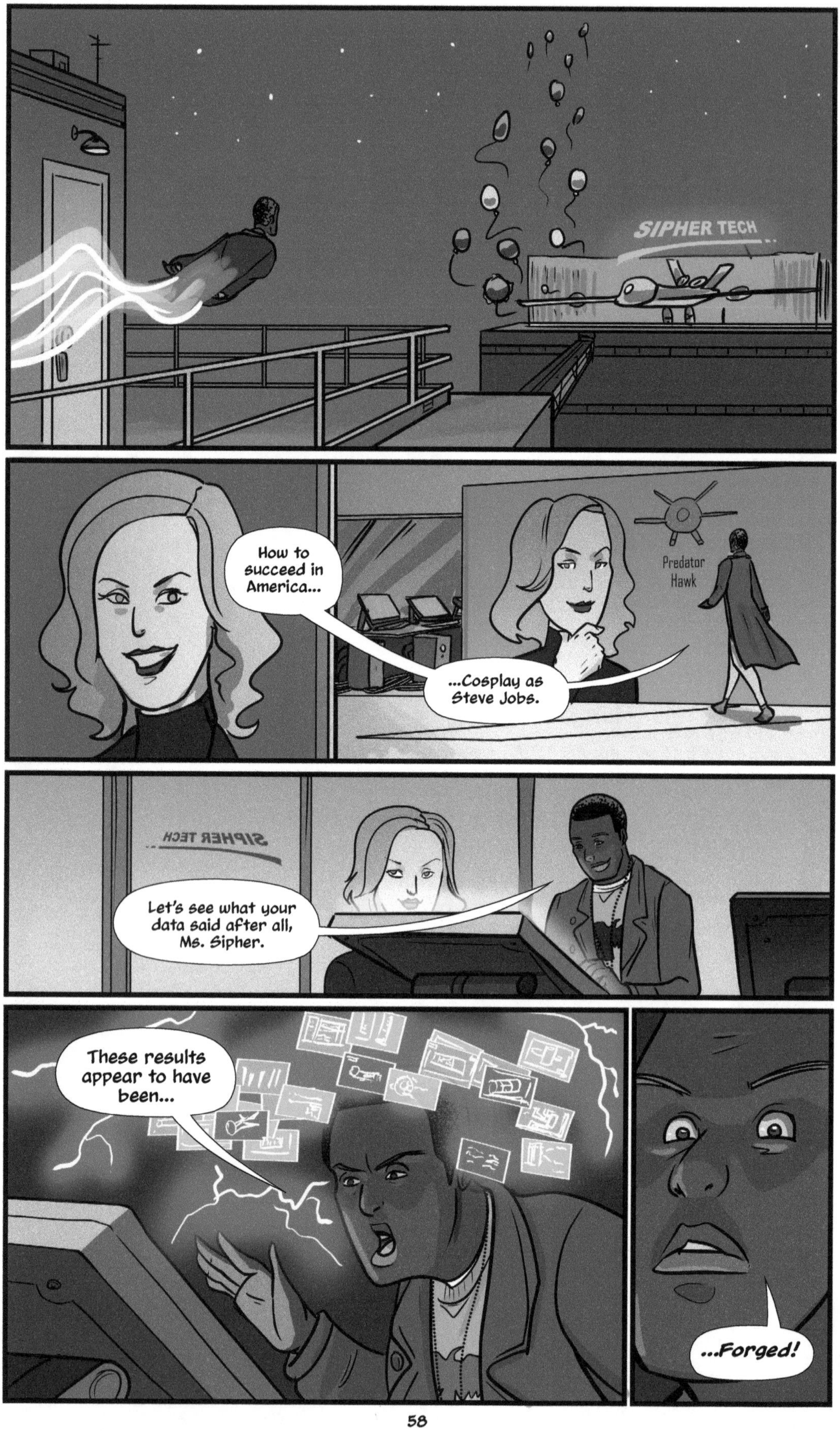
SIPHER TECH
How to succeed in America...
Predator Hawk
...Cosplay as Steve Jobs.
Let's see what your data said after all, Ms. Sipher.
These results appear to have been...
...Forged!

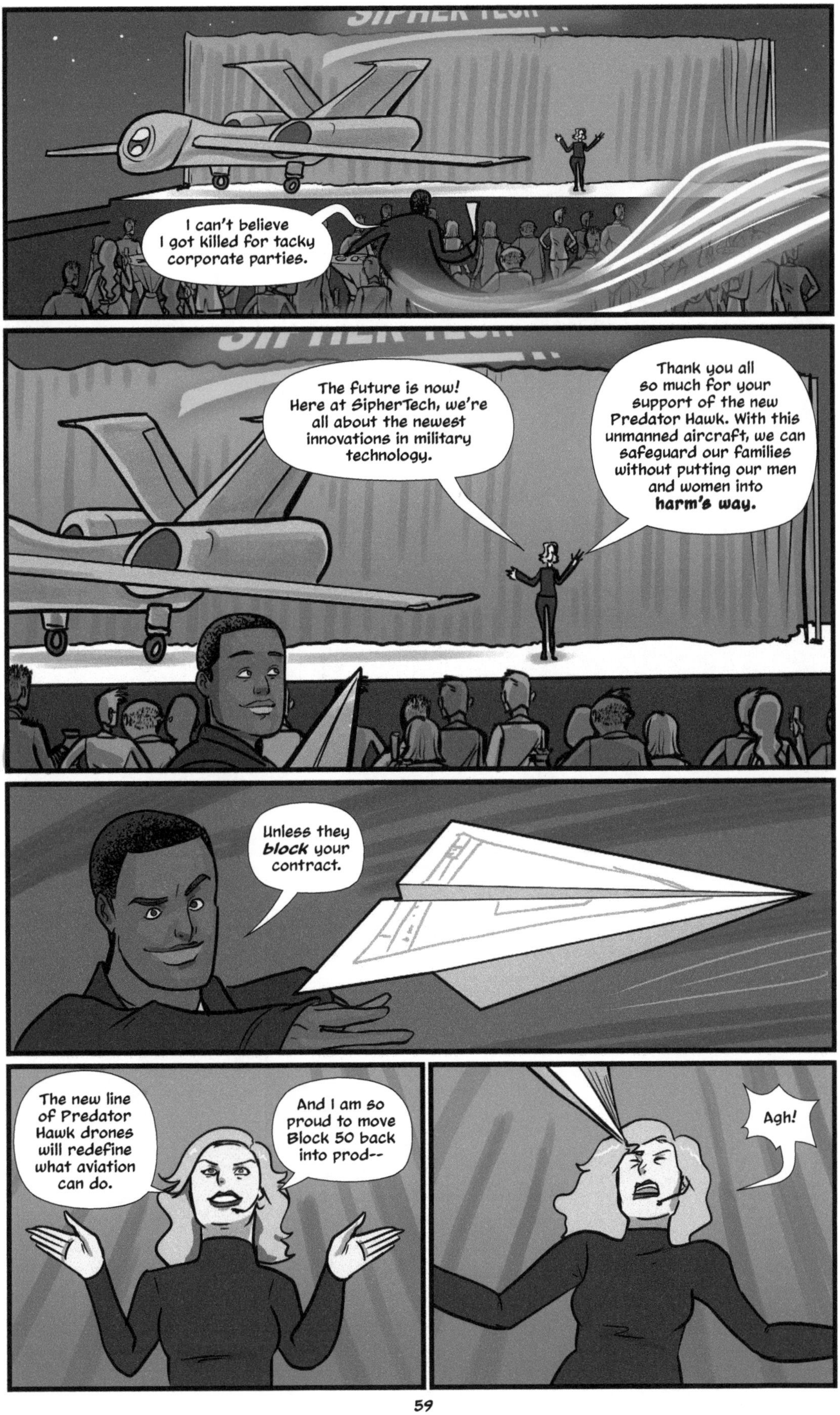
I can't believe I got killed for tacky corporate parties.
The future is now! Here at SipherTech, we're all about the newest innovations in military technology.
Thank you all so much for your support of the new Predator Hawk. With this unmanned aircraft, we can safeguard our families without putting our men and women into **harm's way.**
Unless they ***block*** your contract.
The new line of Predator Hawk drones will redefine what aviation can do.
And I am so proud to move Block 50 back into prod--
Agh!

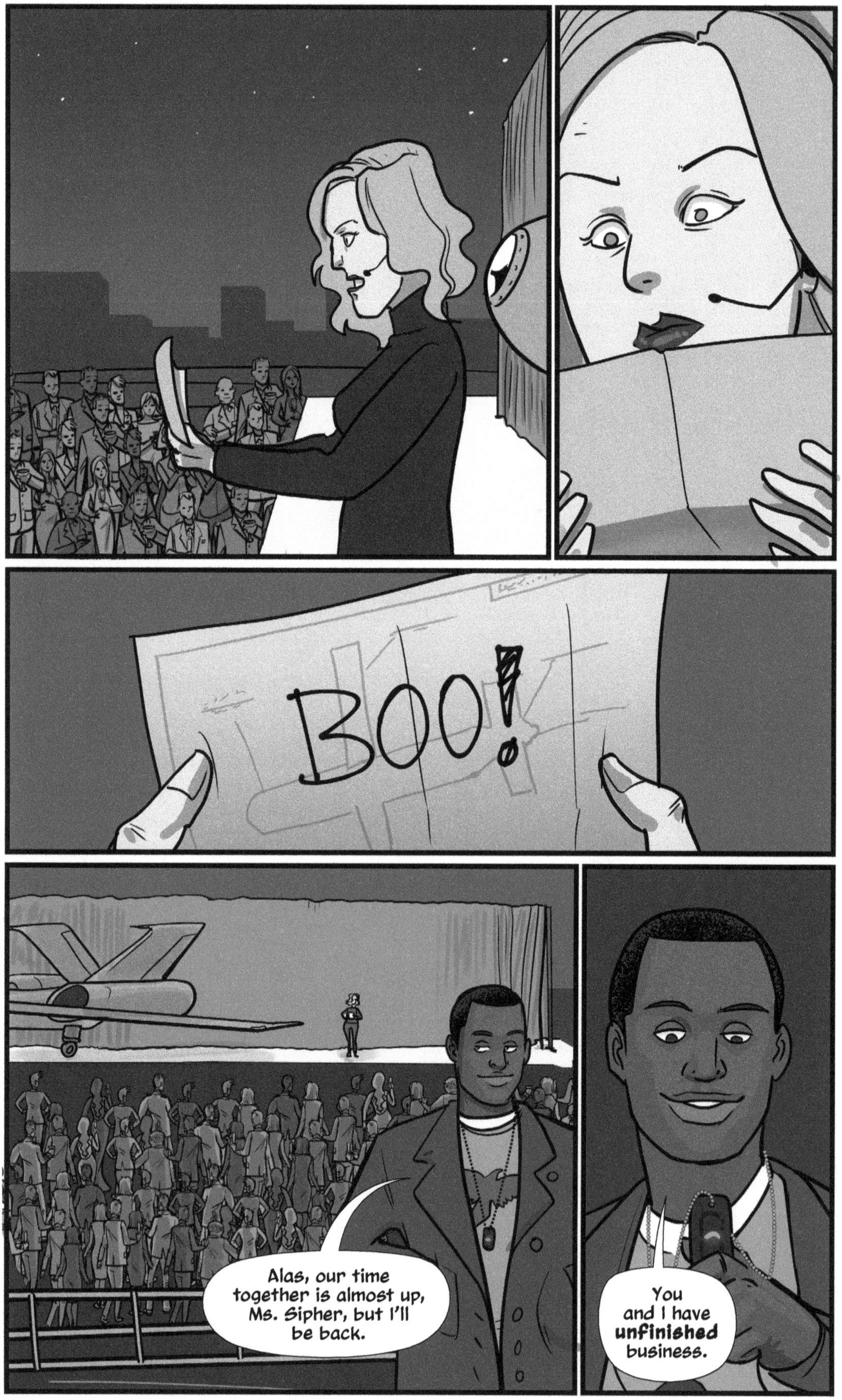
BOO!
Alas, our time together is almost up, Ms. Sipher, but I'll be back.
You and I have **unfinished** business.

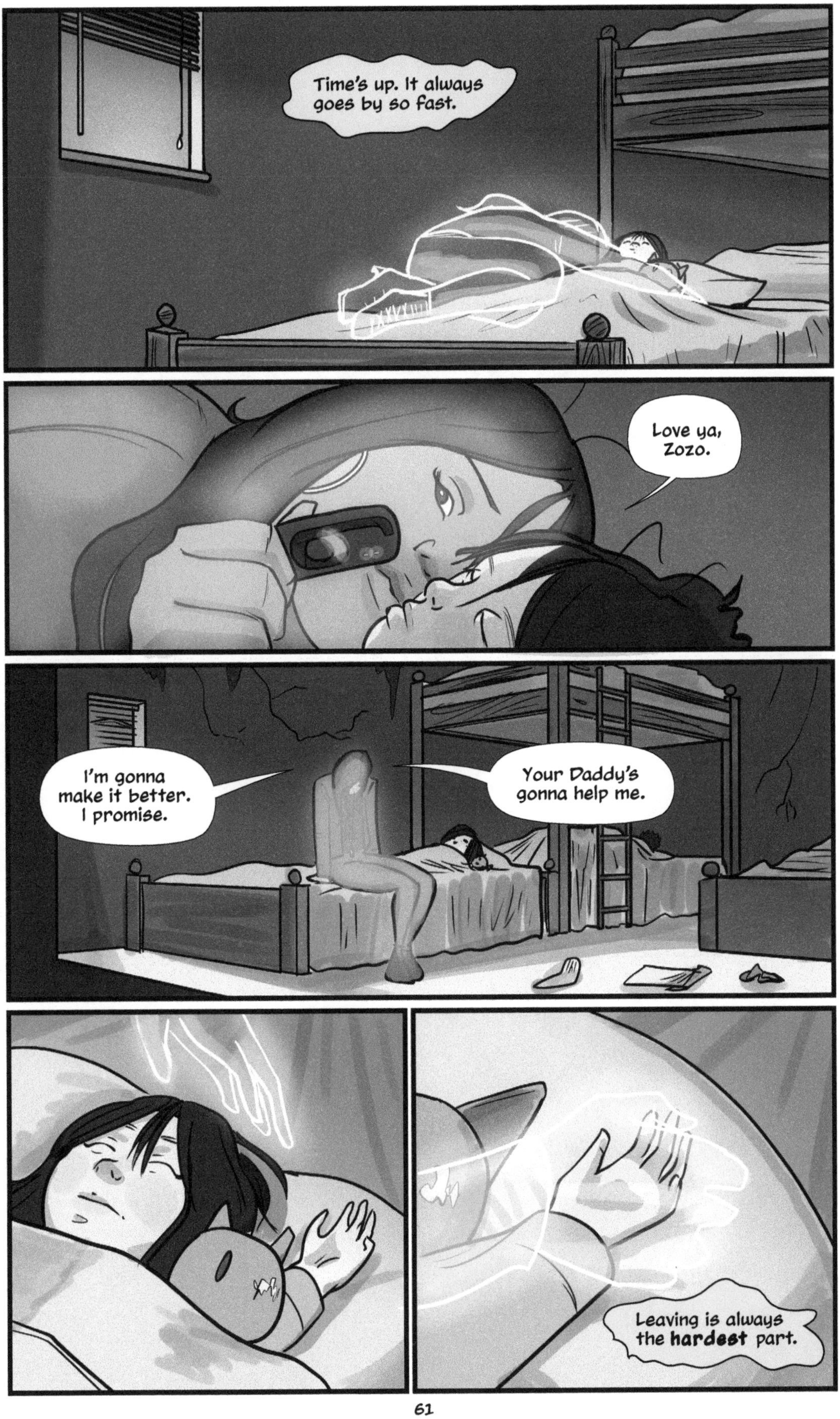
Time's up. It always goes by so fast.
Love ya, Zozo.
I'm gonna make it better. I promise.
Your Daddy's gonna help me.
Leaving is always the **hardest** part.

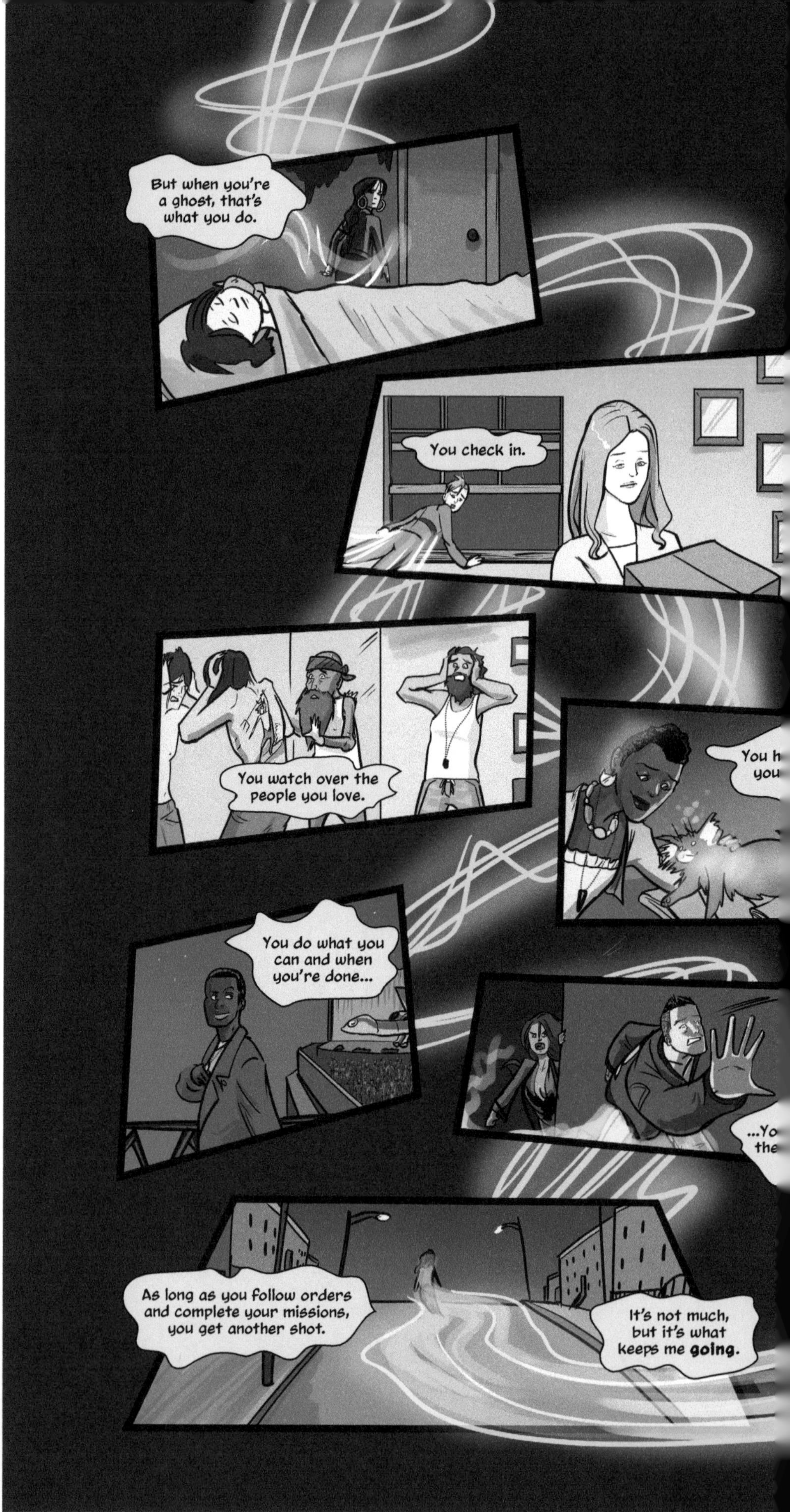

But when you're a ghost, that's what you do.
You check in.
You watch over the people you love.
You do what you can and when you're done...
As long as you follow orders and complete your missions, you get another shot.
It's not much, but it's what keeps me **going**.

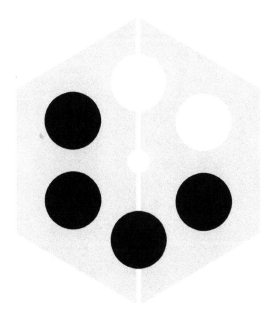

CHAPTER 4
Give Up the Ghost

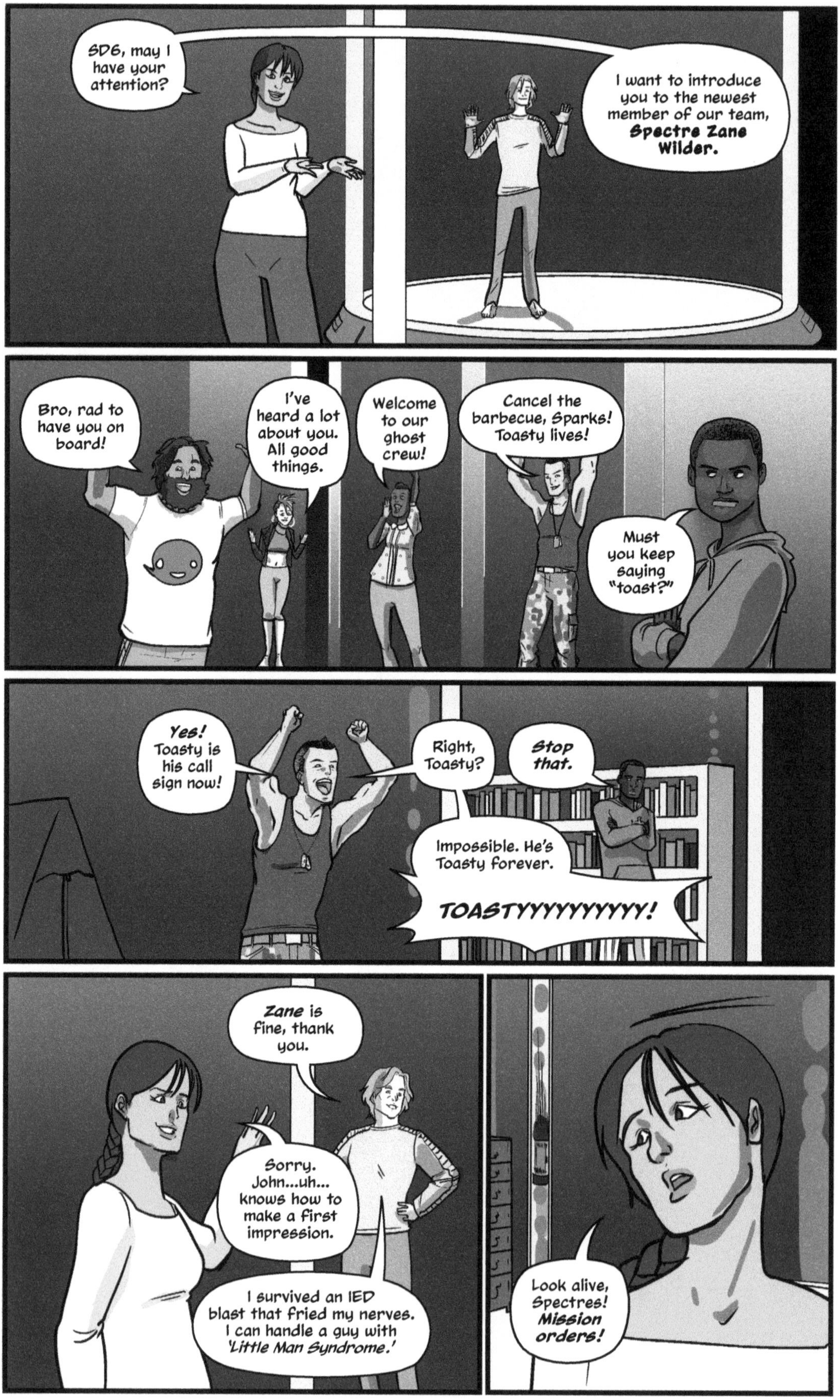
SD6, may I have your attention?
I want to introduce you to the newest member of our team, **Spectre Zane Wilder.**
Bro, rad to have you on board!
I've heard a lot about you. All good things.
Welcome to our ghost crew!
Cancel the barbecue, Sparks! Toasty lives!
Must you keep saying "toast?"
Yes! Toasty is his call sign now!
Right, Toasty?
Stop that.
Impossible. He's Toasty forever.
TOASTYYYYYYYYYY!
Zane is fine, thank you.
Sorry. John...uh... knows how to make a first impression.
I survived an IED blast that fried my nerves. I can handle a guy with *'Little Man Syndrome.'*
Look alive, Spectres! ***Mission orders!***

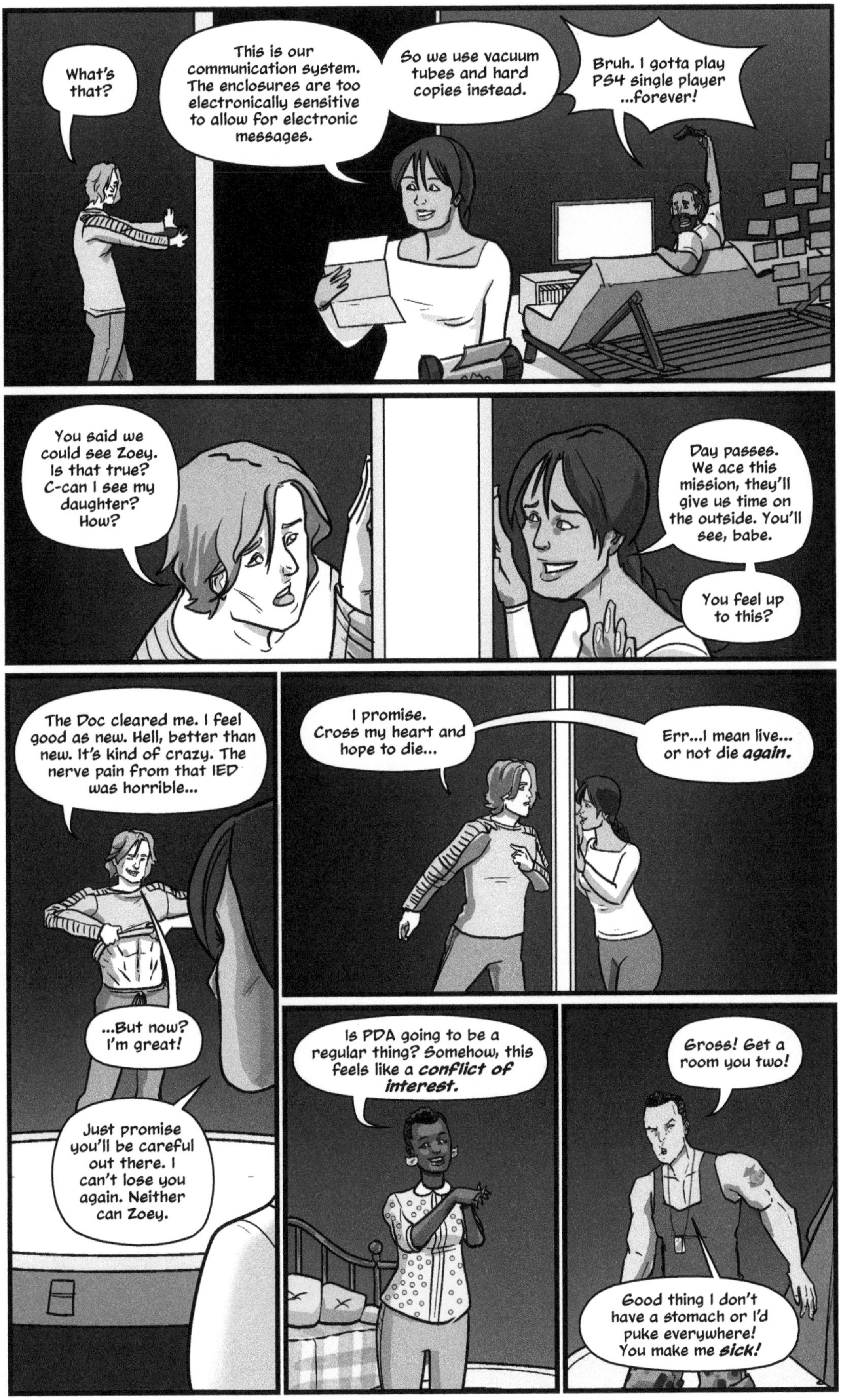
What's that?
This is our communication system. The enclosures are too electronically sensitive to allow for electronic messages.
So we use vacuum tubes and hard copies instead.
Bruh. I gotta play PS4 single player ...forever!
You said we could see Zoey. Is that true? C-can I see my daughter? How?
Day passes. We ace this mission, they'll give us time on the outside. You'll see, babe.
You feel up to this?
The Doc cleared me. I feel good as new. Hell, better than new. It's kind of crazy. The nerve pain from that IED was horrible...
...But now? I'm great!
Just promise you'll be careful out there. I can't lose you again. Neither can Zoey.
I promise. Cross my heart and hope to die...
Err...I mean live... or not die ***again.***
Is PDA going to be a regular thing? Somehow, this feels like a ***conflict of interest.***
Gross! Get a room you two!
Good thing I don't have a stomach or I'd puke everywhere! You make me ***sick!***

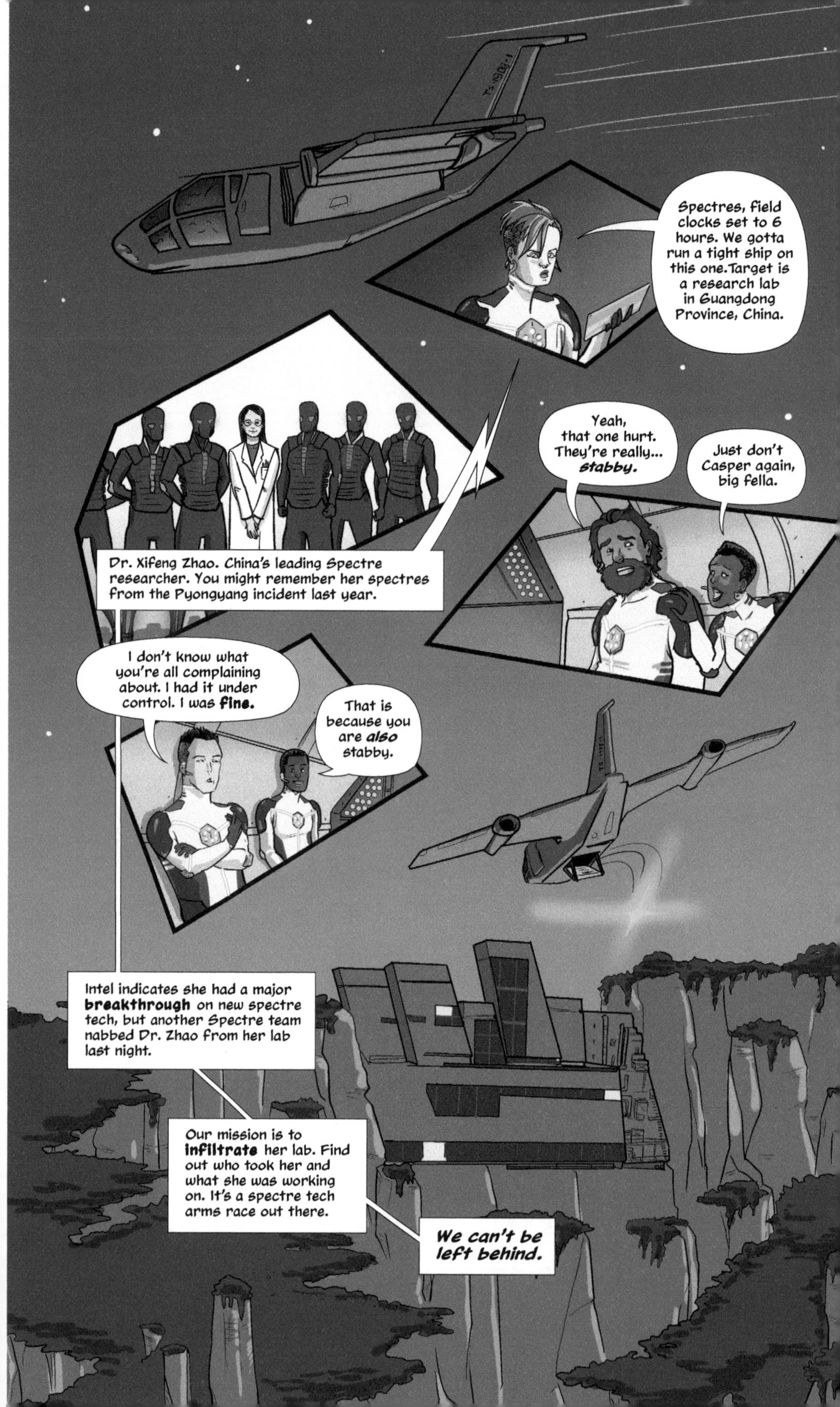
Spectres, field clocks set to 6 hours. We gotta run a tight ship on this one. Target is a research lab in Guangdong Province, China.
Dr. Xifeng Zhao. China's leading Spectre researcher. You might remember her spectres from the Pyongyang incident last year.
Yeah, that one hurt. They're really... *stabby.*
Just don't Casper again, big fella.
I don't know what you're all complaining about. I had it under control. I was **fine.**
That is because you are *also* stabby.
Intel indicates she had a major **breakthrough** on new spectre tech, but another Spectre team nabbed Dr. Zhao from her lab last night.
Our mission is to **infiltrate** her lab. Find out who took her and what she was working on. It's a spectre tech arms race out there.
We can't be left behind.

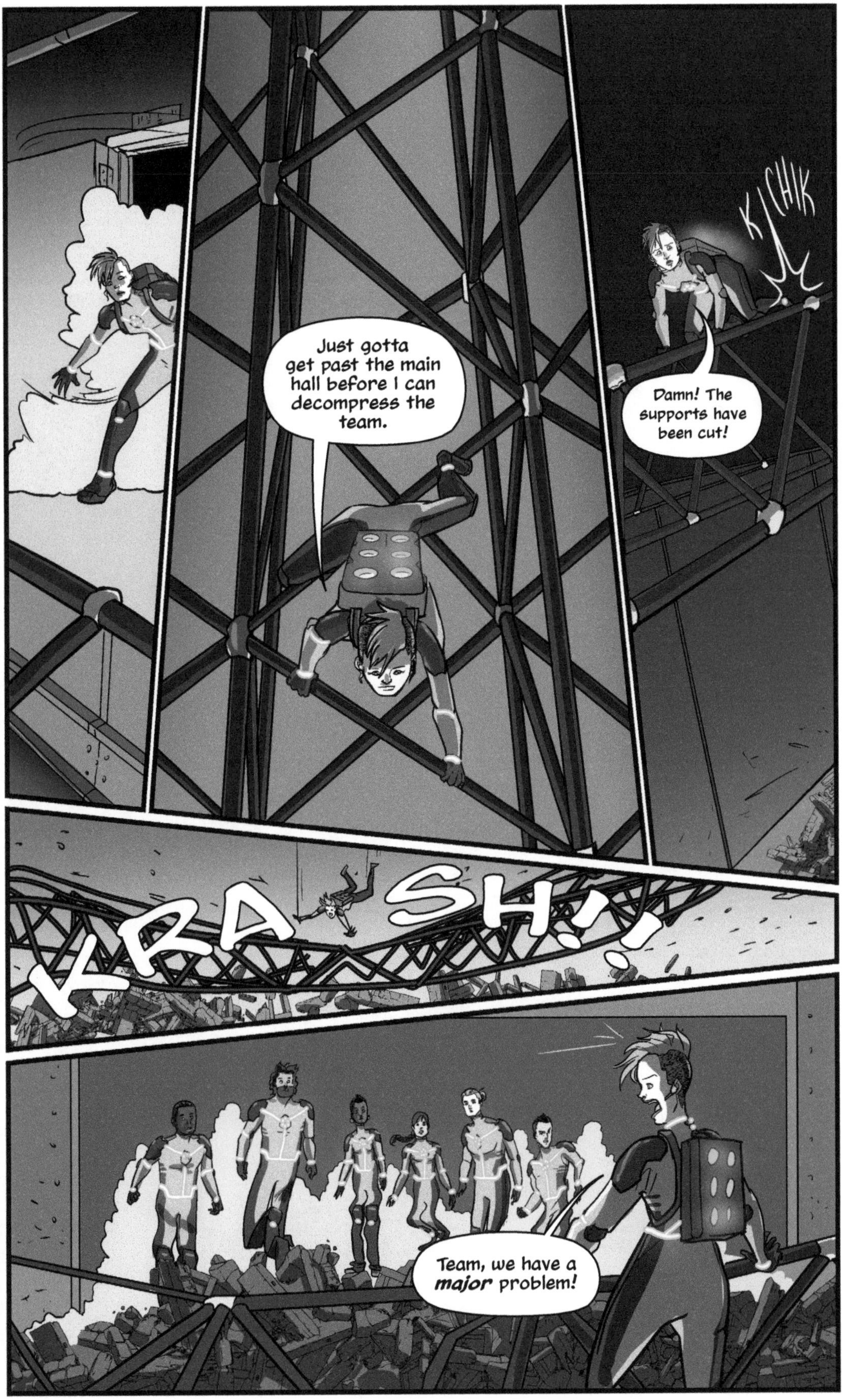
Just gotta get past the main hall before I can decompress the team.
KICHIK
Damn! The supports have been cut!
KRASH!!
Team, we have a *major* problem!

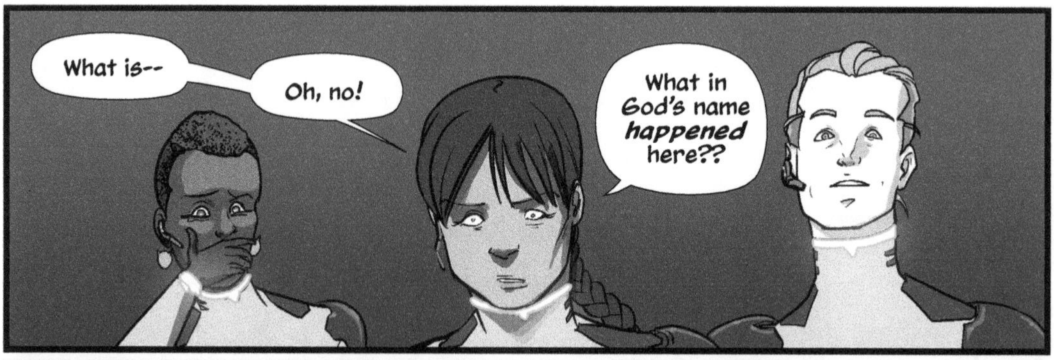
What is--
Oh, no!
What in God's name *happened* here??

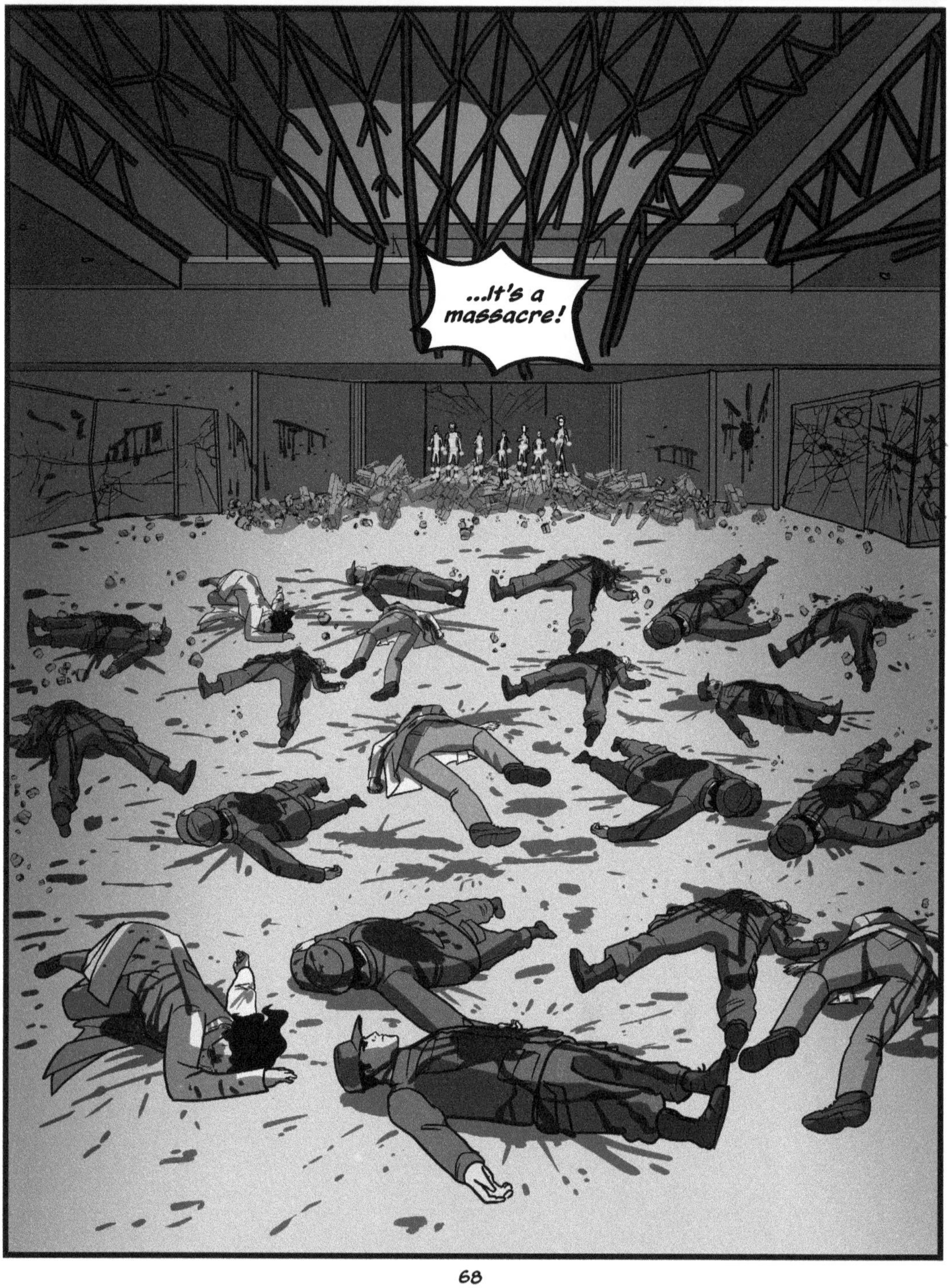
...It's a massacre!

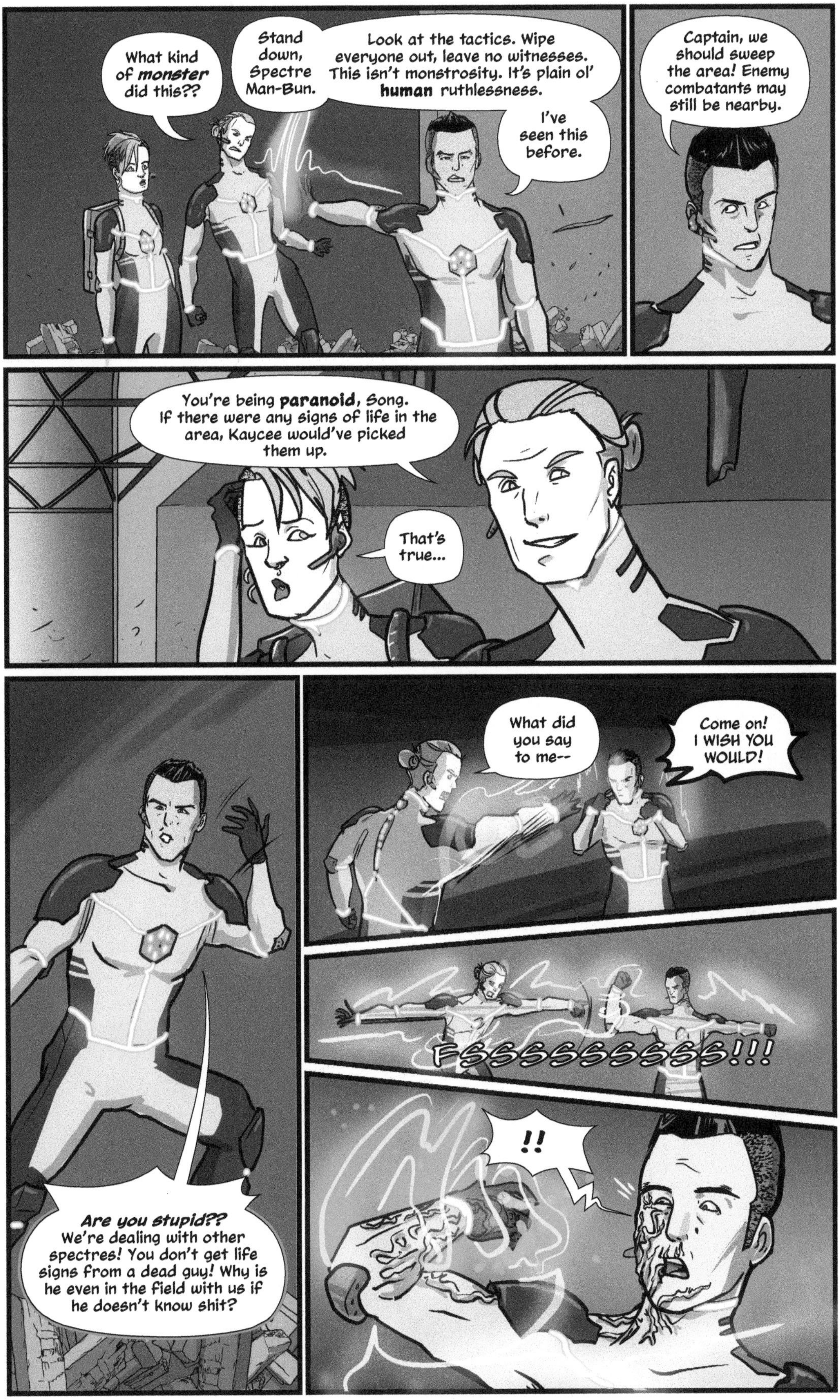
What kind of *monster* did this??
Stand down, Spectre Man-Bun.
Look at the tactics. Wipe everyone out, leave no witnesses. This isn't monstrosity. It's plain ol' **human** ruthlessness.
I've seen this before.
Captain, we should sweep the area! Enemy combatants may still be nearby.
You're being **paranoid**, Song. If there were any signs of life in the area, Kaycee would've picked them up.
That's true...
Are you stupid?? We're dealing with other spectres! You don't get life signs from a dead guy! Why is he even in the field with us if he doesn't know shit?
What did you say to me--
Come on! I WISH YOU WOULD!
FSSSSSSSSSS!!!
!!

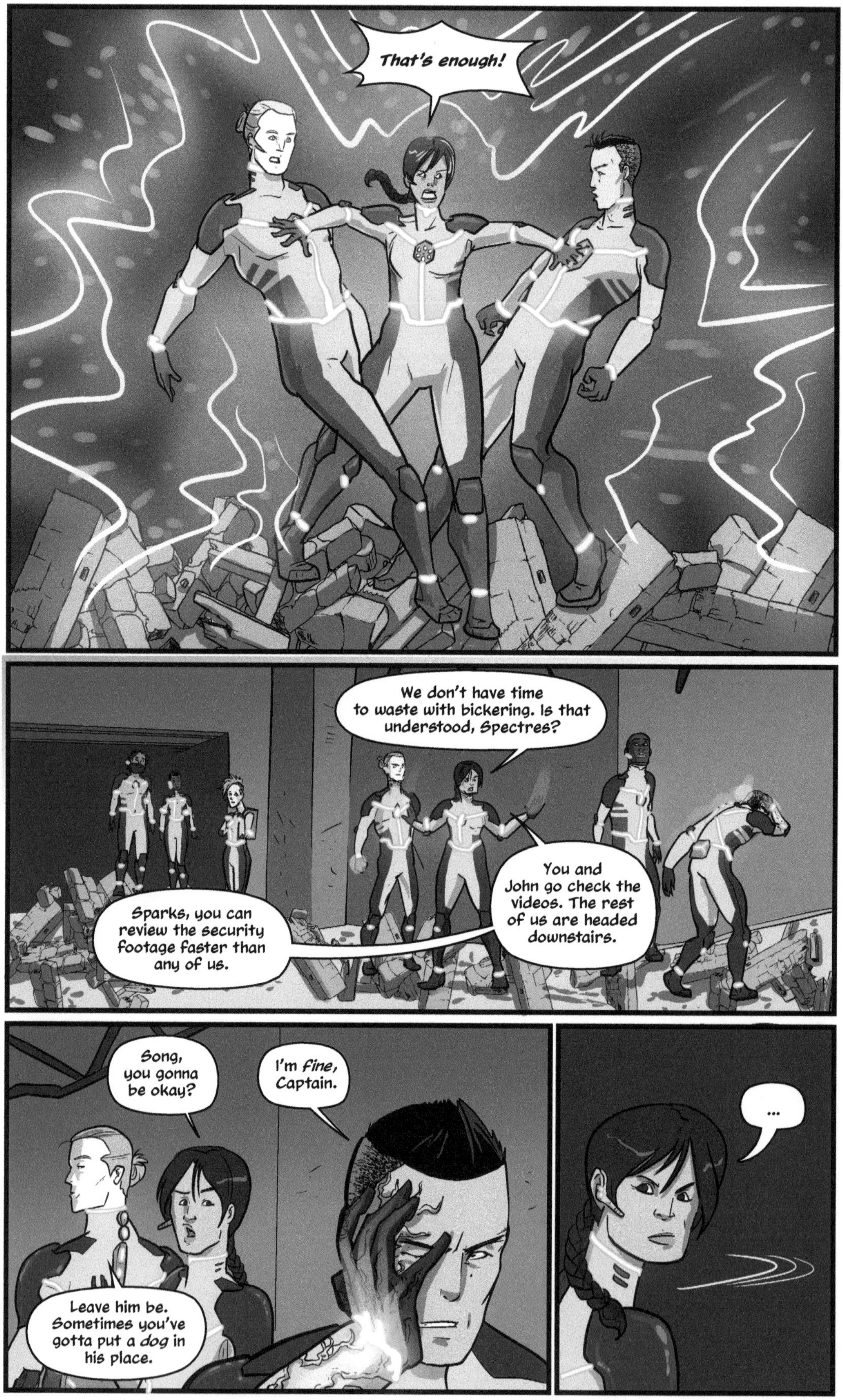
That's enough!
We don't have time to waste with bickering. Is that understood, Spectres?
Sparks, you can review the security footage faster than any of us.
You and John go check the videos. The rest of us are headed downstairs.
Song, you gonna be okay?
I'm *fine*, Captain.
Leave him be. Sometimes you've gotta put a *dog* in his place.
...

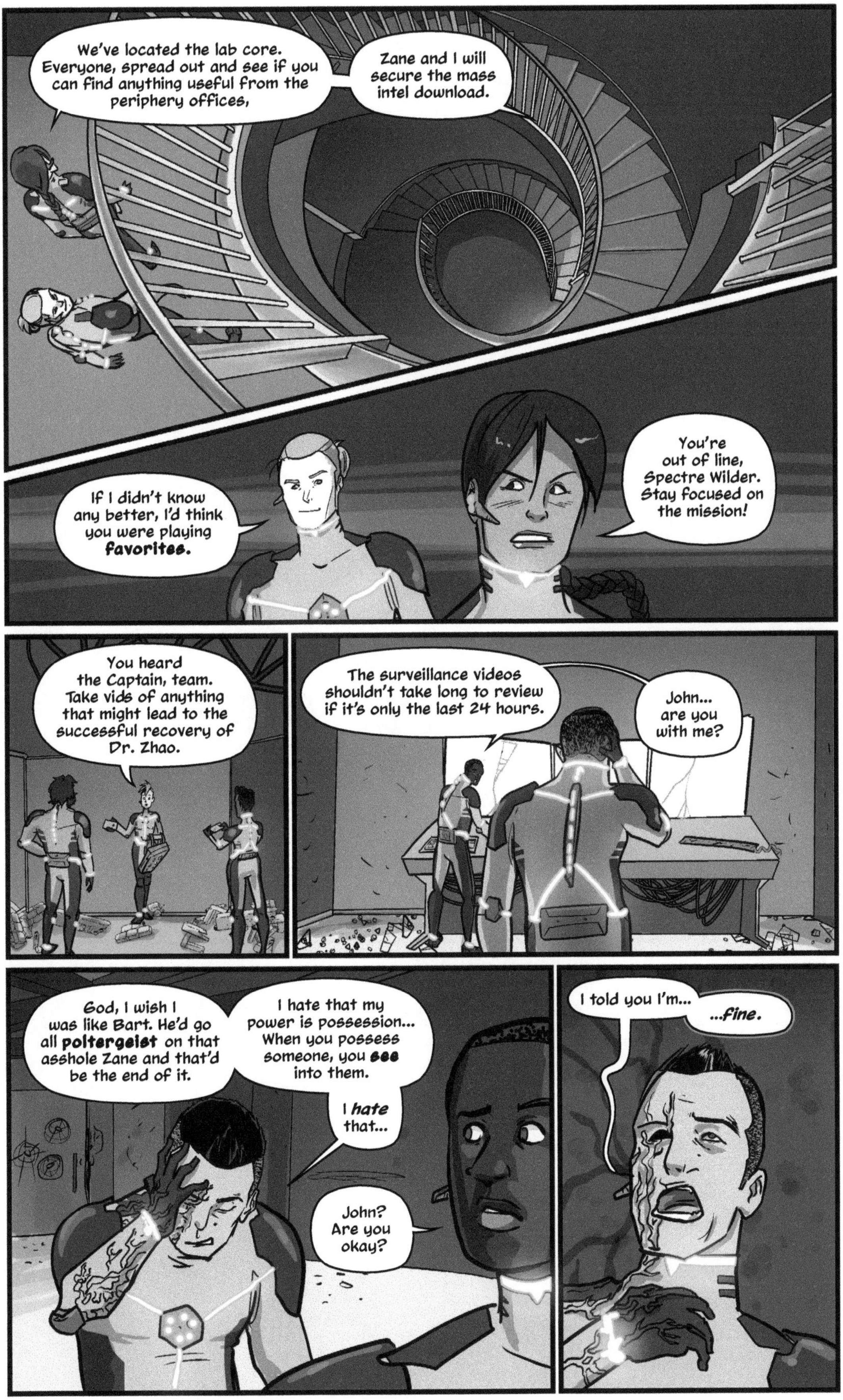
We've located the lab core. Everyone, spread out and see if you can find anything useful from the periphery offices,
Zane and I will secure the mass intel download.
If I didn't know any better, I'd think you were playing **favorites.**
You're out of line, Spectre Wilder. Stay focused on the mission!
You heard the Captain, team. Take vids of anything that might lead to the successful recovery of Dr. Zhao.
The surveillance videos shouldn't take long to review if it's only the last 24 hours.
John... are you with me?
God, I wish I was like Bart. He'd go all **poltergeist** on that asshole Zane and that'd be the end of it.
I hate that my power is possession... When you possess someone, you **see** into them.
I ***hate*** that...
John? Are you okay?
I told you I'm...
...*fine.*

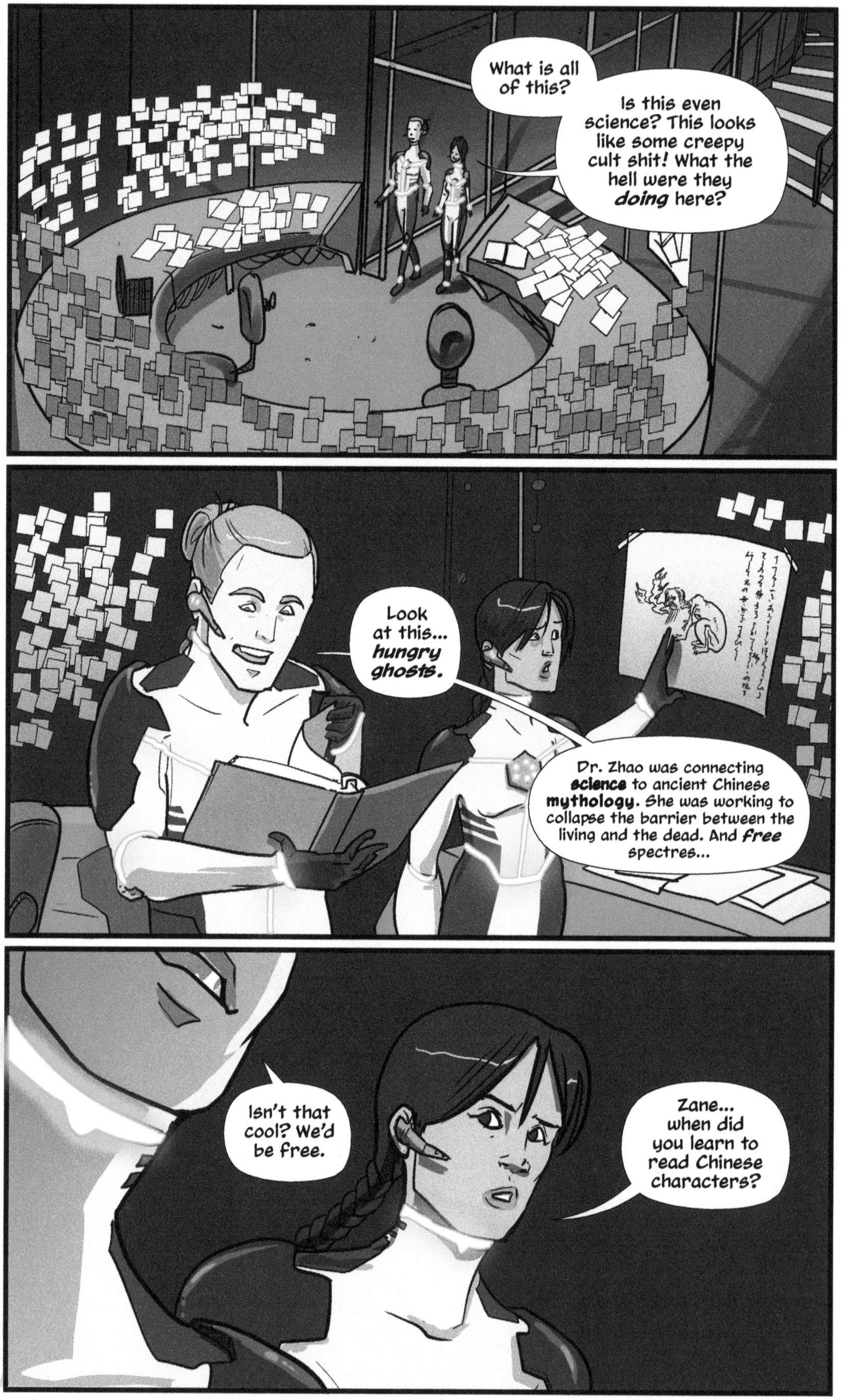
What is all of this?
Is this even science? This looks like some creepy cult shit! What the hell were they *doing* here?
Look at this... ***hungry ghosts***.
Dr. Zhao was connecting **science** to ancient Chinese **mythology**. She was working to collapse the barrier between the living and the dead. And ***free*** spectres...
Isn't that cool? We'd be free.
Zane... when did you learn to read Chinese characters?

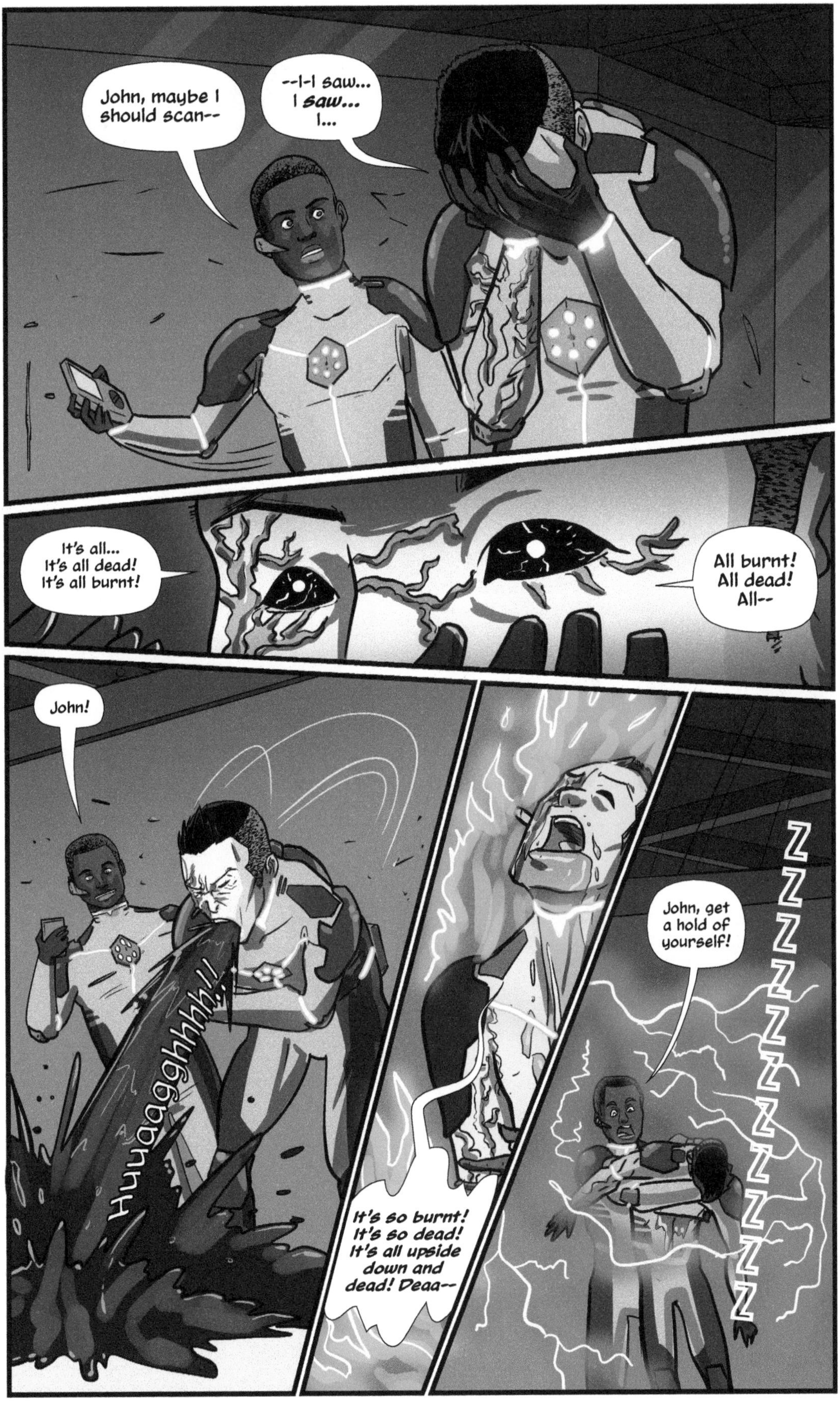
John, maybe I should scan--
--I-I saw... I *saw...* I...
It's all... It's all dead! It's all burnt!
All burnt! All dead! All--
John!
Huuaagghhh!!
It's so burnt! It's so dead! It's all upside down and dead! Deaa--
John, get a hold of yourself!
ZZZZZZZZZZZZ

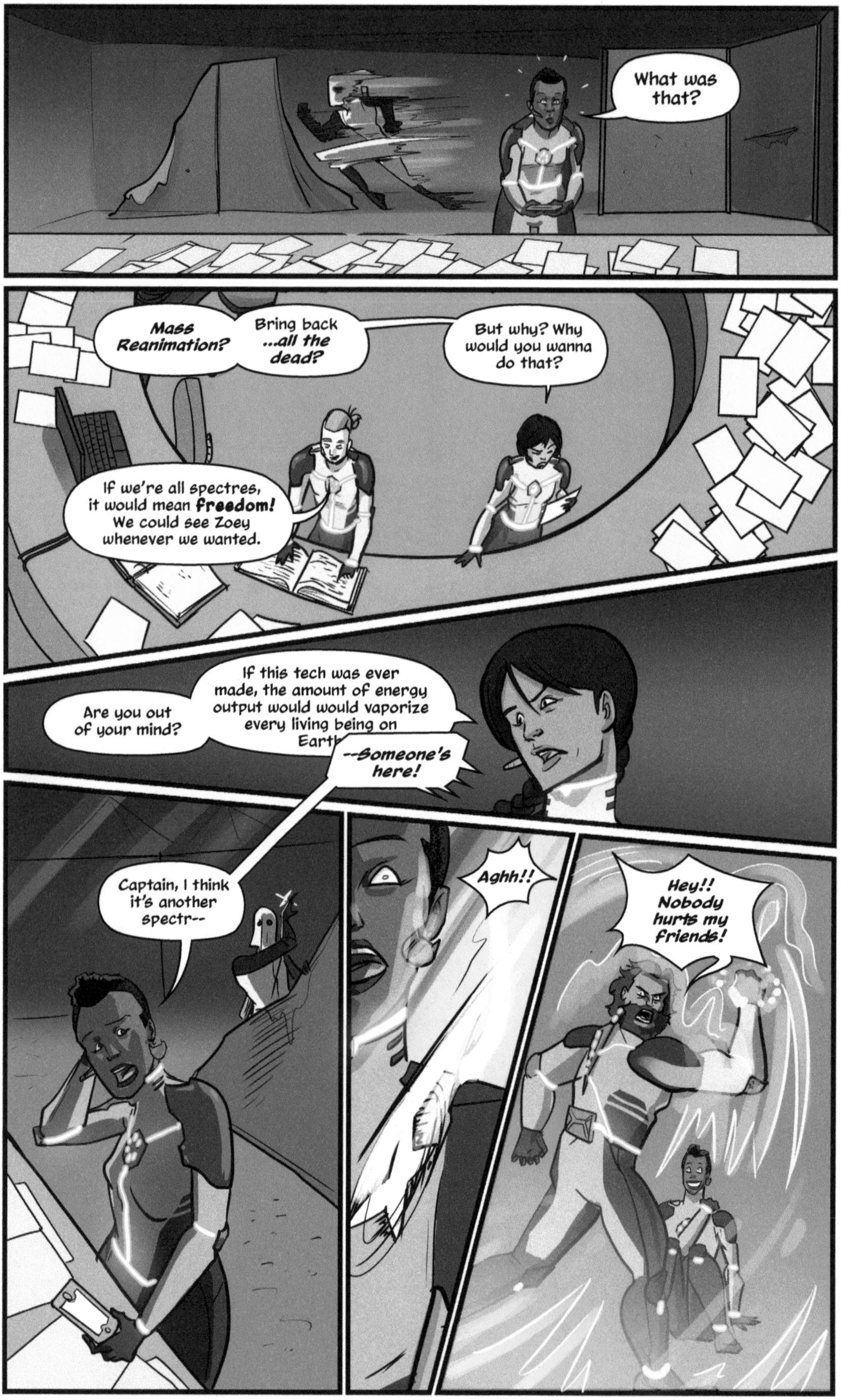
What was that?
Mass Reanimation?
Bring back ...all the dead?
But why? Why would you wanna do that?
If we're all spectres, it would mean freedom! We could see Zoey whenever we wanted.
Are you out of your mind?
If this tech was ever made, the amount of energy output would would vaporize every living being on Earth
--Someone's here!
Captain, I think it's another spectr--
Aghh!!
Hey!! Nobody hurts my friends!

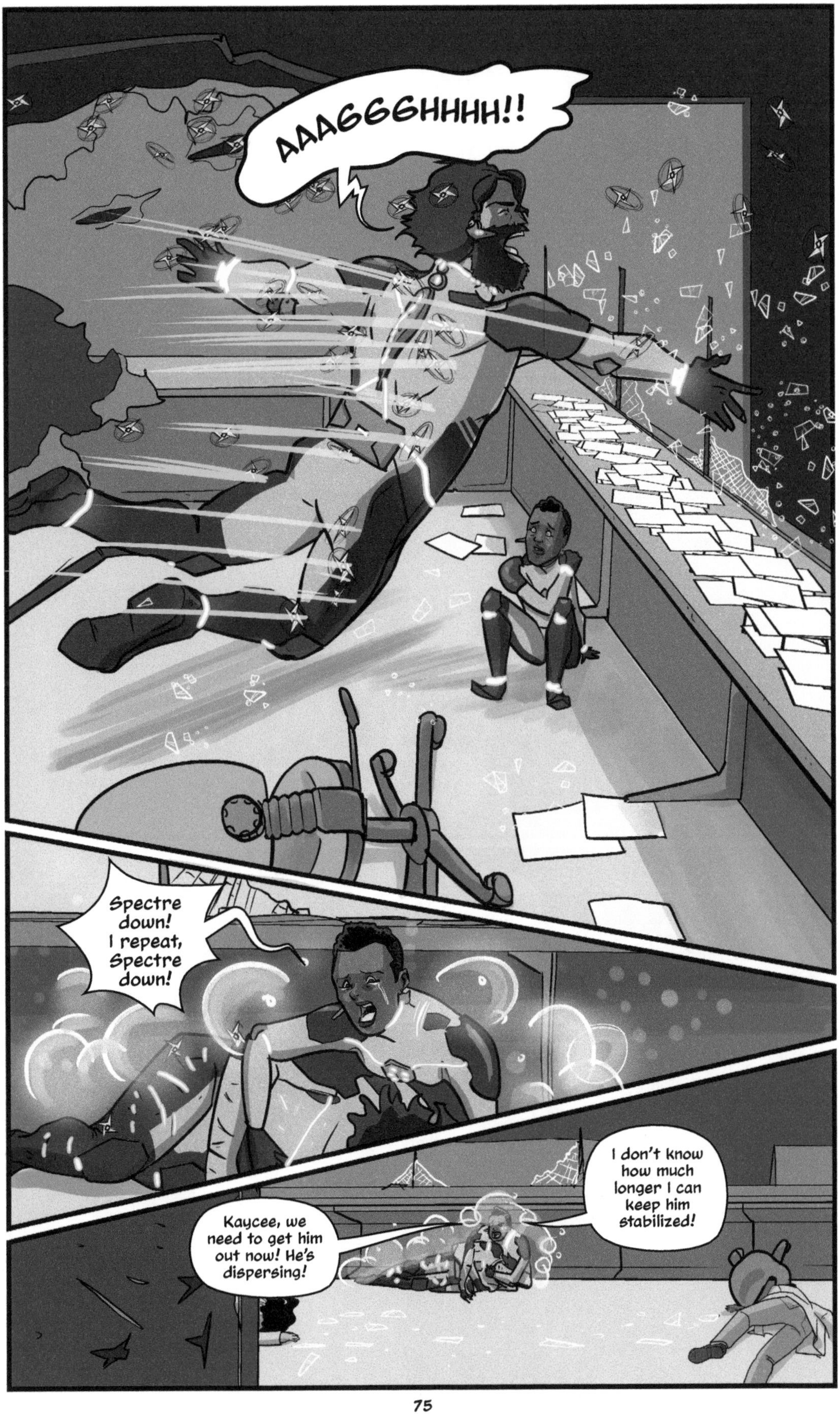
AAAGGGHHHH!!
Spectre down! I repeat, Spectre down!
Kaycee, we need to get him out now! He's dispersing!
I don't know how much longer I can keep him stabilized!

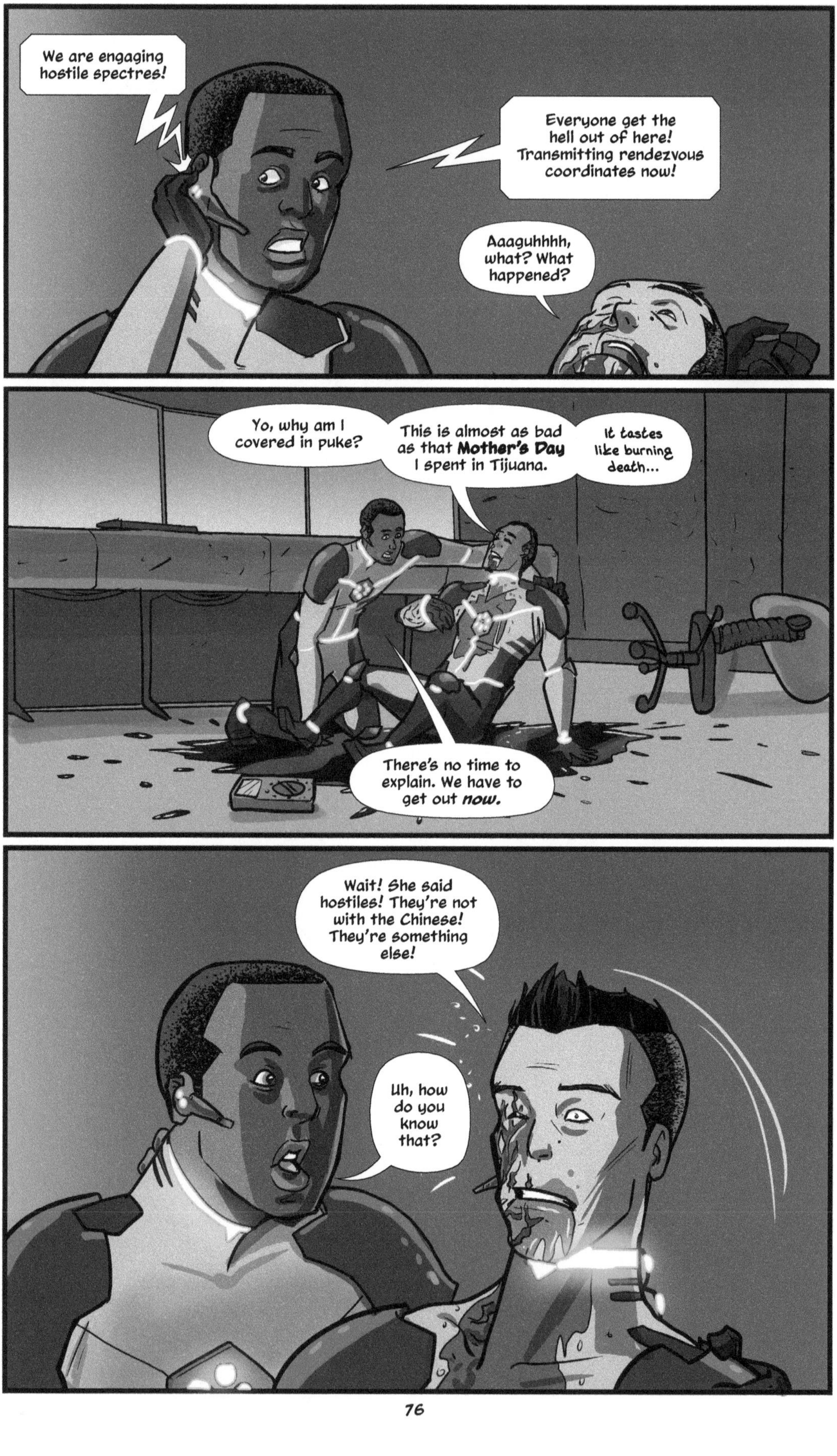
We are engaging hostile spectres!
Everyone get the hell out of here! Transmitting rendezvous coordinates now!
Aaaguhhhh, what? What happened?
Yo, why am I covered in puke?
This is almost as bad as that **Mother's Day** I spent in Tijuana.
It tastes like burning death...
There's no time to explain. We have to get out *now.*
Wait! She said hostiles! They're not with the Chinese! They're something else!
Uh, how do you know that?

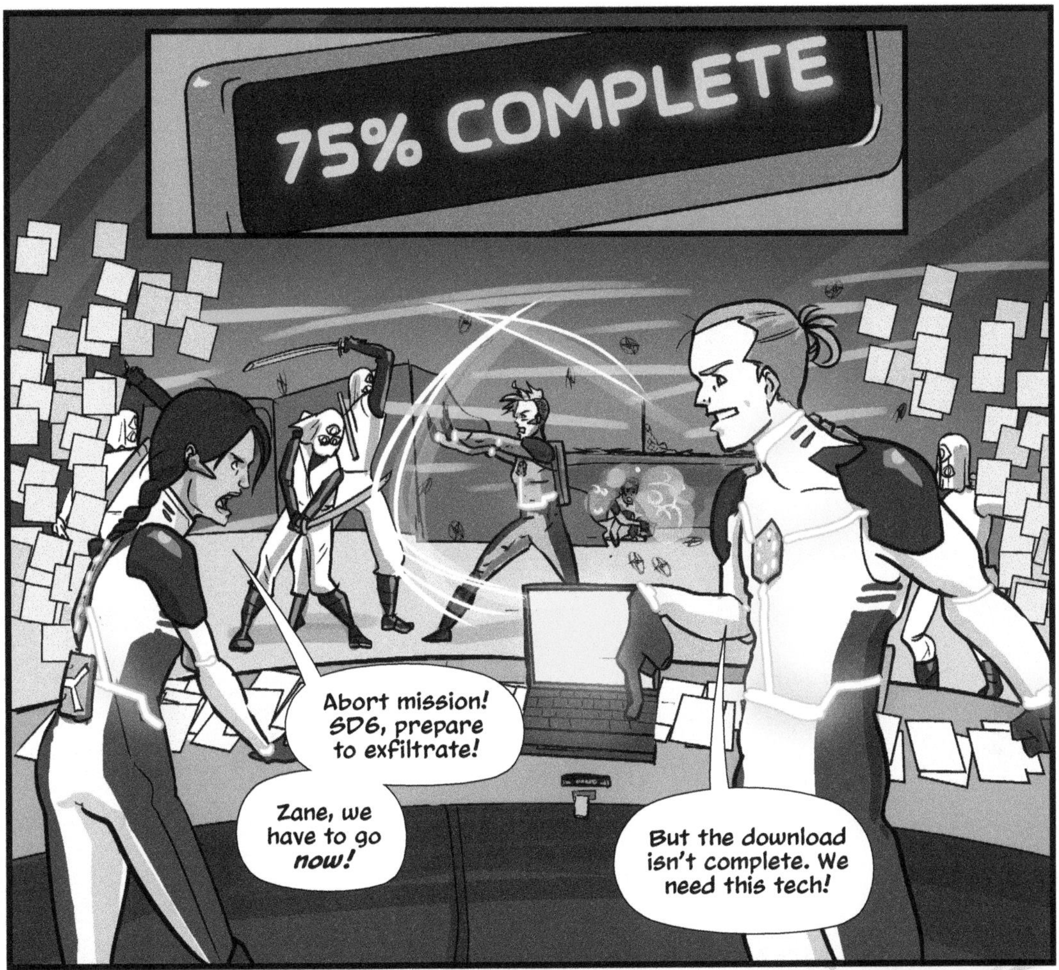
75% COMPLETE
Abort mission! SD6, prepare to exfiltrate!
Zane, we have to go *now!*
But the download isn't complete. We need this tech!

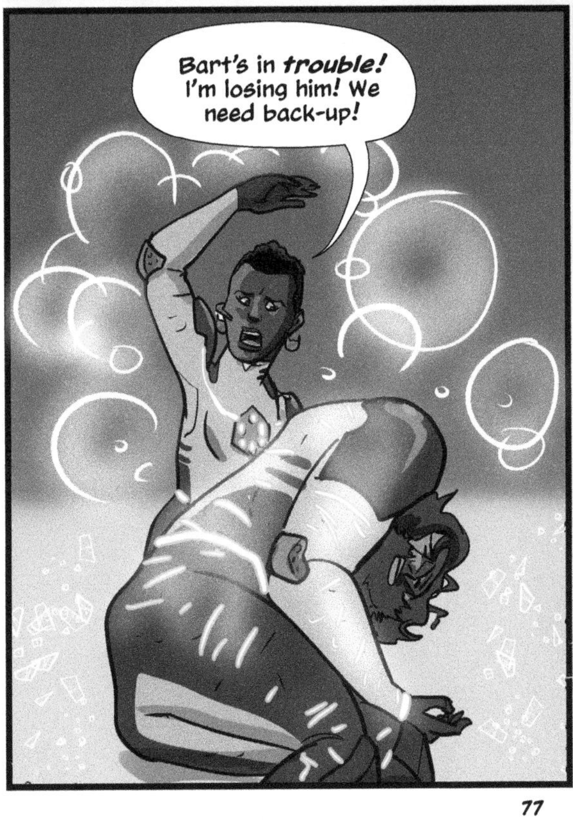
Bart's in *trouble!* I'm losing him! We need back-up!

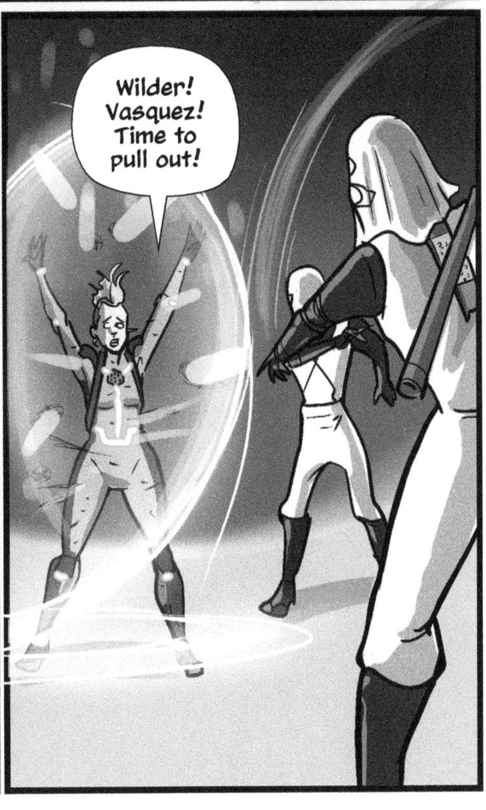
Wilder! Vasquez! Time to pull out!

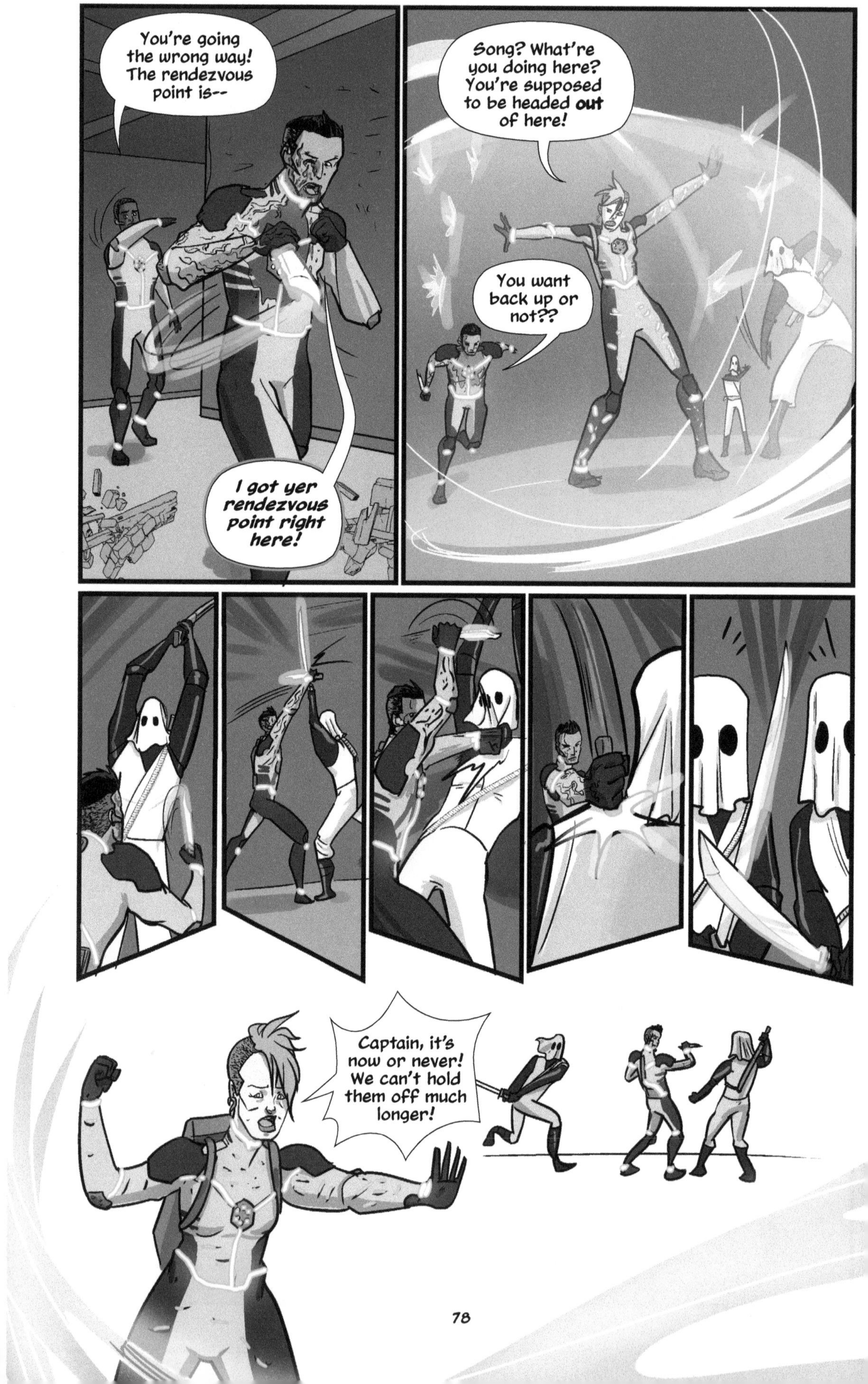
You're going the wrong way! The rendezvous point is--
I got yer rendezvous point right here!
Song? What're you doing here? You're supposed to be headed **out** of here!
You want back up or not??
Captain, it's now or never! We can't hold them off much longer!

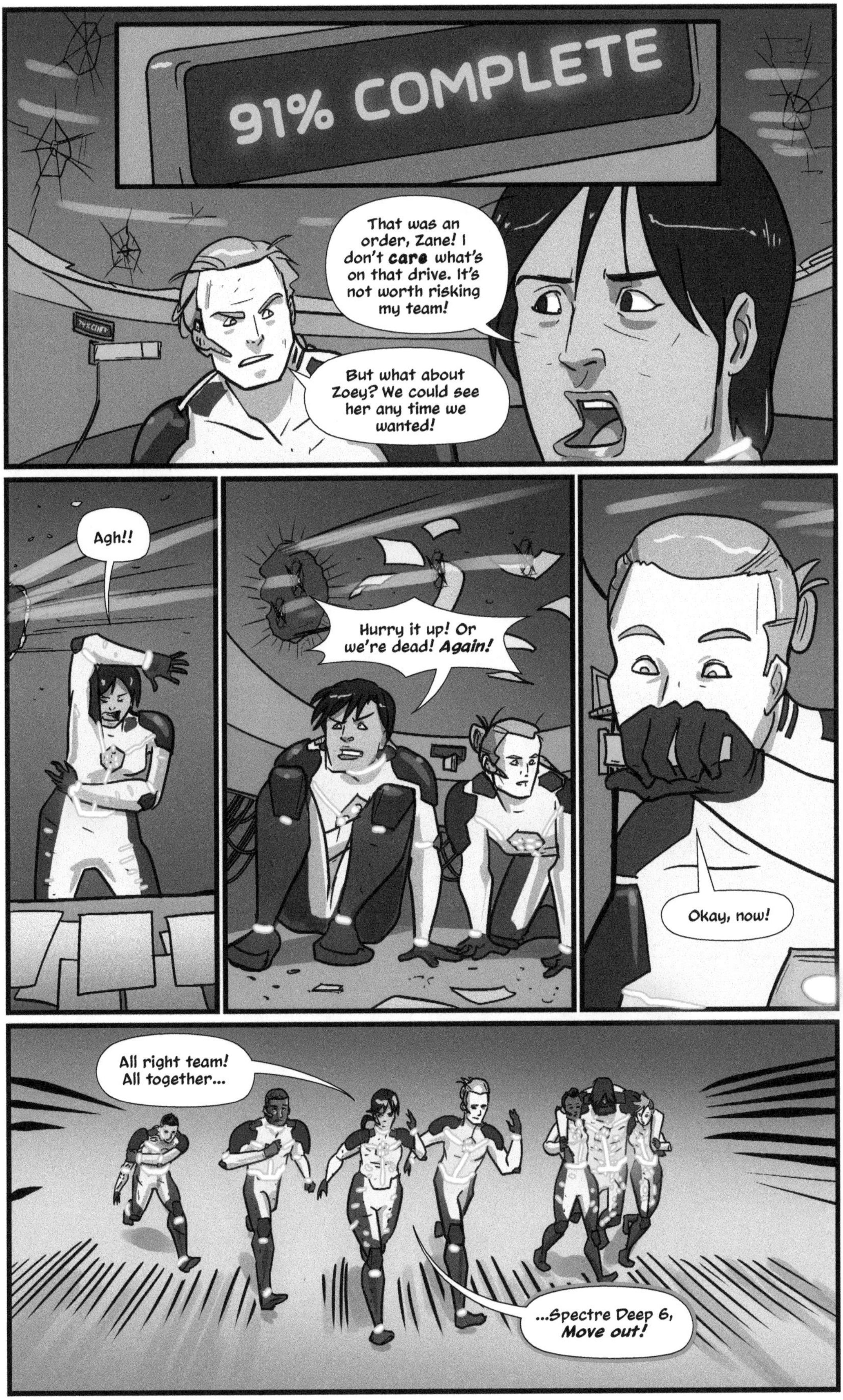
91% COMPLETE
That was an order, Zane! I don't **care** what's on that drive. It's not worth risking my team!
But what about Zoey? We could see her any time we wanted!
Agh!!
Hurry it up! Or we're dead! ***Again!***
Okay, now!
All right team! All together...
...Spectre Deep 6, ***Move out!***

Another few minutes, Bart would have fizzled out.
You're **lucky** you got back when you did.
Cap, I didn't Casper... I swear...
I know, big fella. Just rest and save your strength.
Spectre, get yourself patched up. You're hurt, too.
I know.

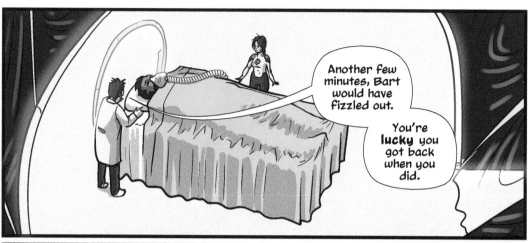

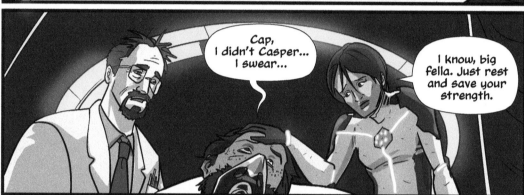

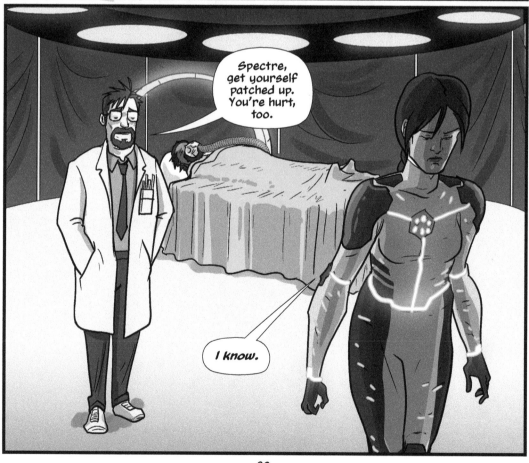

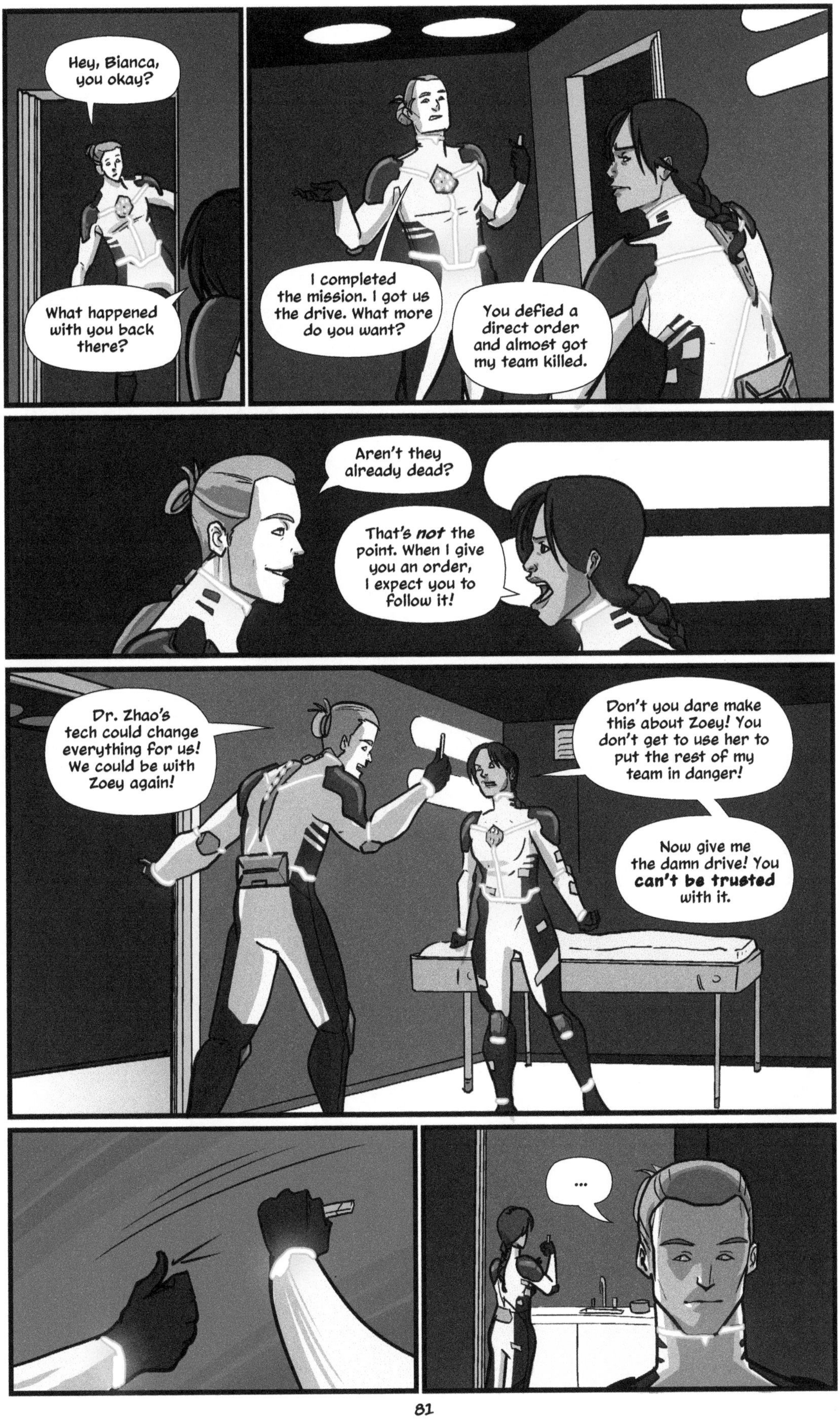
Hey, Bianca, you okay?
What happened with you back there?
I completed the mission. I got us the drive. What more do you want?
You defied a direct order and almost got my team killed.
Aren't they already dead?
That's *not* the point. When I give you an order, I expect you to follow it!
Dr. Zhao's tech could change everything for us! We could be with Zoey again!
Don't you dare make this about Zoey! You don't get to use her to put the rest of my team in danger!
Now give me the damn drive! You **can't be trusted** with it.
...

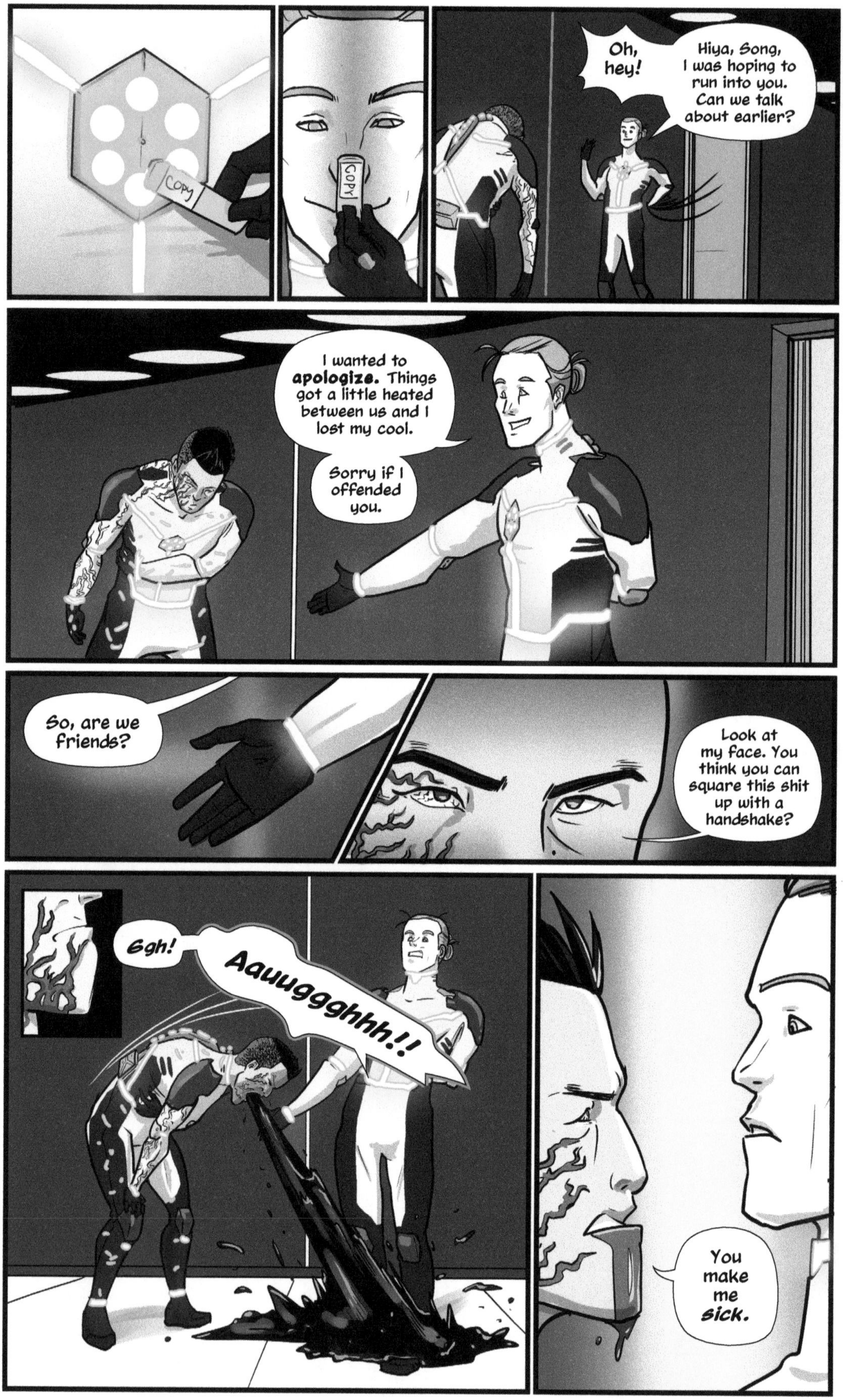
COPY
COPY
Oh, hey!
Hiya, Song, I was hoping to run into you. Can we talk about earlier?
I wanted to **apologize.** Things got a little heated between us and I lost my cool.
Sorry if I offended you.
So, are we friends?
Look at my face. You think you can square this shit up with a handshake?
Ggh!
Aauuggghhh!!
You make me *sick.*

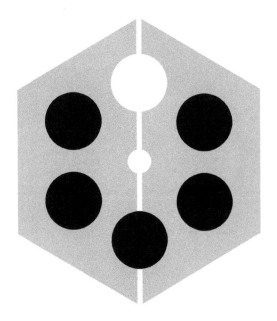

CHAPTER 5
Everybody Haunts II

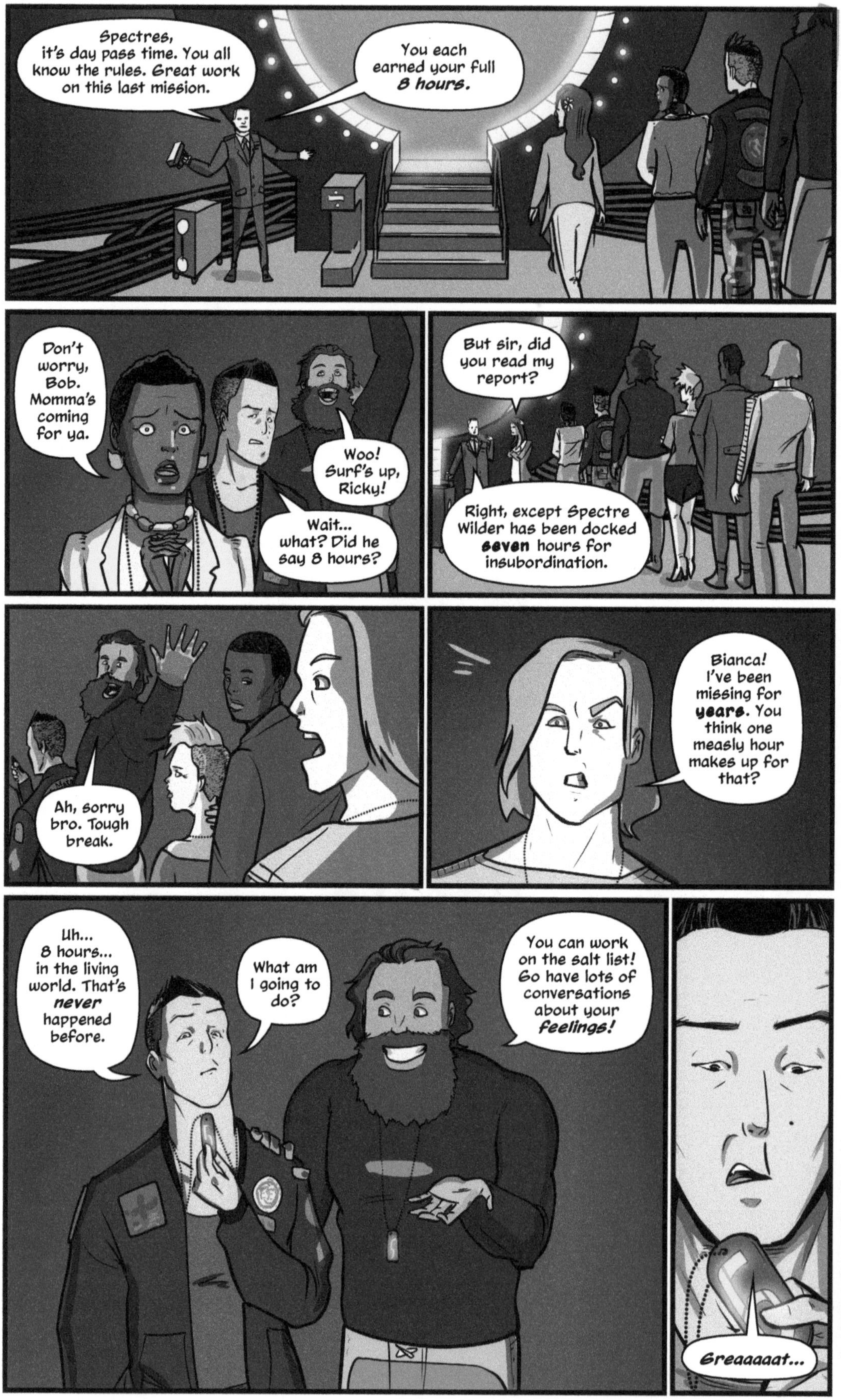

Spectres, it's day pass time. You all know the rules. Great work on this last mission.
You each earned your full *8 hours.*
Don't worry, Bob. Momma's coming for ya.
Woo! Surf's up, Ricky!
Wait... what? Did he say 8 hours?
But sir, did you read my report?
Right, except Spectre Wilder has been docked **seven** hours for insubordination.
Ah, sorry bro. Tough break.
Bianca! I've been missing for **years**. You think one measly hour makes up for that?
Uh... 8 hours... in the living world. That's *never* happened before.
What am I going to do?
You can work on the salt list! Go have lots of conversations about your *feelings!*
Greaaaaat...

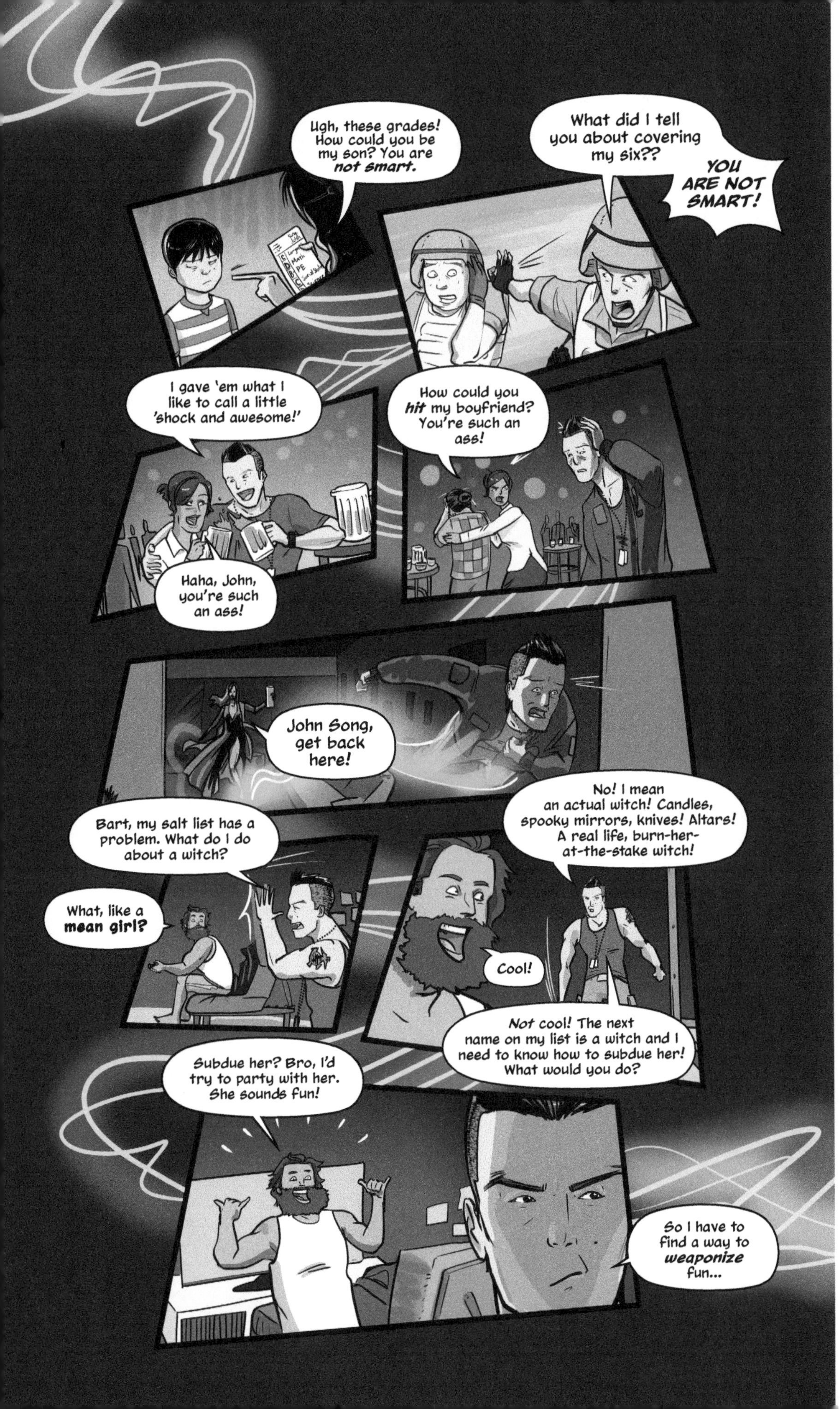

Ugh, these grades! How could you be my son? You are *not smart.*
What did I tell you about covering my six??
YOU ARE NOT SMART!
I gave 'em what I like to call a little 'shock and awesome!'
Haha, John, you're such an ass!
How could you *hit* my boyfriend? You're such an ass!
John Song, get back here!
Bart, my salt list has a problem. What do I do about a witch?
What, like a **mean girl?**
No! I mean an actual witch! Candles, spooky mirrors, knives! Altars! A real life, burn-her-at-the-stake witch!
Cool!
Not cool! The next name on my list is a witch and I need to know how to subdue her! What would you do?
Subdue her? Bro, I'd try to party with her. She sounds fun!
So I have to find a way to *weaponize* fun...

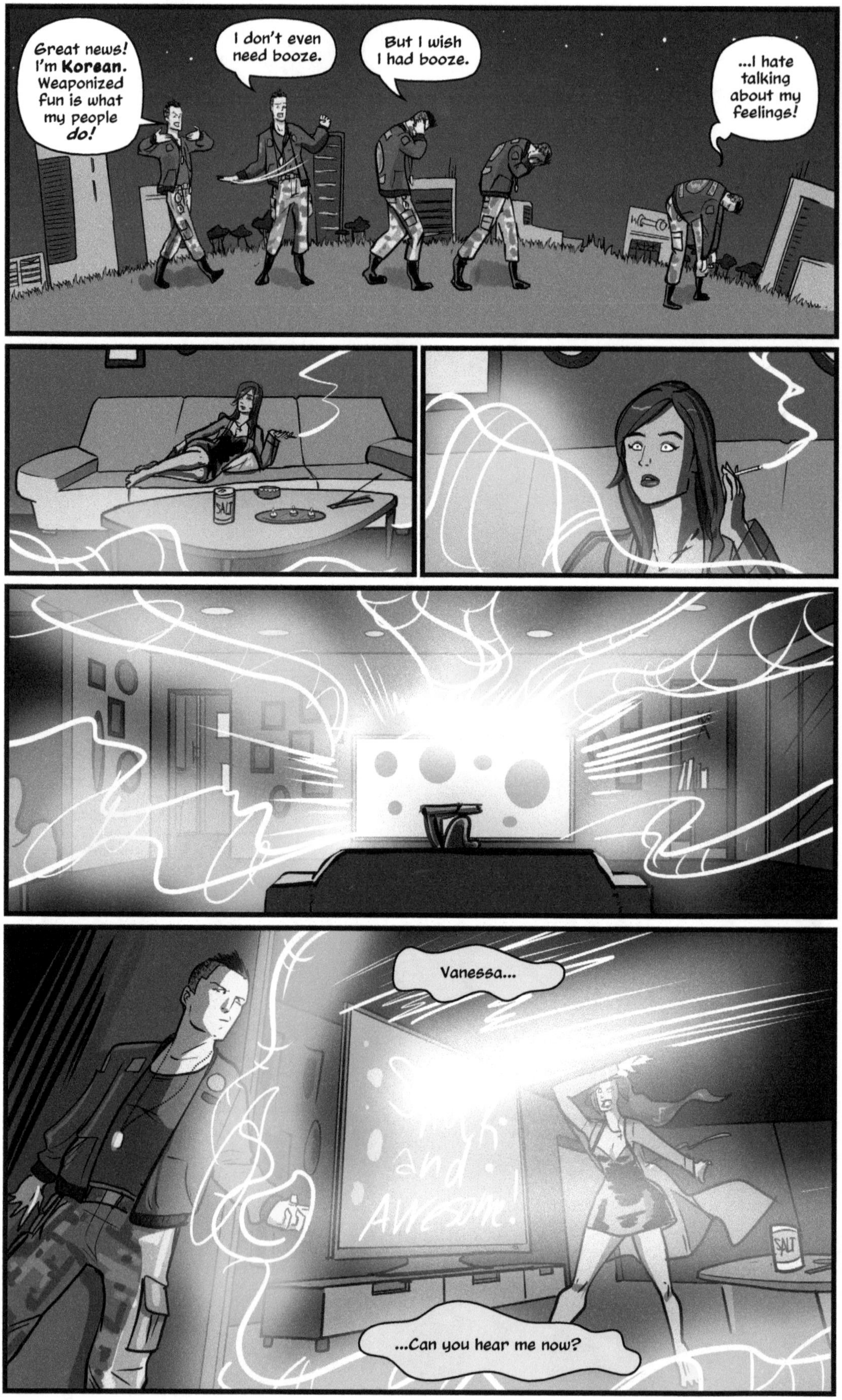
Great news! I'm **Korean**. Weaponized fun is what my people *do!*
I don't even need booze.
But I wish I had booze.
...I hate talking about my feelings!
Vanessa...
...Can you hear me now?

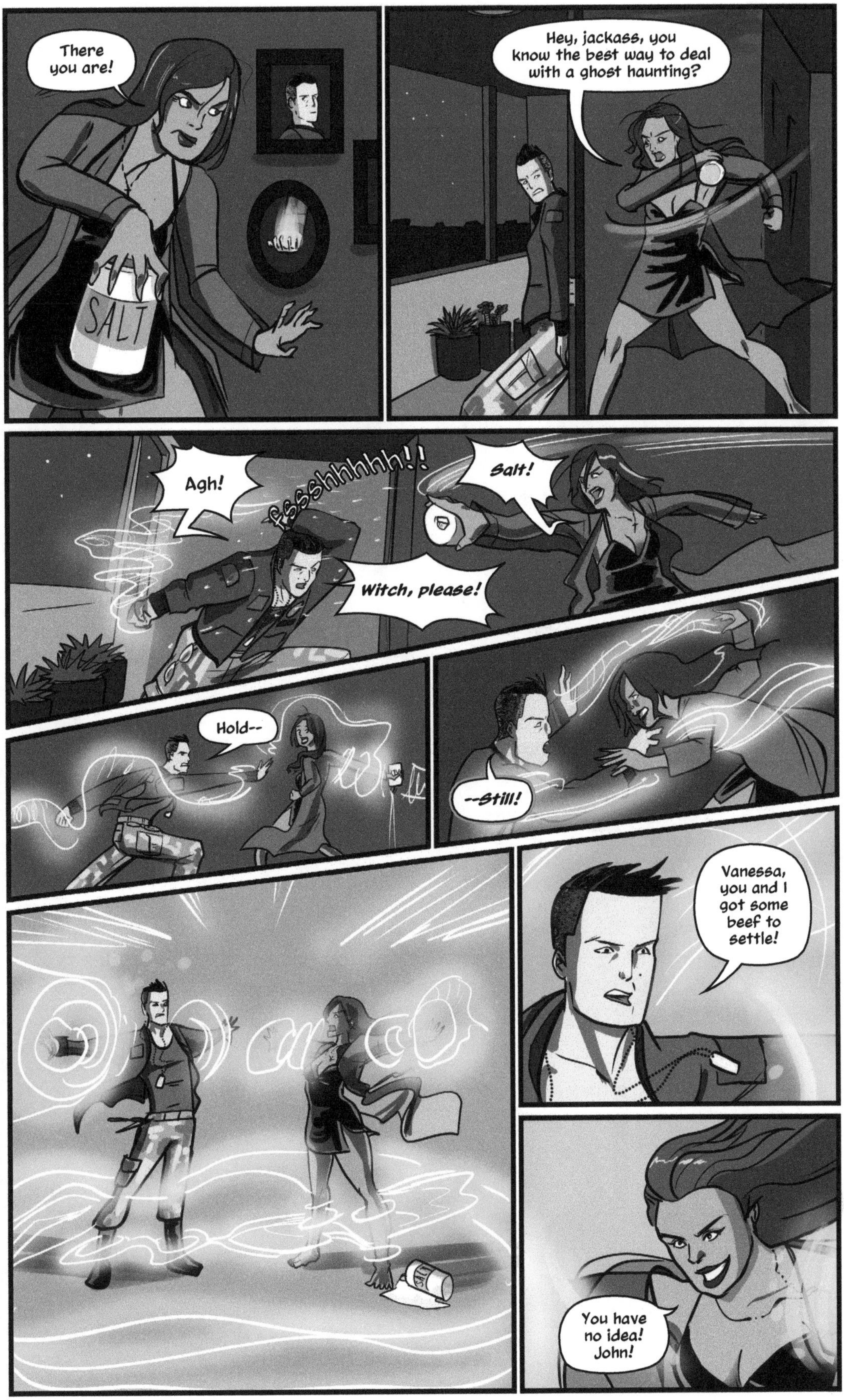
There you are!
Hey, jackass, you know the best way to deal with a ghost haunting?
Agh!
FSSSHHHHH!!
Salt!
Witch, please!
Hold--
--Still!
Vanessa, you and I got some beef to settle!
You have no idea! John!

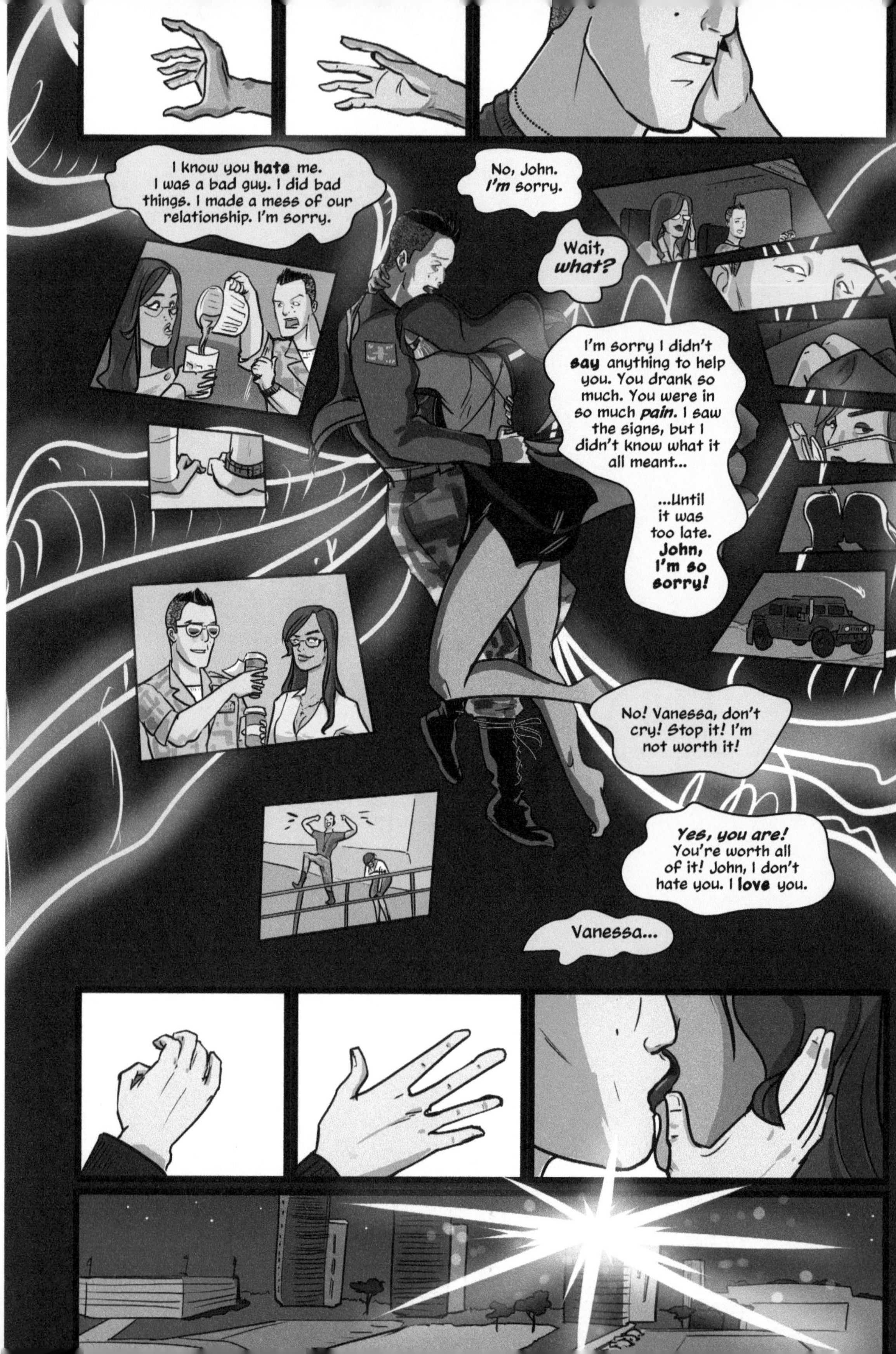
I know you **hate** me. I was a bad guy. I did bad things. I made a mess of our relationship. I'm sorry.
No, John. ***I'm*** sorry.
Wait, ***what?***
I'm sorry I didn't **say** anything to help you. You drank so much. You were in so much ***pain***. I saw the signs, but I didn't know what it all meant...
...Until it was too late. **John, I'm so sorry!**
No! Vanessa, don't cry! Stop it! I'm not worth it!
Yes, you are! You're worth all of it! John, I don't hate you. I **love** you.
Vanessa...

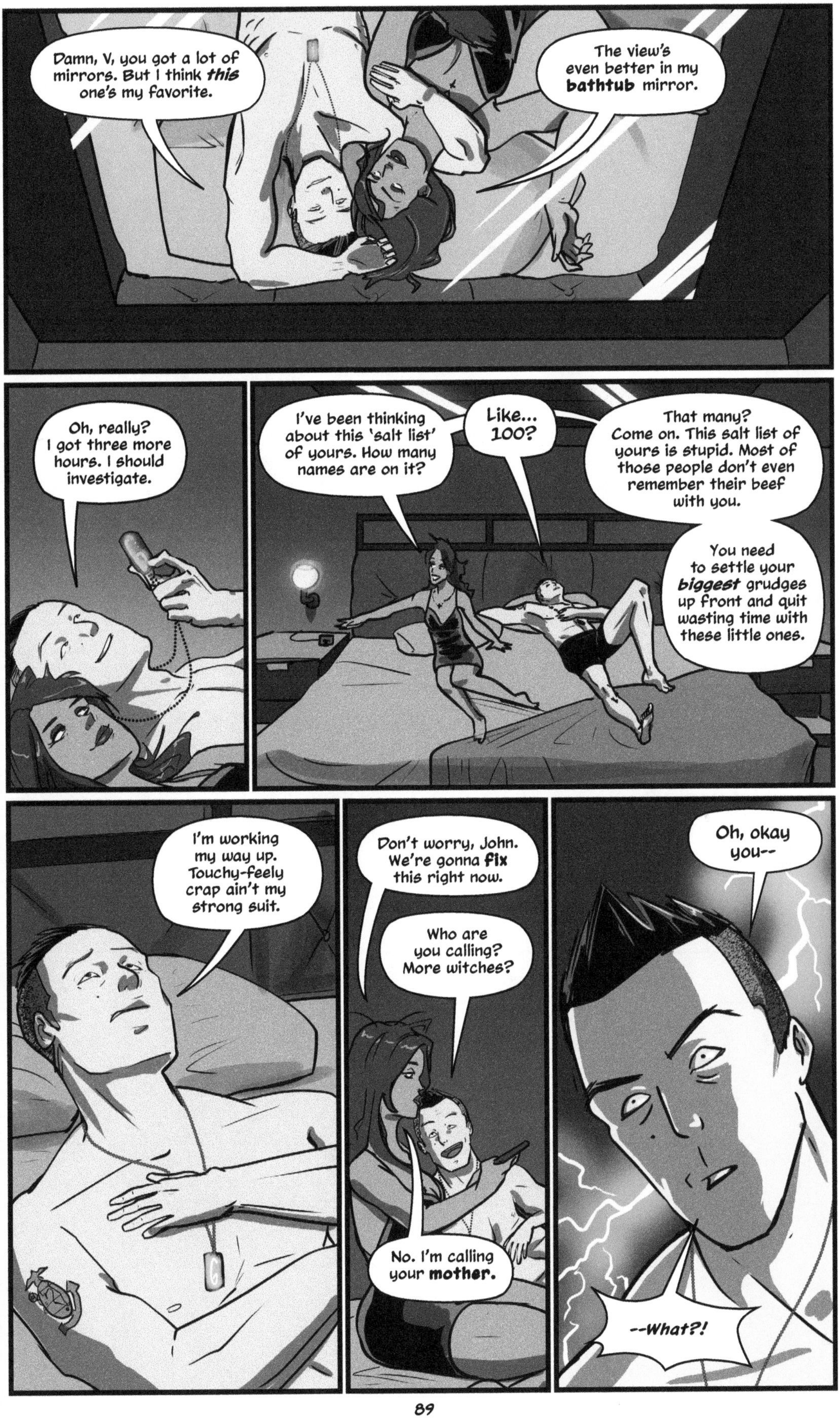
Damn, V, you got a lot of mirrors. But I think *this* one's my favorite.
The view's even better in my **bathtub** mirror.
Oh, really? I got three more hours. I should investigate.
I've been thinking about this 'salt list' of yours. How many names are on it?
Like... 100?
That many? Come on. This salt list of yours is stupid. Most of those people don't even remember their beef with you.
You need to settle your *biggest* grudges up front and quit wasting time with these little ones.
I'm working my way up. Touchy-feely crap ain't my strong suit.
Don't worry, John. We're gonna **fix** this right now.
Who are you calling? More witches?
No. I'm calling your **mother.**
Oh, okay you--
--*What?!*

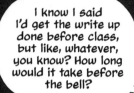

I know I said I'd get the write up done before class, but like, whatever, you know? How long would it take before the bell?

Maybe it's better if I do the lab write ups...

...for the rest of the year.

Come on, Sparks. From what you tell me, there's no way everyone's happy at SipherTech. You've gotta have a little troublemaker in there.

Someone's gotta be looking to blow the whistle. If they get your data packet, they can send it out to the media.

Kim, calling the media is not like calling in an airstrike--

I *love* airstrikes!

Exposure is a long, drawn out process. Sandra Sipher has already proven she's willing to take out whistleblowers. I can't risk someone else dying on my account.

I have enough **roommates.**

But it takes a two-faced *liar* to build a case against someone like Sandra Sipher. It takes time and receipts.

You need someone who can play the dutiful employee while slowly destroying them.

You sound like you've done this before.

I might've systematically **poisoned** some people.

I don't hate the idea of a turncoat...

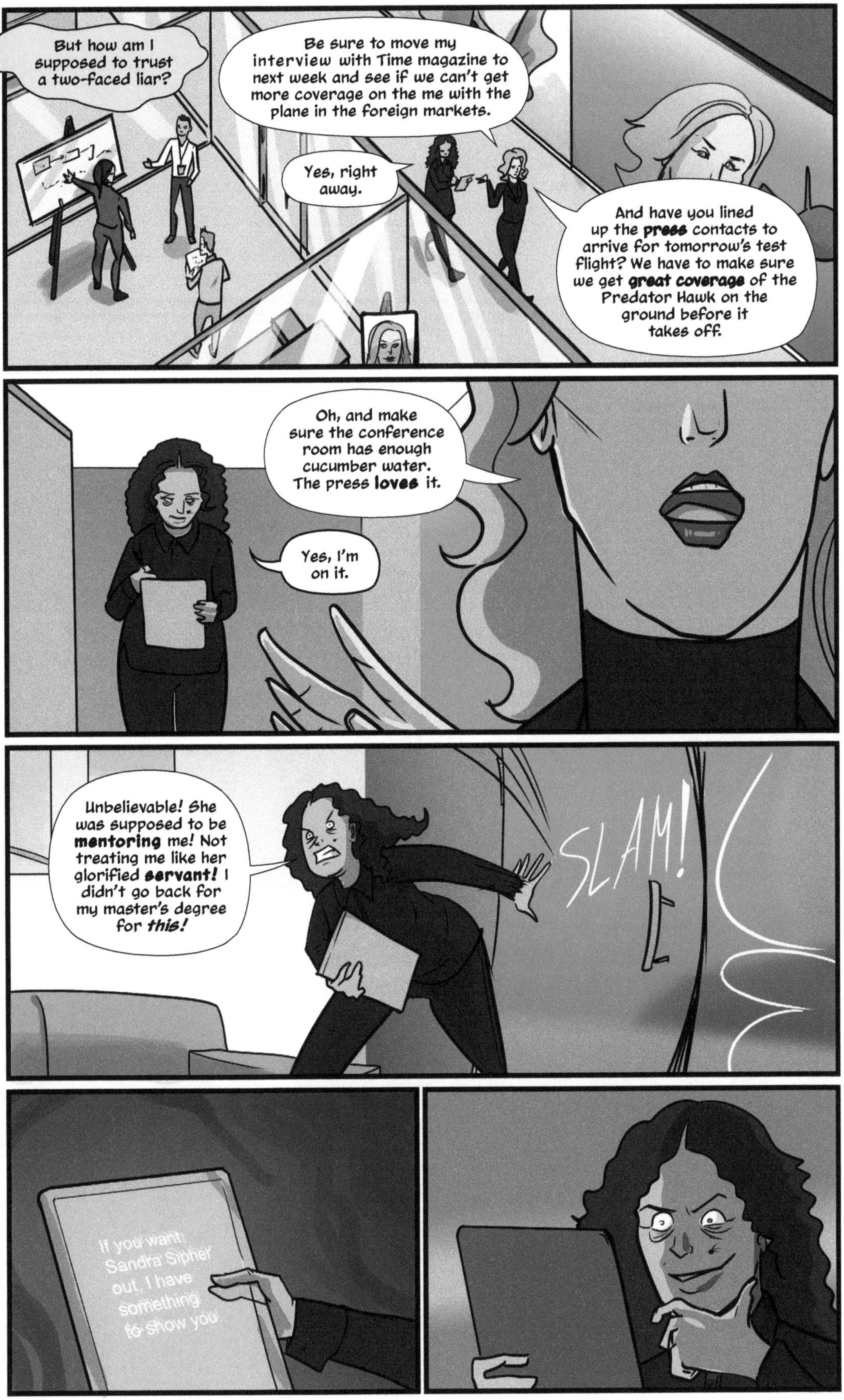
But how am I supposed to trust a two-faced liar?
Be sure to move my interview with Time magazine to next week and see if we can't get more coverage on the me with the plane in the foreign markets.
Yes, right away.
And have you lined up the **press** contacts to arrive for tomorrow's test flight? We have to make sure we get **great coverage** of the Predator Hawk on the ground before it takes off.
Oh, and make sure the conference room has enough cucumber water. The press **loves** it.
Yes, I'm on it.
Unbelievable! She was supposed to be **mentoring** me! Not treating me like her glorified **servant!** I didn't go back for my master's degree for ***this!***
SLAM!
If you want Sandra Sipher out, I have something to show you.

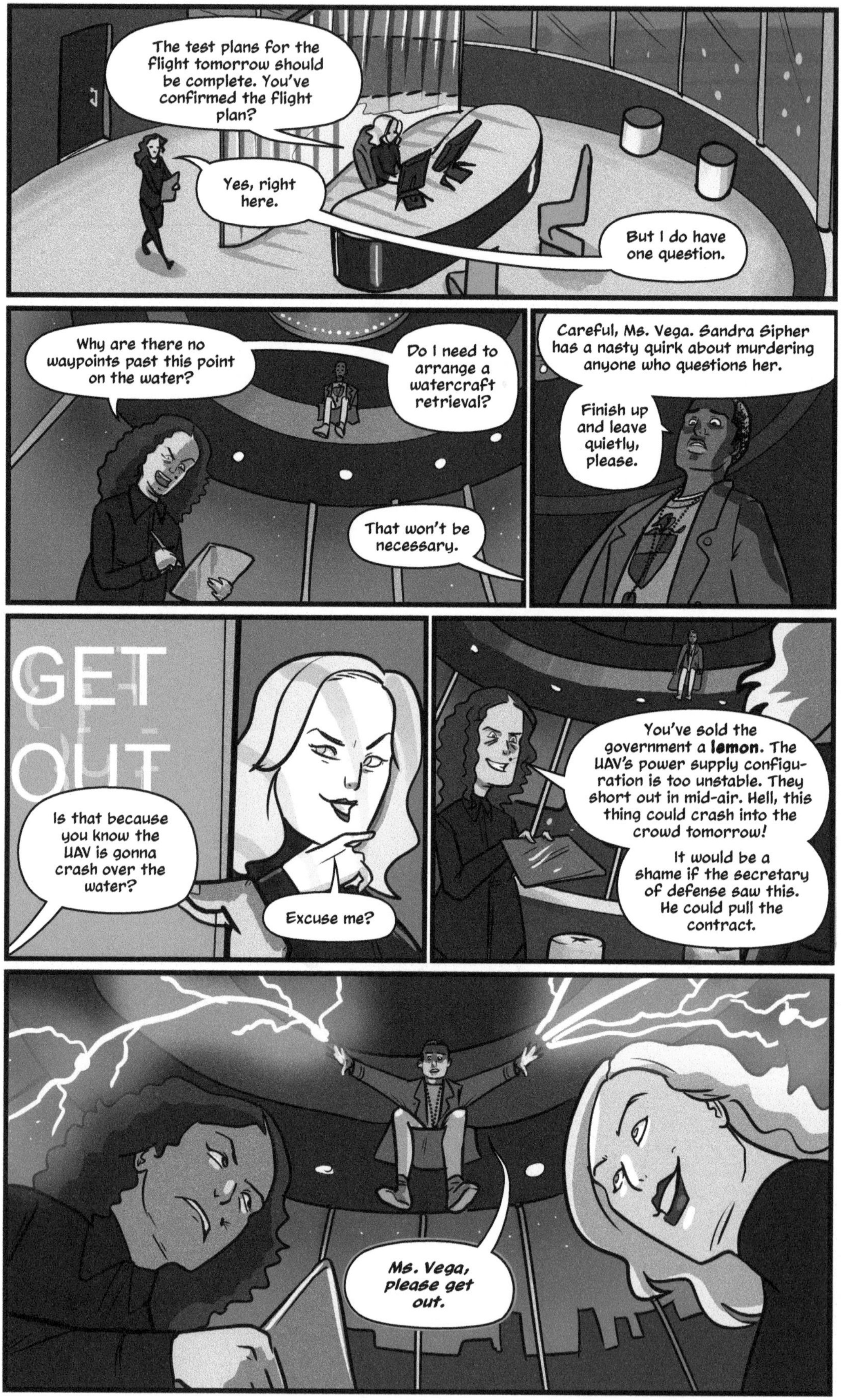

The test plans for the flight tomorrow should be complete. You've confirmed the flight plan?
Yes, right here.
But I do have one question.
Why are there no waypoints past this point on the water?
Do I need to arrange a watercraft retrieval?
That won't be necessary.
Careful, Ms. Vega. Sandra Sipher has a nasty quirk about murdering anyone who questions her.
Finish up and leave quietly, please.
GET OUT
Is that because you know the UAV is gonna crash over the water?
Excuse me?
You've sold the government a **lemon**. The UAV's power supply configuration is too unstable. They short out in mid-air. Hell, this thing could crash into the crowd tomorrow!
It would be a shame if the secretary of defense saw this. He could pull the contract.
Ms. Vega, please get out.

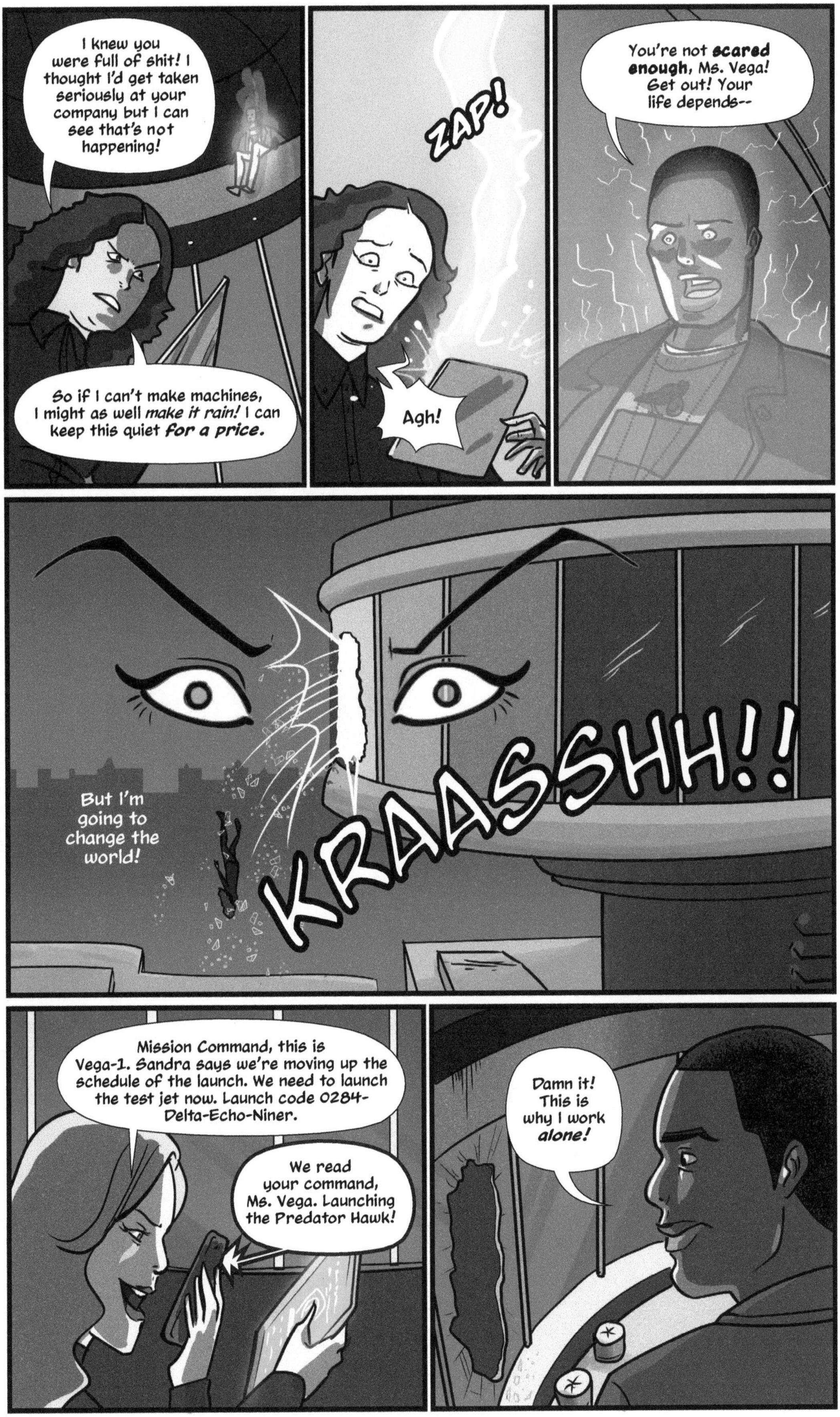

I knew you were full of shit! I thought I'd get taken seriously at your company but I can see that's not happening!
So if I can't make machines, I might as well *make it rain!* I can keep this quiet **for a price.**
ZAP!
Agh!
You're not **scared enough**, Ms. Vega! Get out! Your life depends--
But I'm going to change the world!
KRAASSHH!!
Mission Command, this is Vega-1. Sandra says we're moving up the schedule of the launch. We need to launch the test jet now. Launch code 0284-Delta-Echo-Niner.
We read your command, Ms. Vega. Launching the Predator Hawk!
Damn it! This is why I work *alone!*

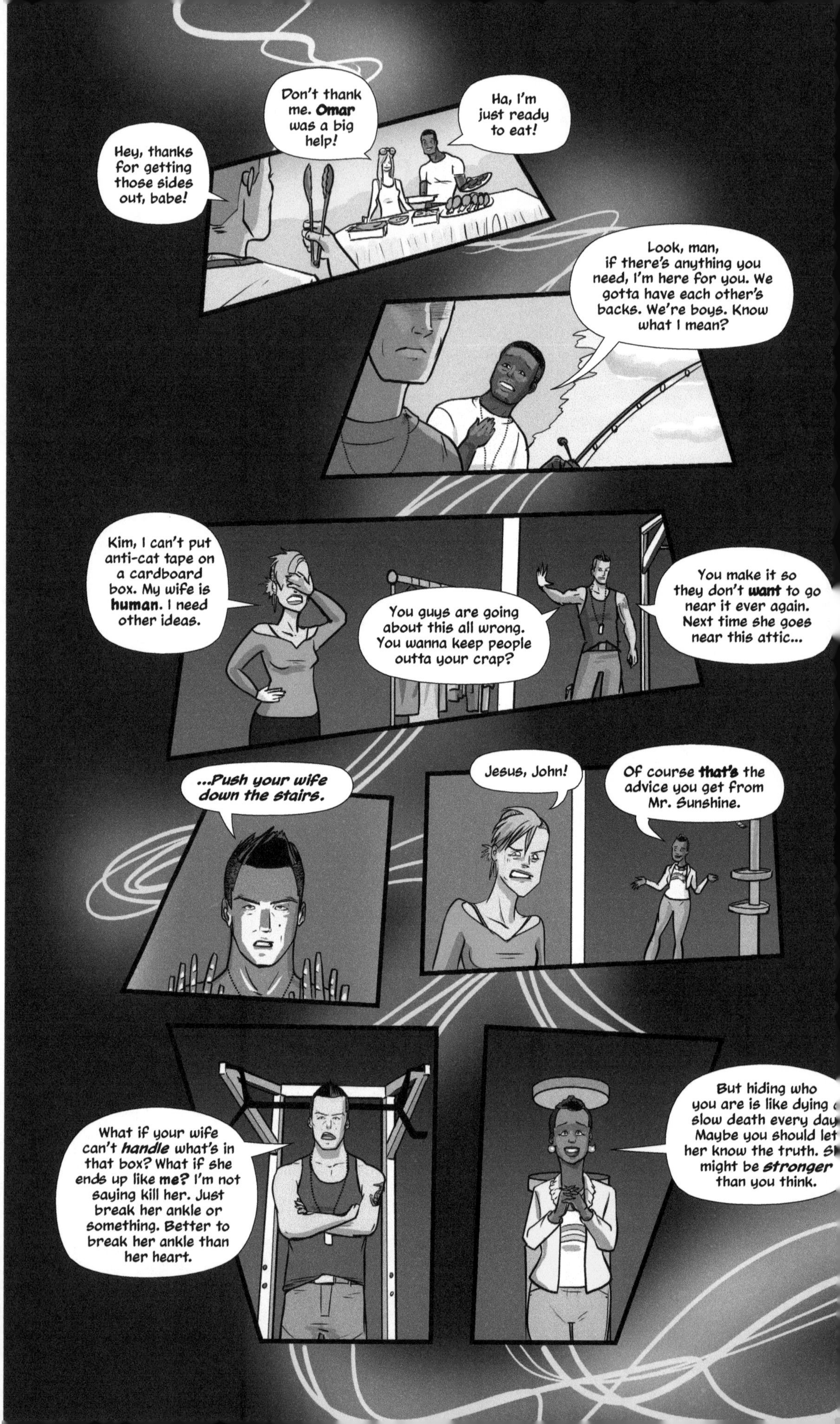
Hey, thanks for getting those sides out, babe!
Don't thank me. **Omar** was a big help!
Ha, I'm just ready to eat!
Look, man, if there's anything you need, I'm here for you. We gotta have each other's backs. We're boys. Know what I mean?
Kim, I can't put anti-cat tape on a cardboard box. My wife is **human**. I need other ideas.
You guys are going about this all wrong. You wanna keep people outta your crap?
You make it so they don't **want** to go near it ever again. Next time she goes near this attic...
...Push your wife down the stairs.
Jesus, John!
Of course **that's** the advice you get from Mr. Sunshine.
What if your wife can't ***handle*** what's in that box? What if she ends up like **me?** I'm not saying kill her. Just break her ankle or something. Better to break her ankle than her heart.
But hiding who you are is like dying slow death every day Maybe you should let her know the truth. might be ***stronger*** than you think.

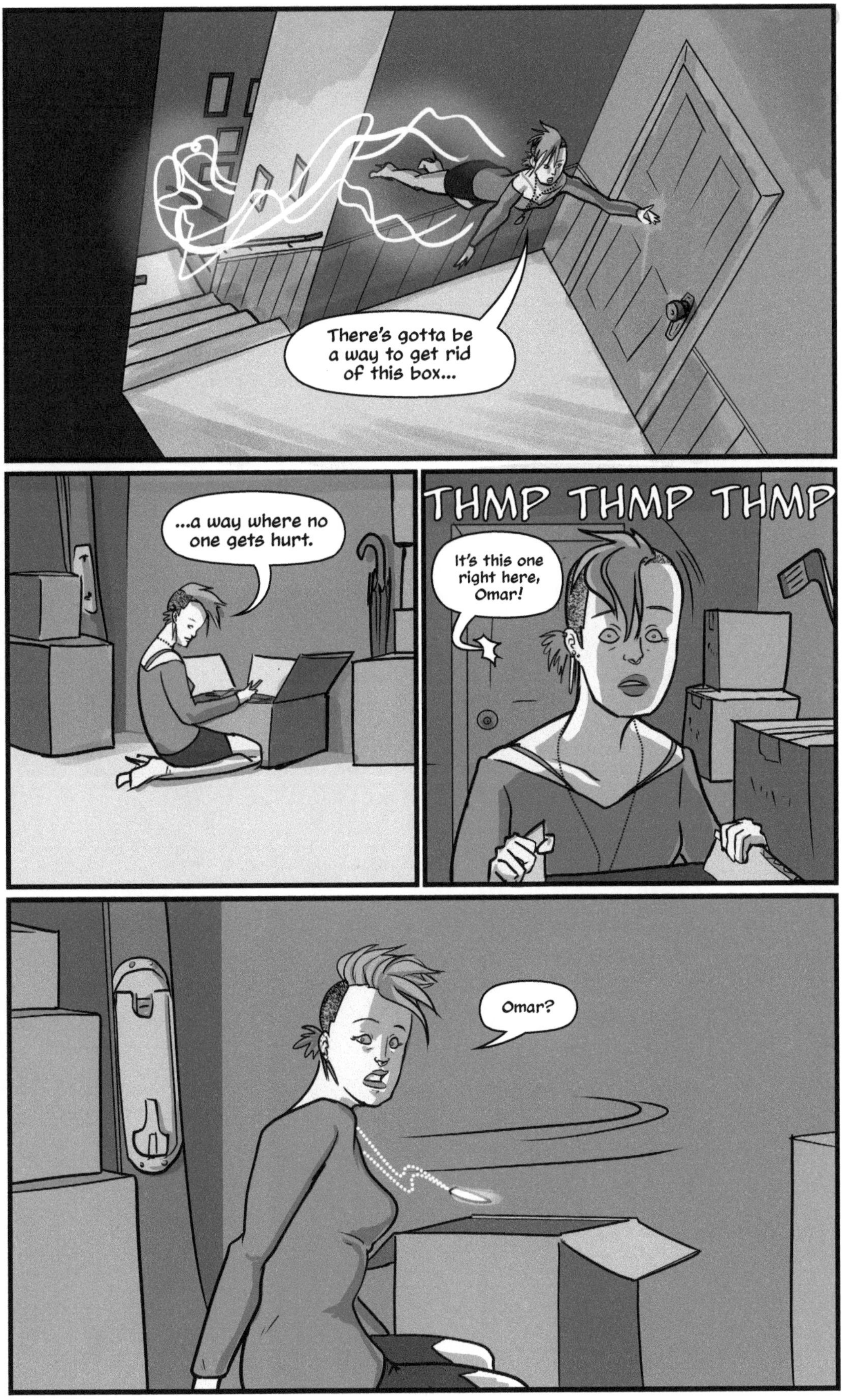
There's gotta be a way to get rid of this box...
...a way where no one gets hurt.
THMP THMP THMP
It's this one right here, Omar!
Omar?

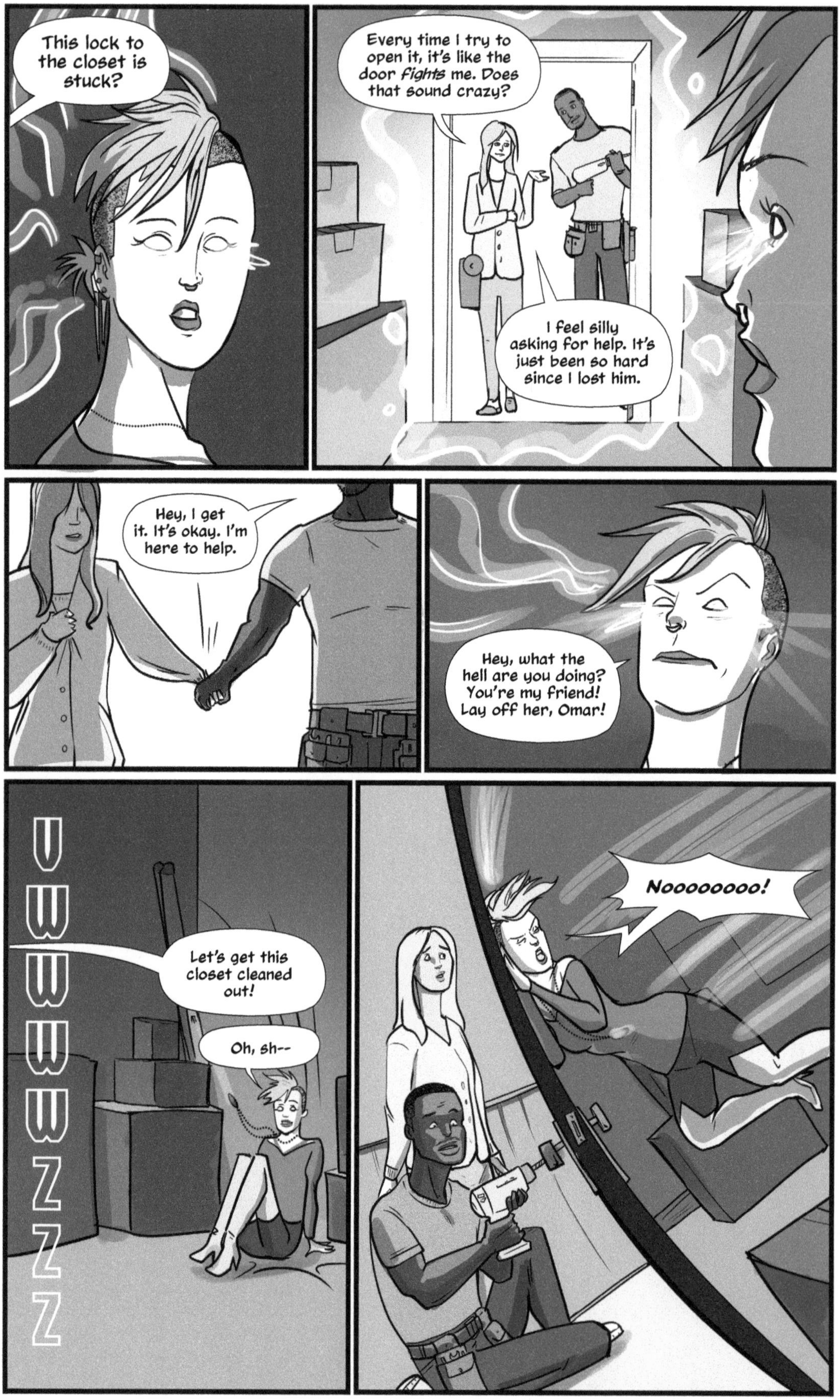

This lock to the closet is stuck?
Every time I try to open it, it's like the door *fights* me. Does that sound crazy?
I feel silly asking for help. It's just been so hard since I lost him.
Hey, I get it. It's okay. I'm here to help.
Hey, what the hell are you doing? You're my friend! Lay off her, Omar!
UWWWWWZZZ
Let's get this closet cleaned out!
Oh, sh--
Noooooooo!

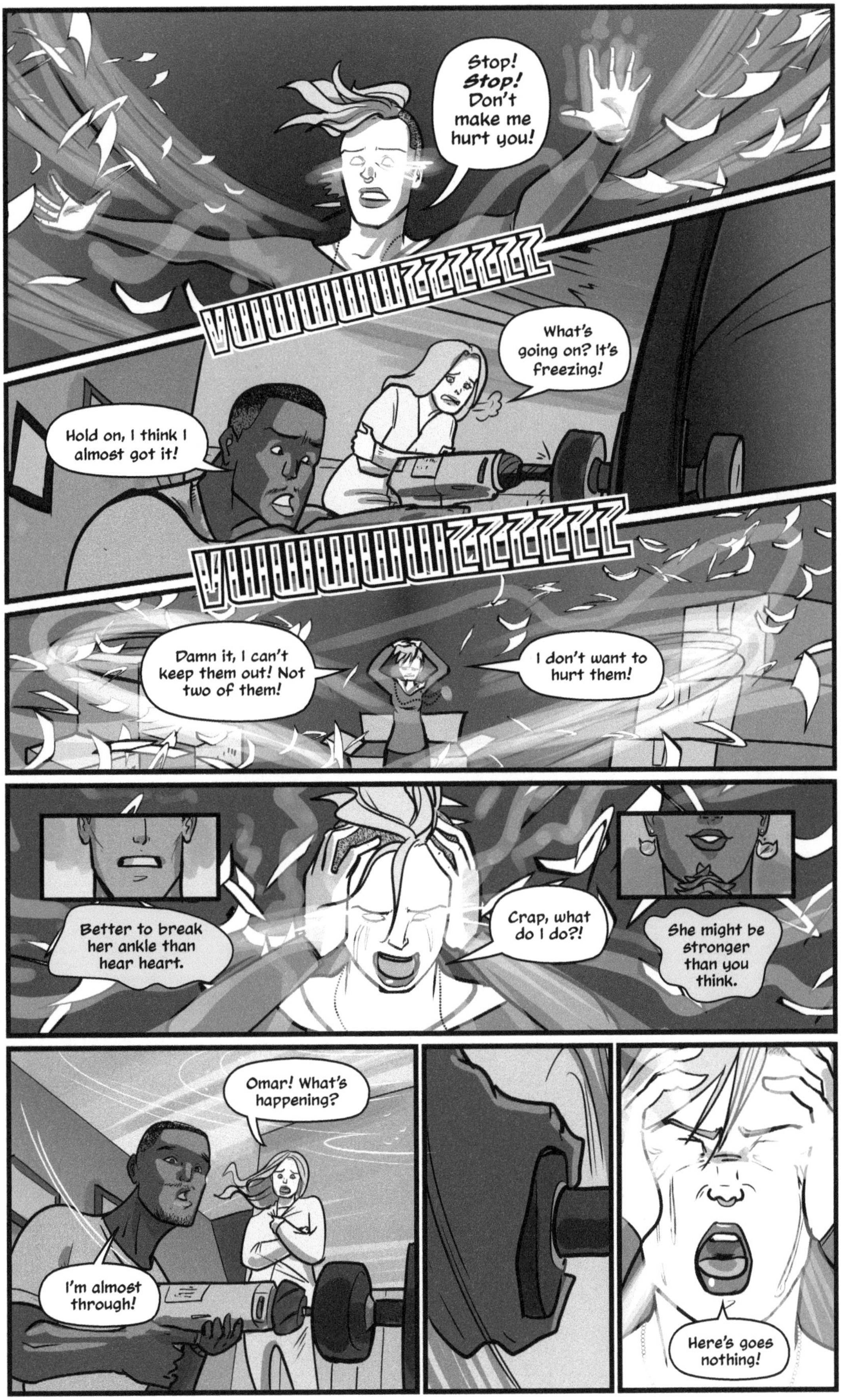
Stop! *Stop!* Don't make me hurt you!
VWWWWWWZZZZZZ
What's going on? It's freezing!
Hold on, I think I almost got it!
VWWWWWWWZZZZZZZ
Damn it, I can't keep them out! Not two of them!
I don't want to hurt them!
Better to break her ankle than hear heart.
Crap, what do I do?!
She might be stronger than you think.
Omar! What's happening?
I'm almost through!
Here's goes nothing!

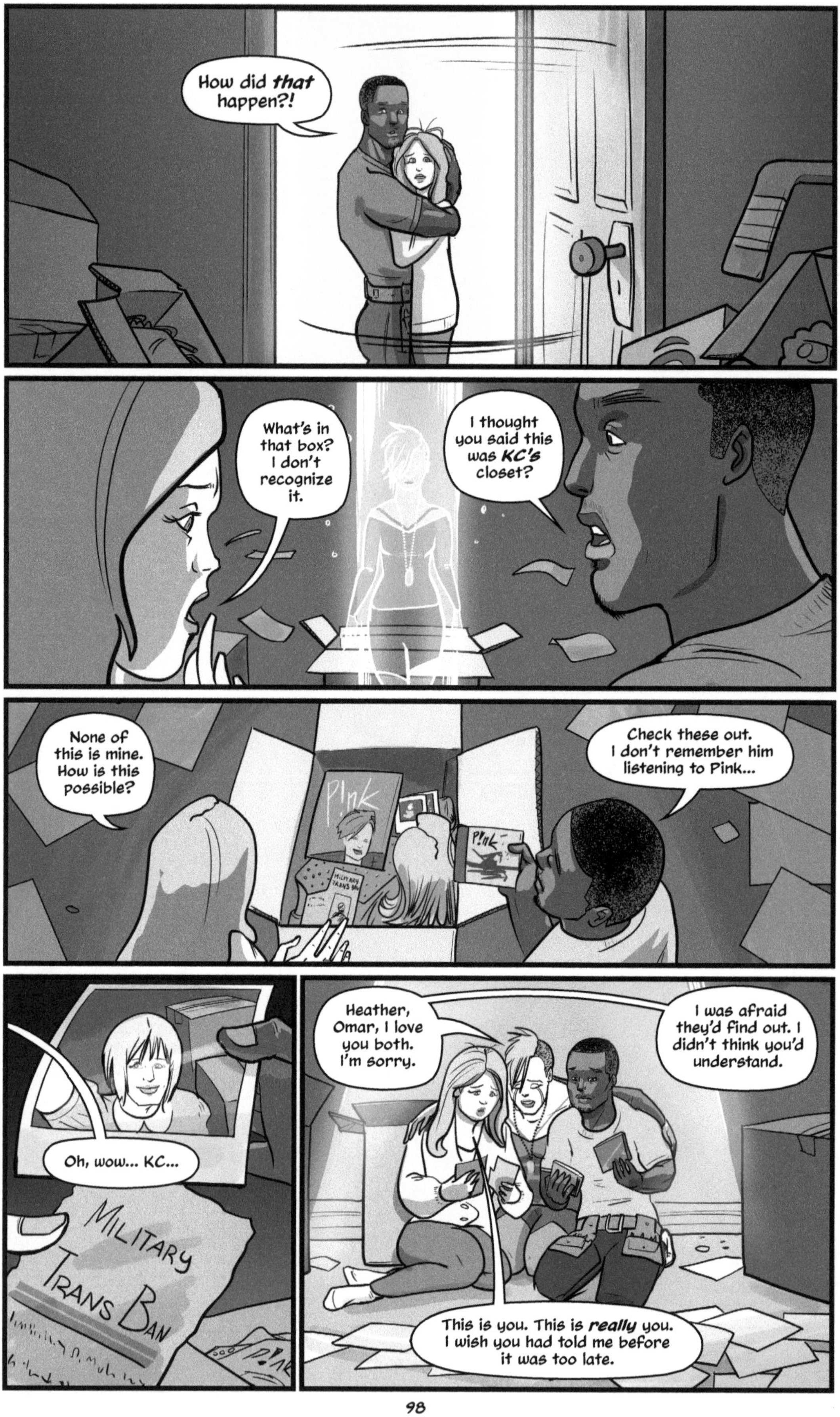
How did *that* happen?!
What's in that box? I don't recognize it.
I thought you said this was *KC's* closet?
None of this is mine. How is this possible?
P!nk
Check these out. I don't remember him listening to Pink...
Oh, wow... KC...
MILITARY TRANS BAN
Heather, Omar, I love you both. I'm sorry.
I was afraid they'd find out. I didn't think you'd understand.
This is you. This is *really* you. I wish you had told me before it was too late.

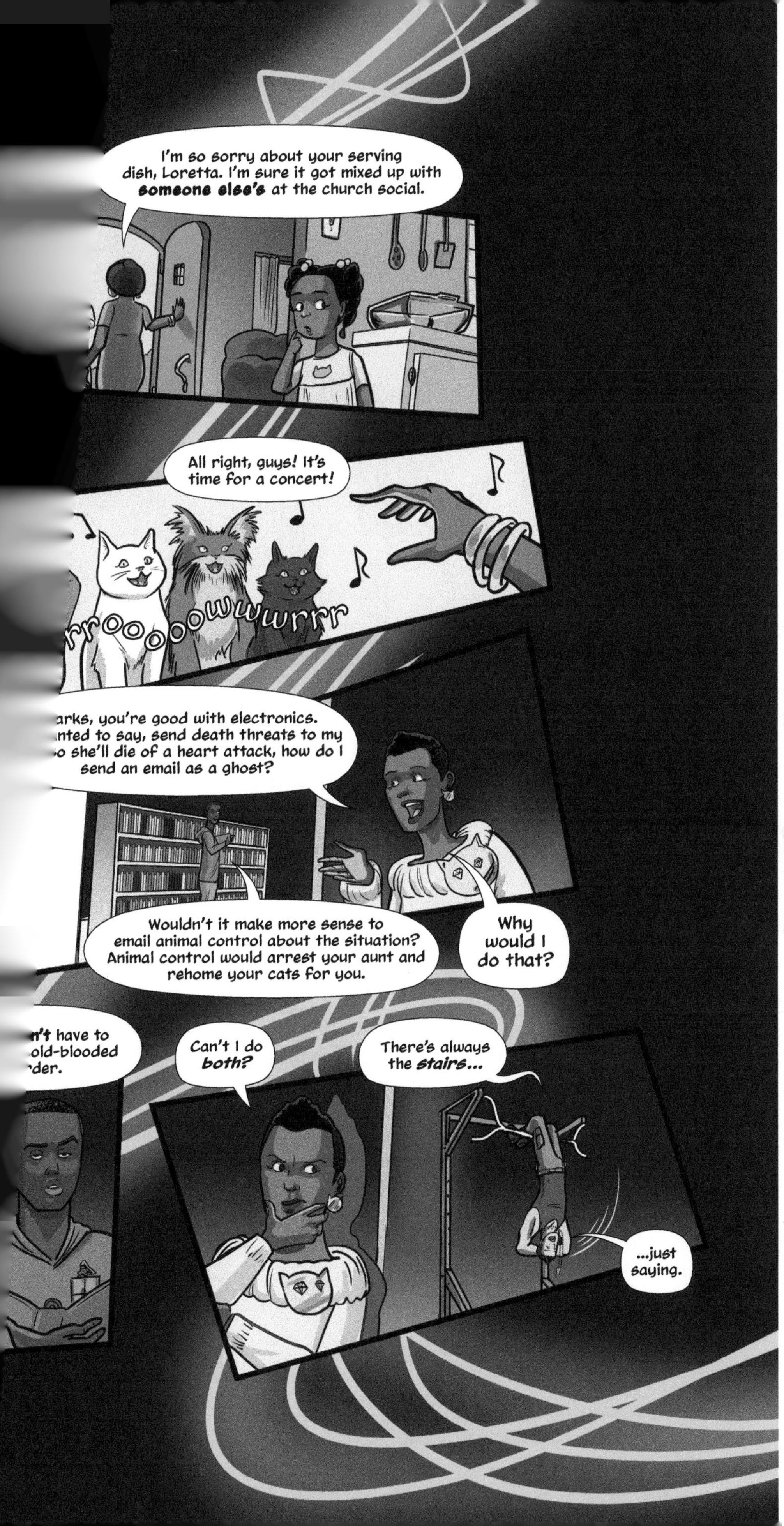
I'm so sorry about your serving dish, Loretta. I'm sure it got mixed up with **someone else's** at the church social.
All right, guys! It's time for a concert!
rrooooooowwurrr
arks, you're good with electronics. anted to say, send death threats to my o she'll die of a heart attack, how do I send an email as a ghost?
Wouldn't it make more sense to email animal control about the situation? Animal control would arrest your aunt and rehome your cats for you.
Why would I do that?
n't have to old-blooded rder.
Can't I do ***both?***
There's always the ***stairs...***
...just saying.

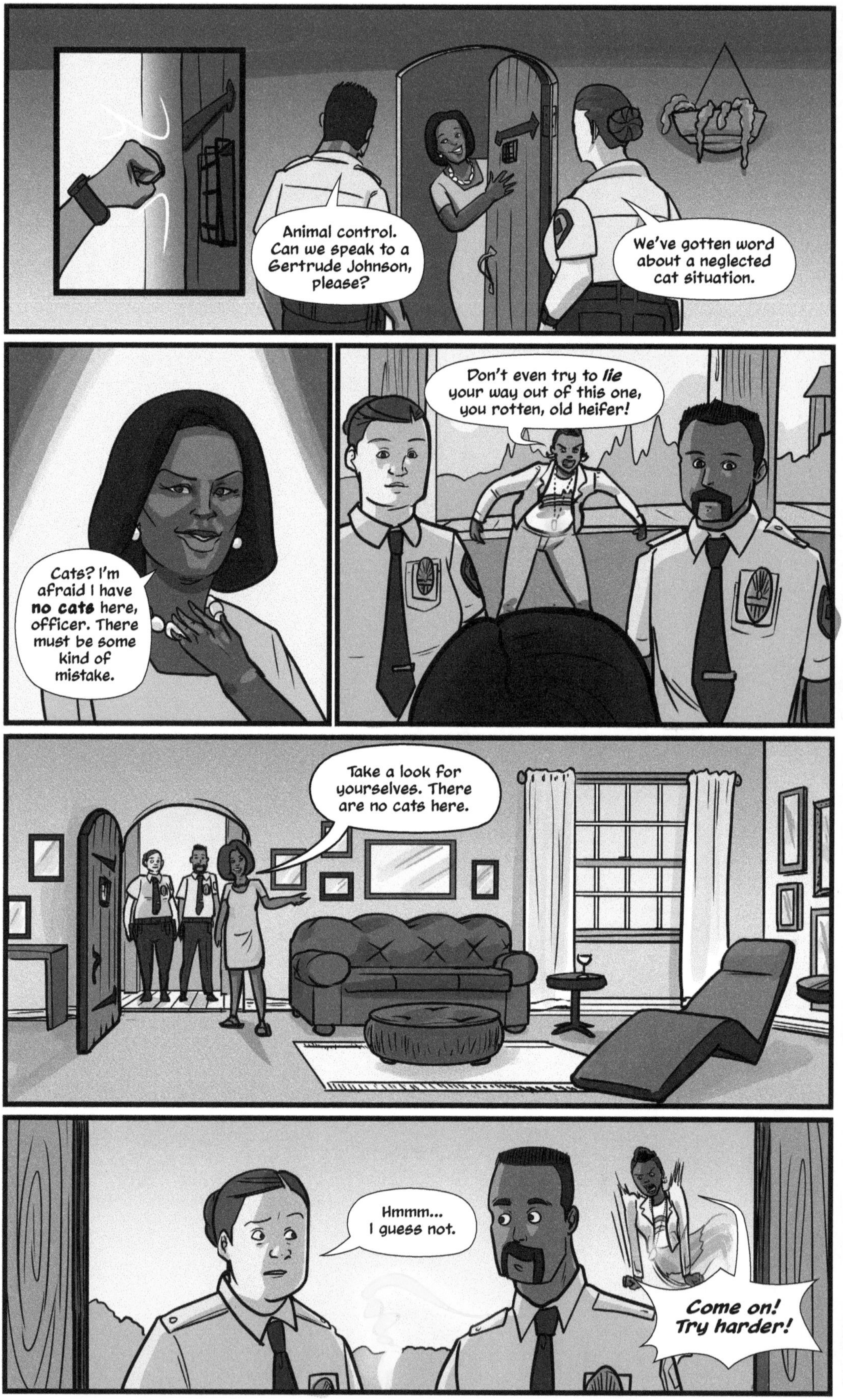

Animal control. Can we speak to a Gertrude Johnson, please?
We've gotten word about a neglected cat situation.
Cats? I'm afraid I have **no cats** here, officer. There must be some kind of mistake.
Don't even try to ***lie*** your way out of this one, you rotten, old heifer!
Take a look for yourselves. There are no cats here.
Hmmm... I guess not.
Come on! Try harder!

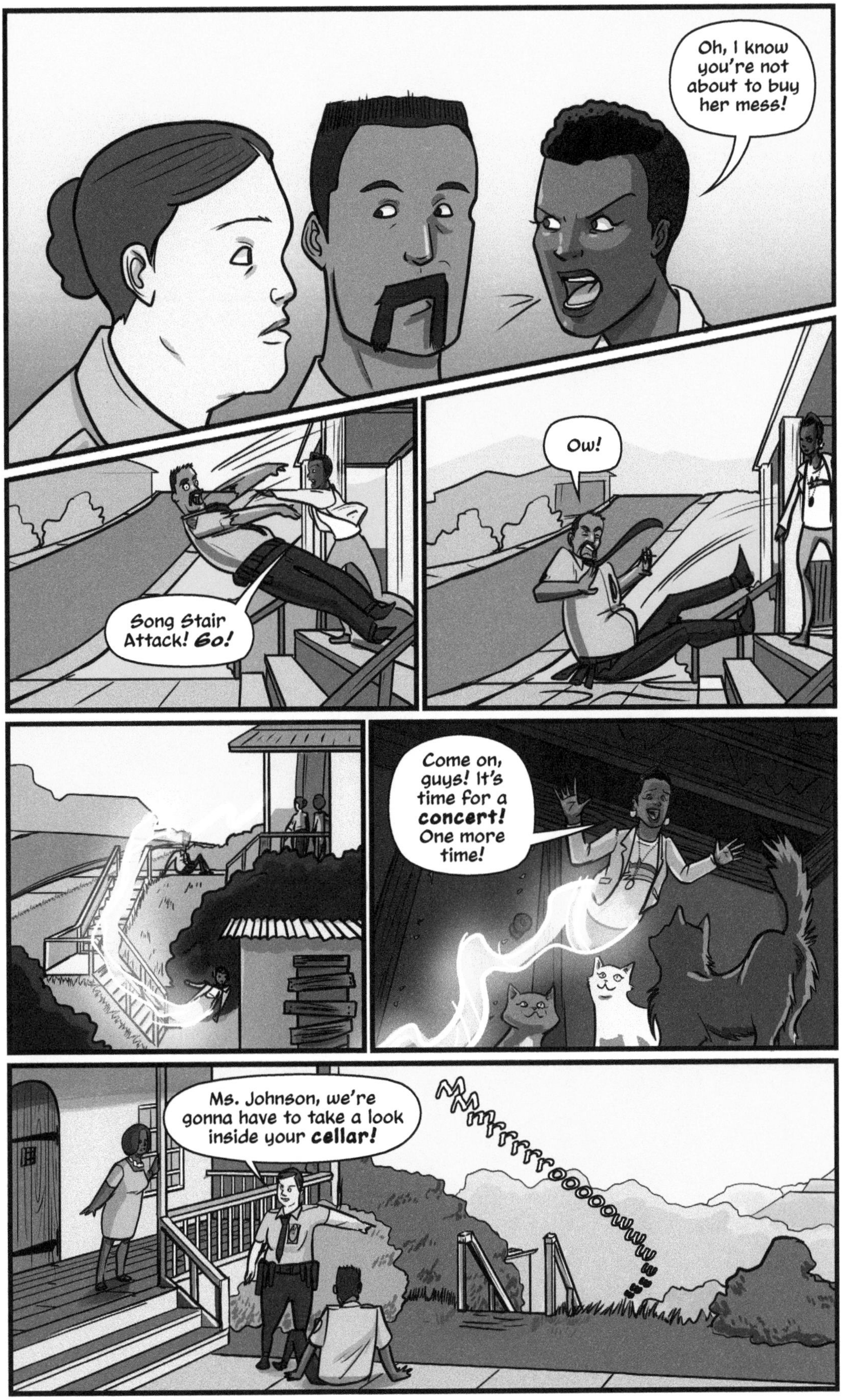
Oh, I know you're not about to buy her mess!
Song Stair Attack! Go!
Ow!
Come on, guys! It's time for a concert! One more time!
Ms. Johnson, we're gonna have to take a look inside your cellar!
MMrrrrrroooooowwww

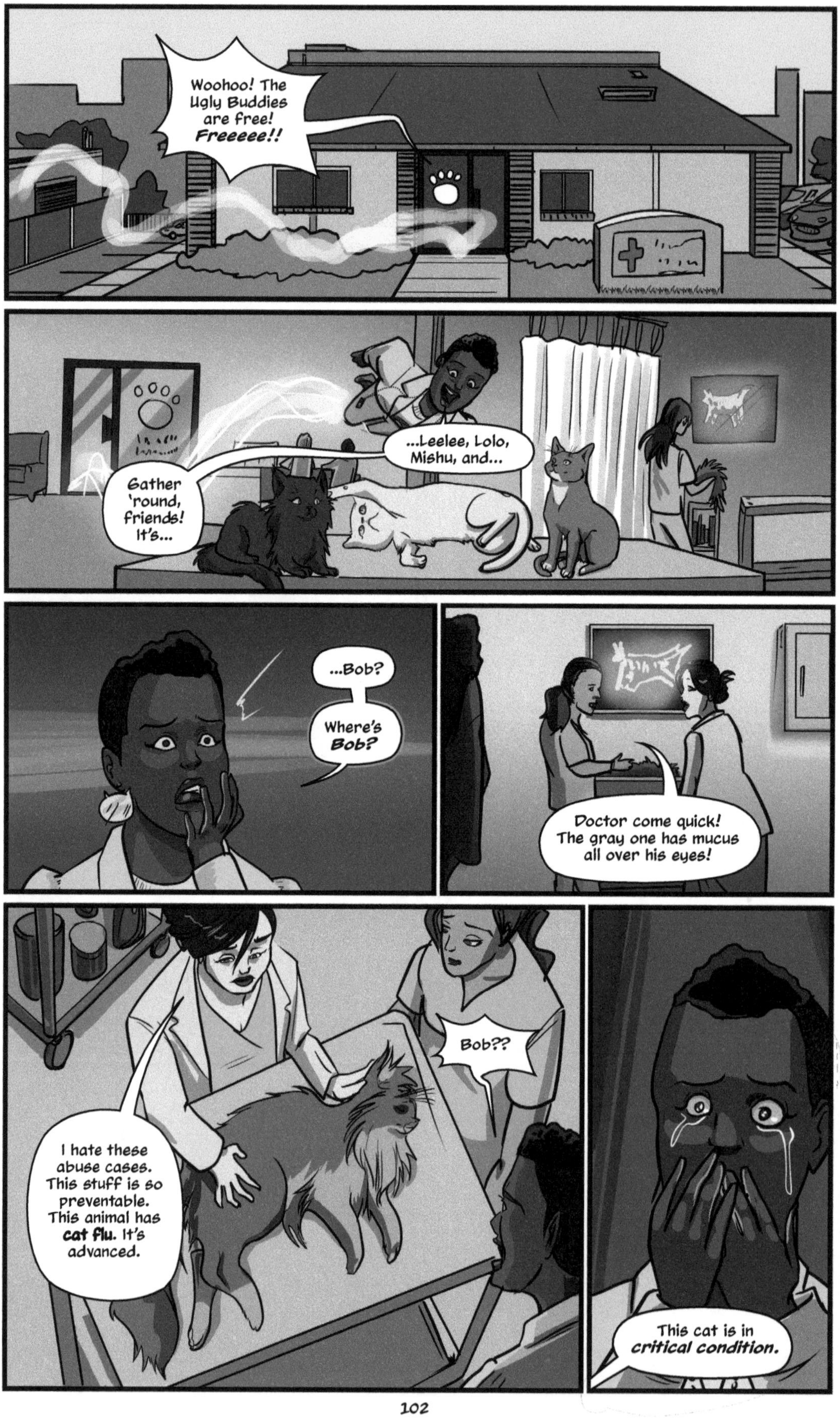

Woohoo! The Ugly Buddies are free! **Freeeee!!**
Gather 'round, friends! It's...
...Leelee, Lolo, Mishu, and...
...Bob?
Where's **Bob?**
Doctor come quick! The gray one has mucus all over his eyes!
I hate these abuse cases. This stuff is so preventable. This animal has **cat flu.** It's advanced.
Bob??
This cat is in ***critical condition.***

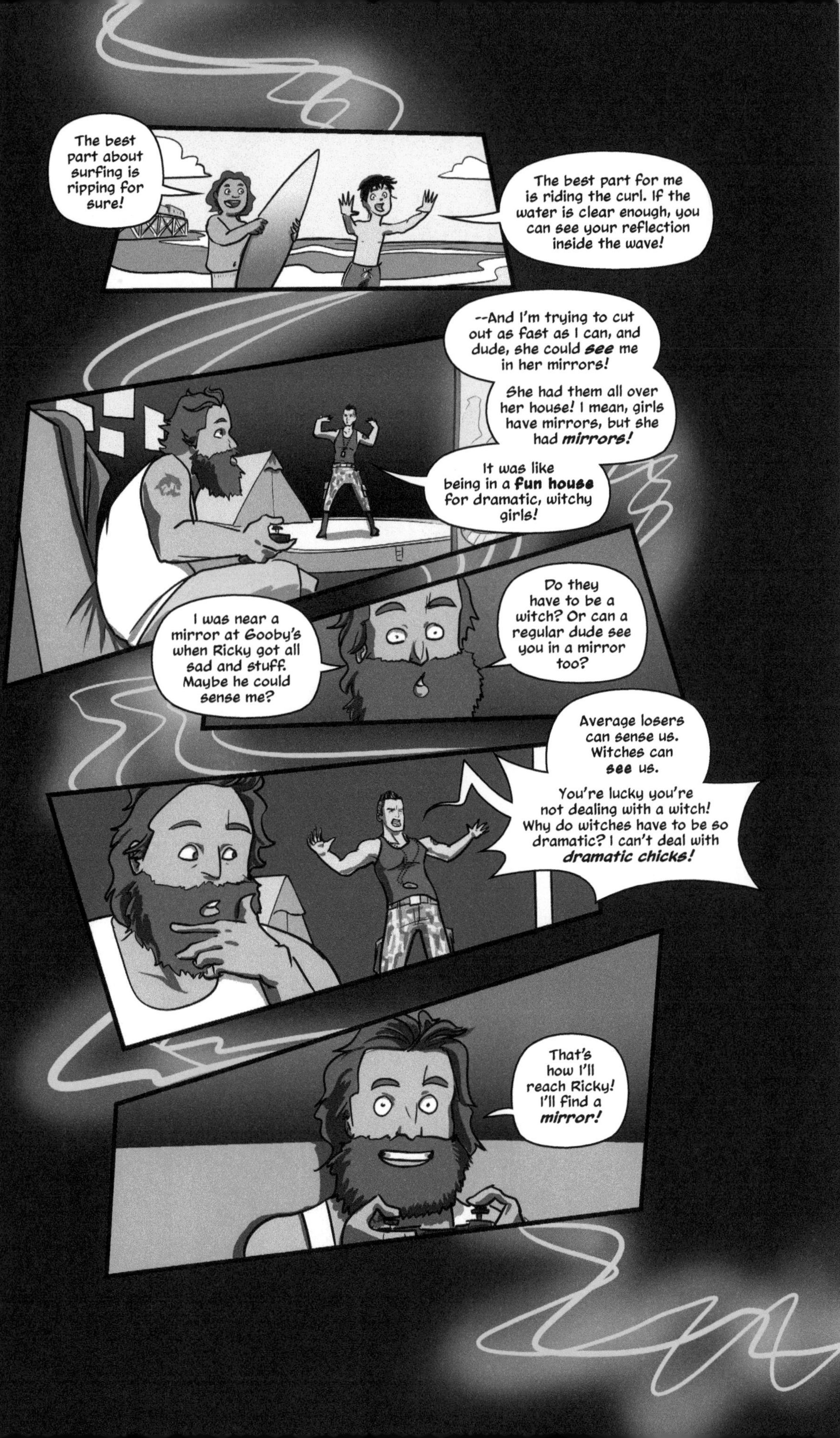
The best part about surfing is ripping for sure!
The best part for me is riding the curl. If the water is clear enough, you can see your reflection inside the wave!
--And I'm trying to cut out as fast as I can, and dude, she could *see* me in her mirrors!
She had them all over her house! I mean, girls have mirrors, but she had *mirrors!*
It was like being in a **fun house** for dramatic, witchy girls!
I was near a mirror at Gooby's when Ricky got all sad and stuff. Maybe he could sense me?
Do they have to be a witch? Or can a regular dude see you in a mirror too?
Average losers can sense us. Witches can **see** us.
You're lucky you're not dealing with a witch! Why do witches have to be so dramatic? I can't deal with ***dramatic chicks!***
That's how I'll reach Ricky! I'll find a ***mirror!***

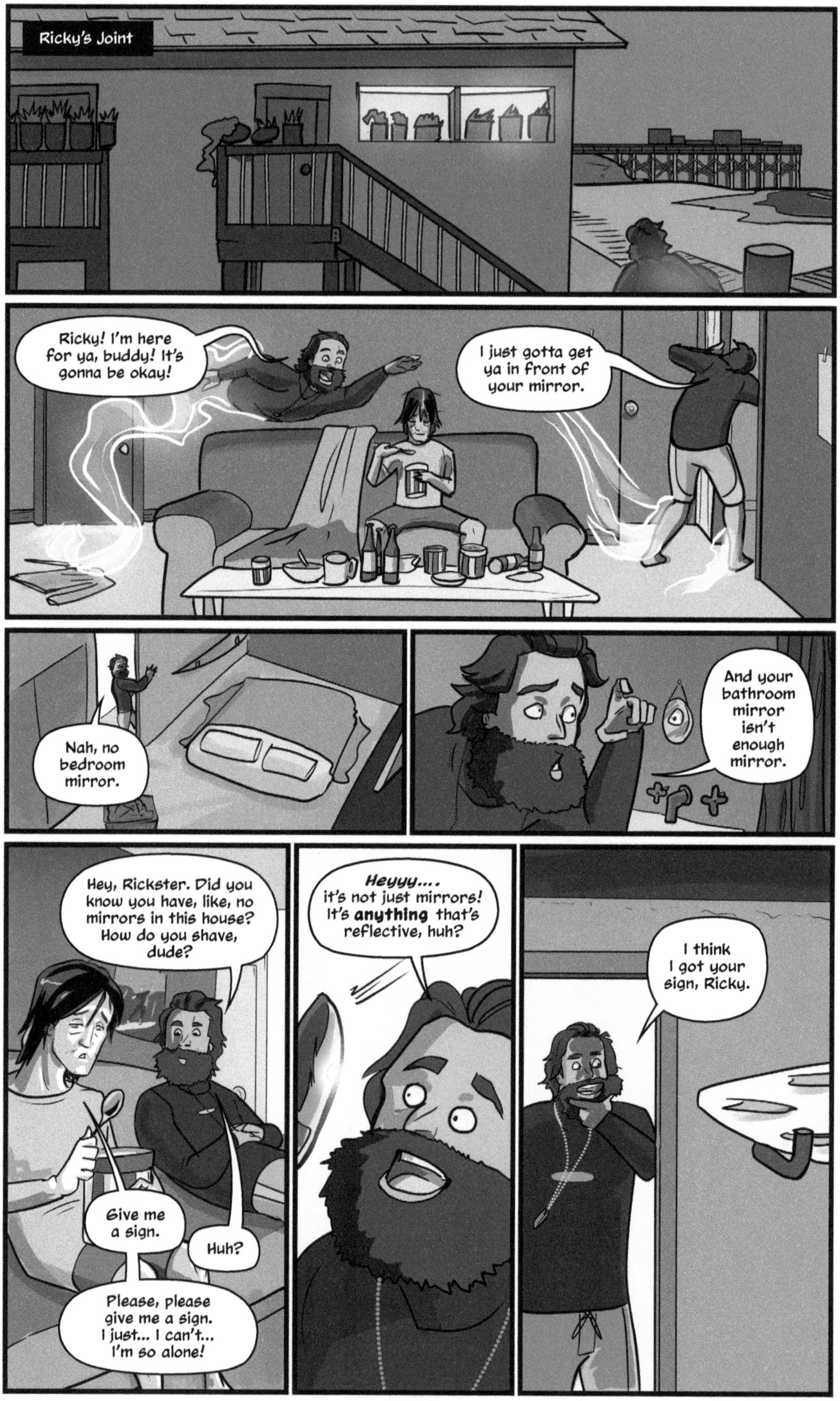
Ricky's Joint
Ricky! I'm here for ya, buddy! It's gonna be okay!
I just gotta get ya in front of your mirror.
Nah, no bedroom mirror.
And your bathroom mirror isn't enough mirror.
Hey, Rickster. Did you know you have, like, no mirrors in this house? How do you shave, dude?
Give me a sign.
Huh?
Please, please give me a sign. I just... I can't... I'm so alone!
Heyyy.... it's not just mirrors! It's **anything** that's reflective, huh?
I think I got your sign, Ricky.

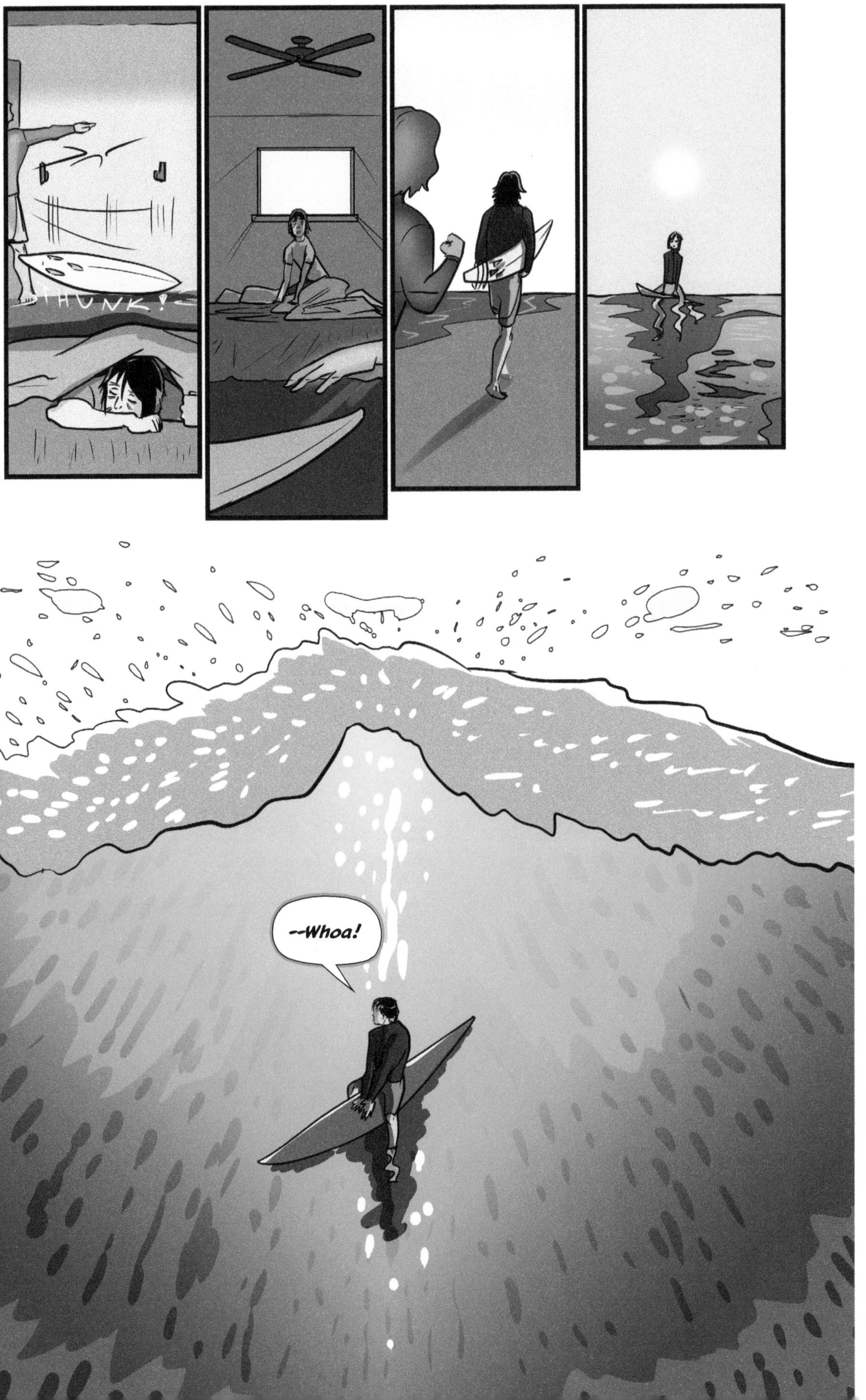
THUNK!
--Whoa!

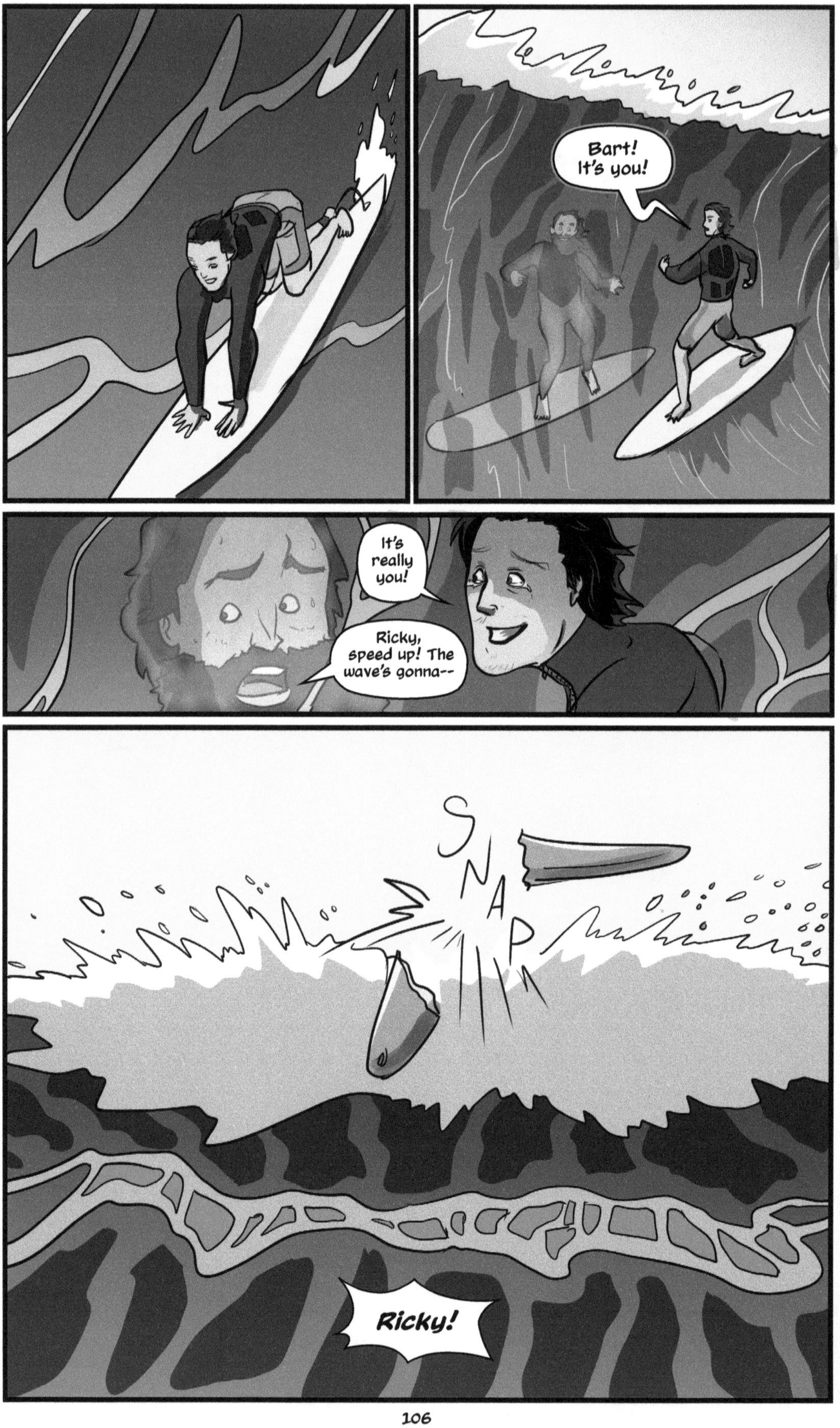
Bart! It's you!
It's really you!
Ricky, speed up! The wave's gonna--
SNAP
Ricky!

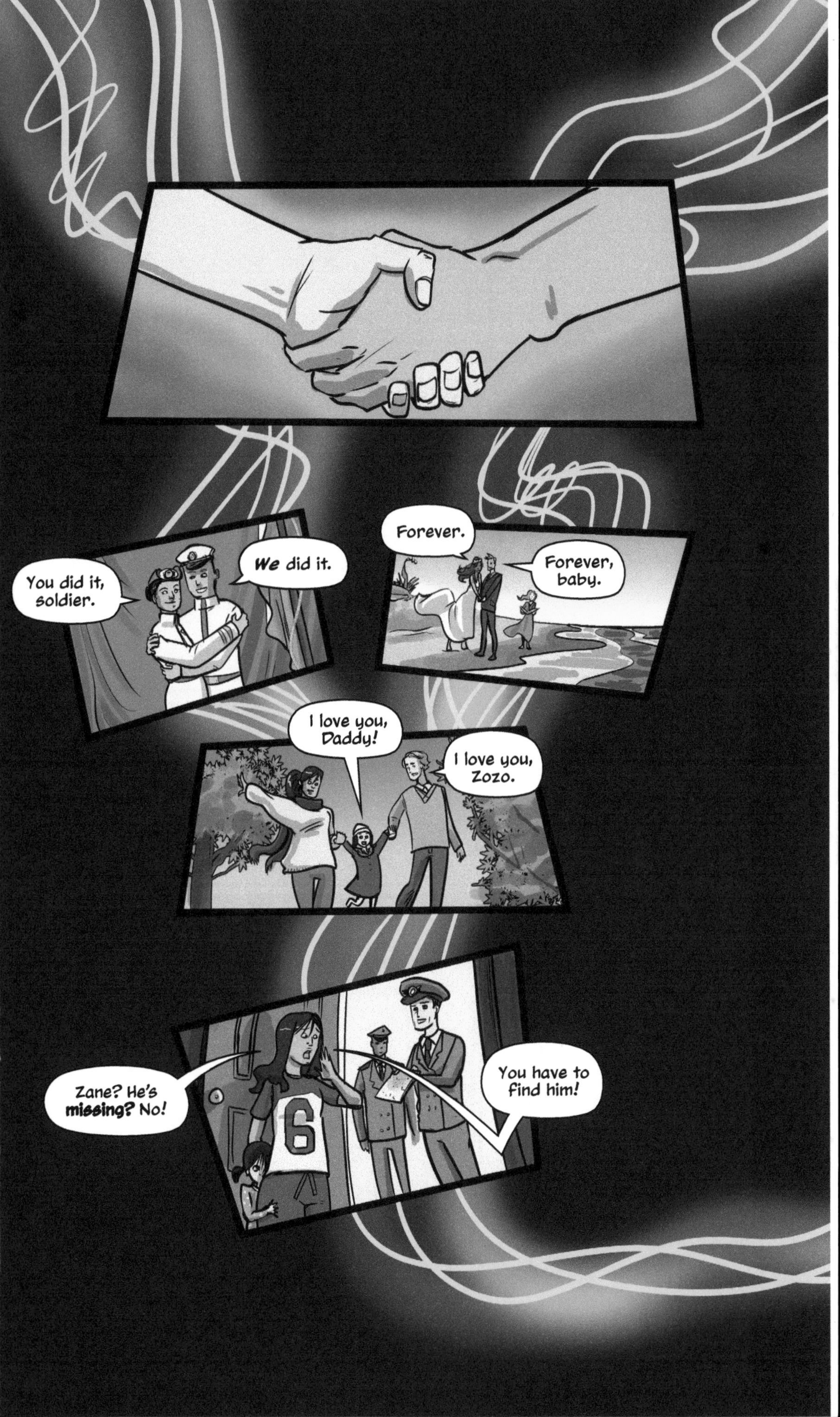
You did it, soldier.
We did it.
Forever.
Forever, baby.
I love you, Daddy!
I love you, Zozo.
Zane? He's **missing?** No!
You have to find him!

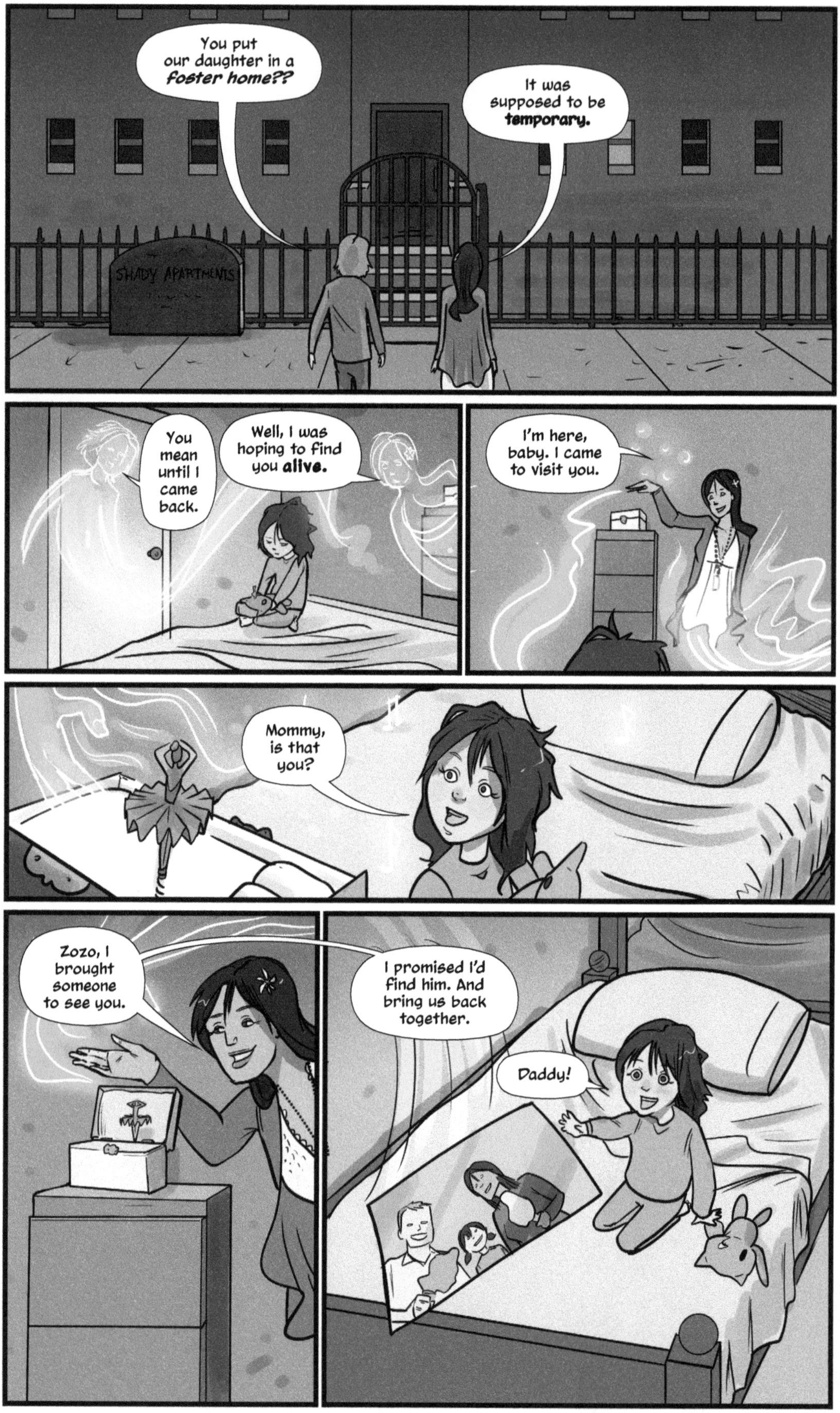

You put our daughter in a *foster home??*
It was supposed to be **temporary.**
SHADY APARTMENTS
You mean until I came back.
Well, I was hoping to find you **alive.**
I'm here, baby. I came to visit you.
Mommy, is that you?
Zozo, I brought someone to see you.
I promised I'd find him. And bring us back together.
Daddy!

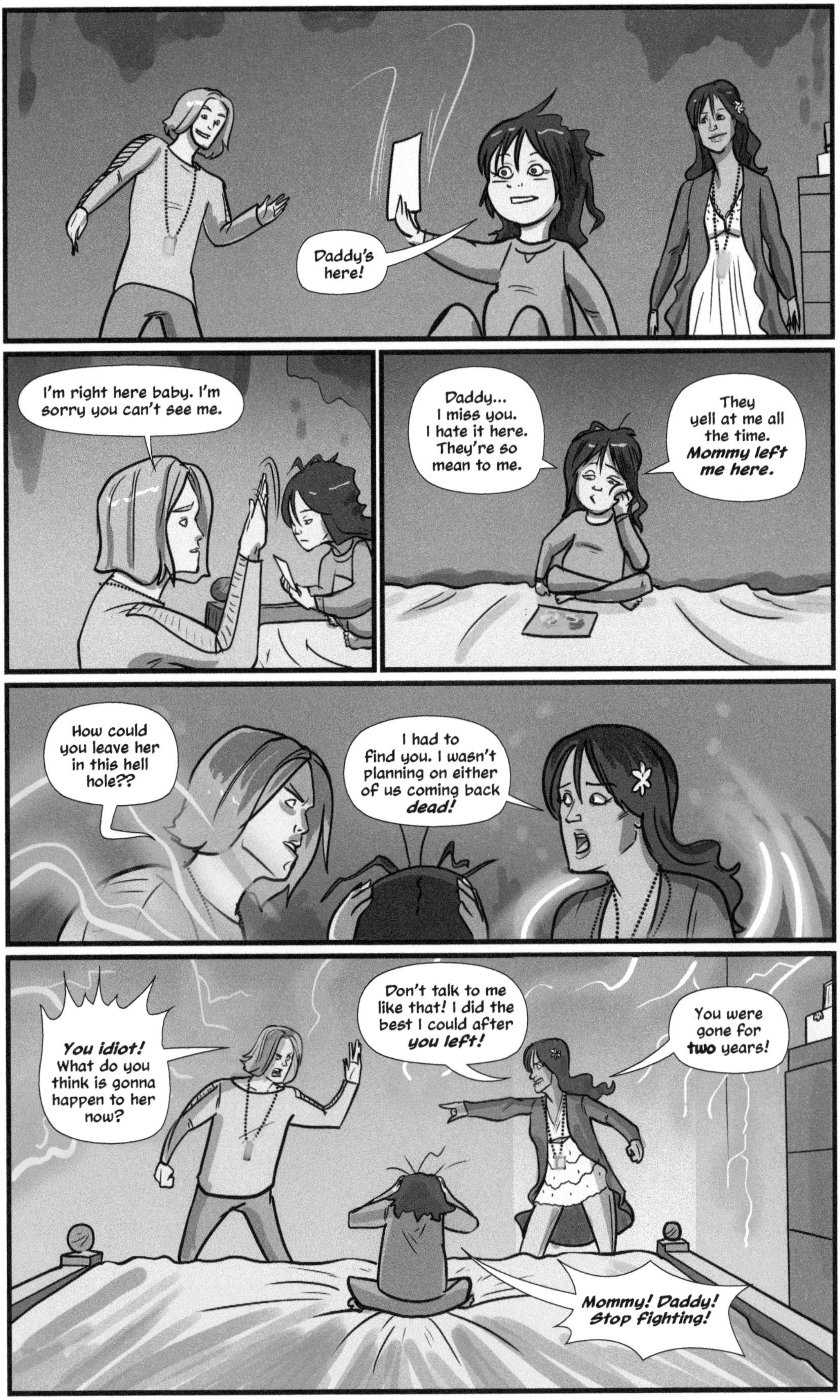
Daddy's here!
I'm right here baby. I'm sorry you can't see me.
Daddy... I miss you. I hate it here. They're so mean to me.
They yell at me all the time. *Mommy left me here.*
How could you leave her in this hell hole??
I had to find you. I wasn't planning on either of us coming back *dead!*
You idiot! What do you think is gonna happen to her now?
Don't talk to me like that! I did the best I could after *you left!*
You were gone for **two** years!
Mommy! Daddy! Stop fighting!

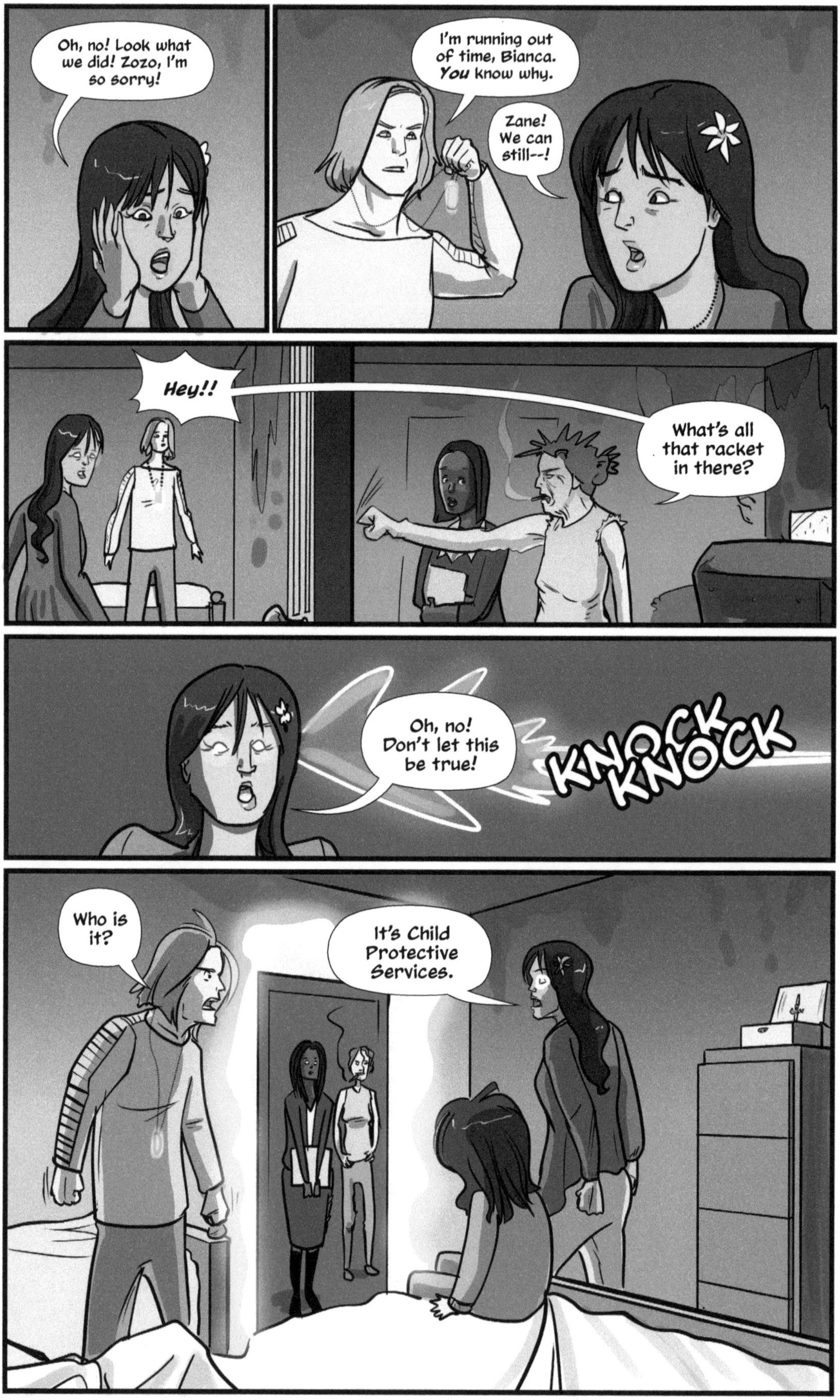
Oh, no! Look what we did! Zozo, I'm so sorry!
I'm running out of time, Bianca. *You* know why.
Zane! We can still--!
Hey!!
What's all that racket in there?
Oh, no! Don't let this be true!
KNOCK KNOCK
Who is it?
It's Child Protective Services.

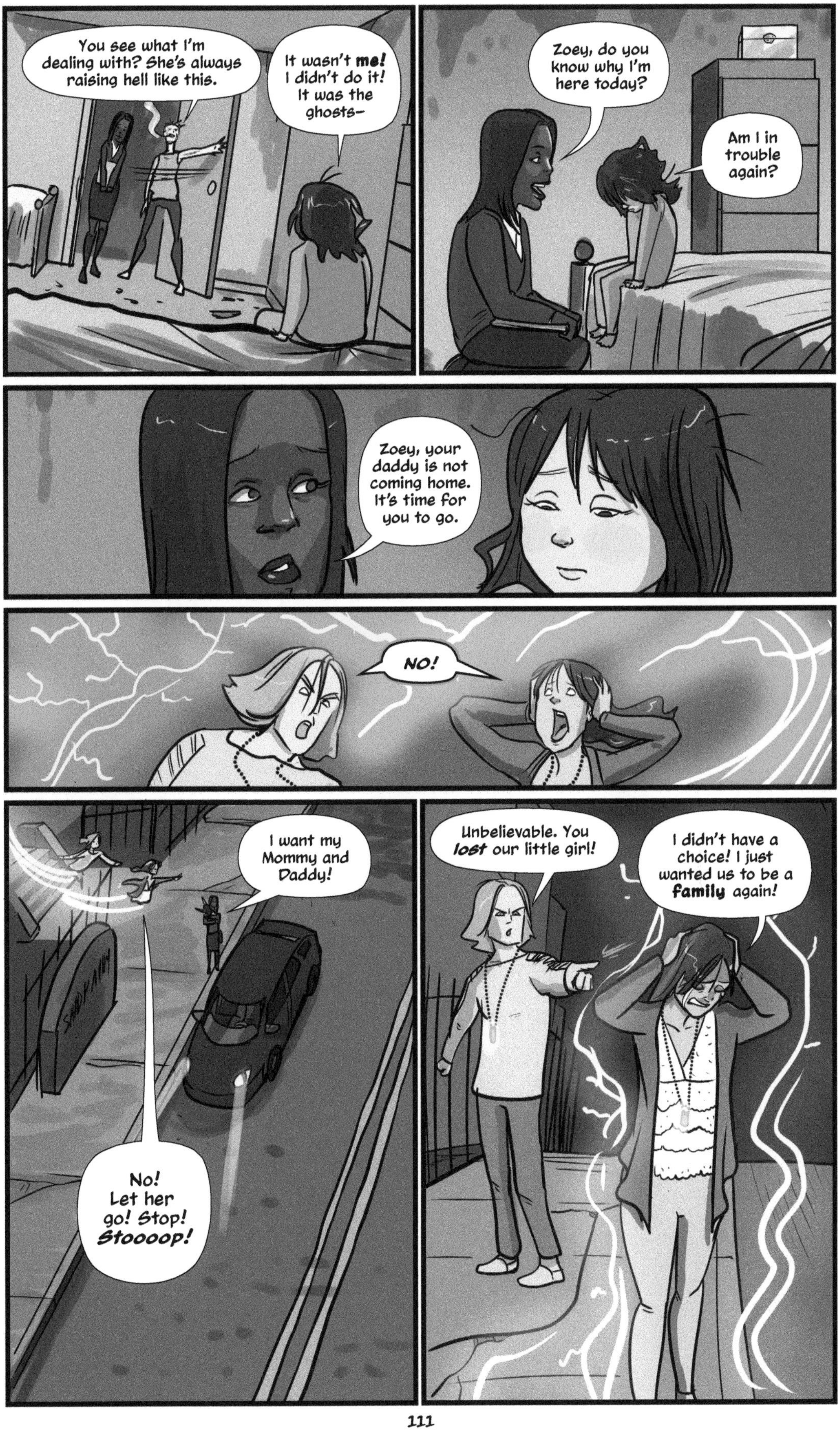

You see what I'm dealing with? She's always raising hell like this.
It wasn't **me!** I didn't do it! It was the ghosts-
Zoey, do you know why I'm here today?
Am I in trouble again?
Zoey, your daddy is not coming home. It's time for you to go.
NO!
I want my Mommy and Daddy!
No! Let her go! Stop! *Stoooop!*
Unbelievable. You ***lost*** our little girl!
I didn't have a choice! I just wanted us to be a **family** again!

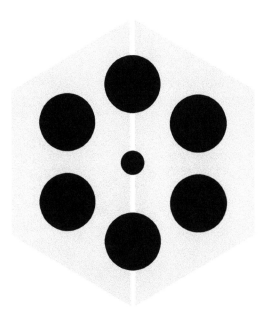

CHAPTER 6
Deep Sixed

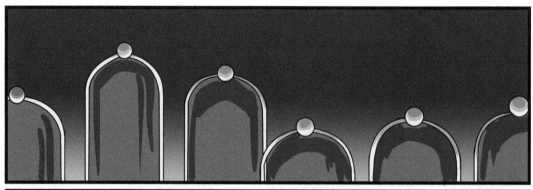

Bob...

Heather...

I take it **nobody** had a good haunt.

How 'bout you, John? Did you at least make **nice** with your witch?

What do you mean 'make nice?' I didn't make nice with anyone!

Definitely not for five hours straight!

Shut up!

I might have a girlfriend now.

Zane? Come on! You can't ignore me **forever.** I did the best I could!

Forever. That's the one thing I've got **left.**

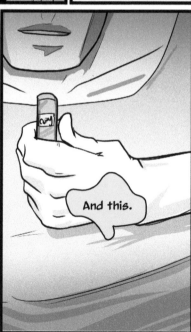

And this.

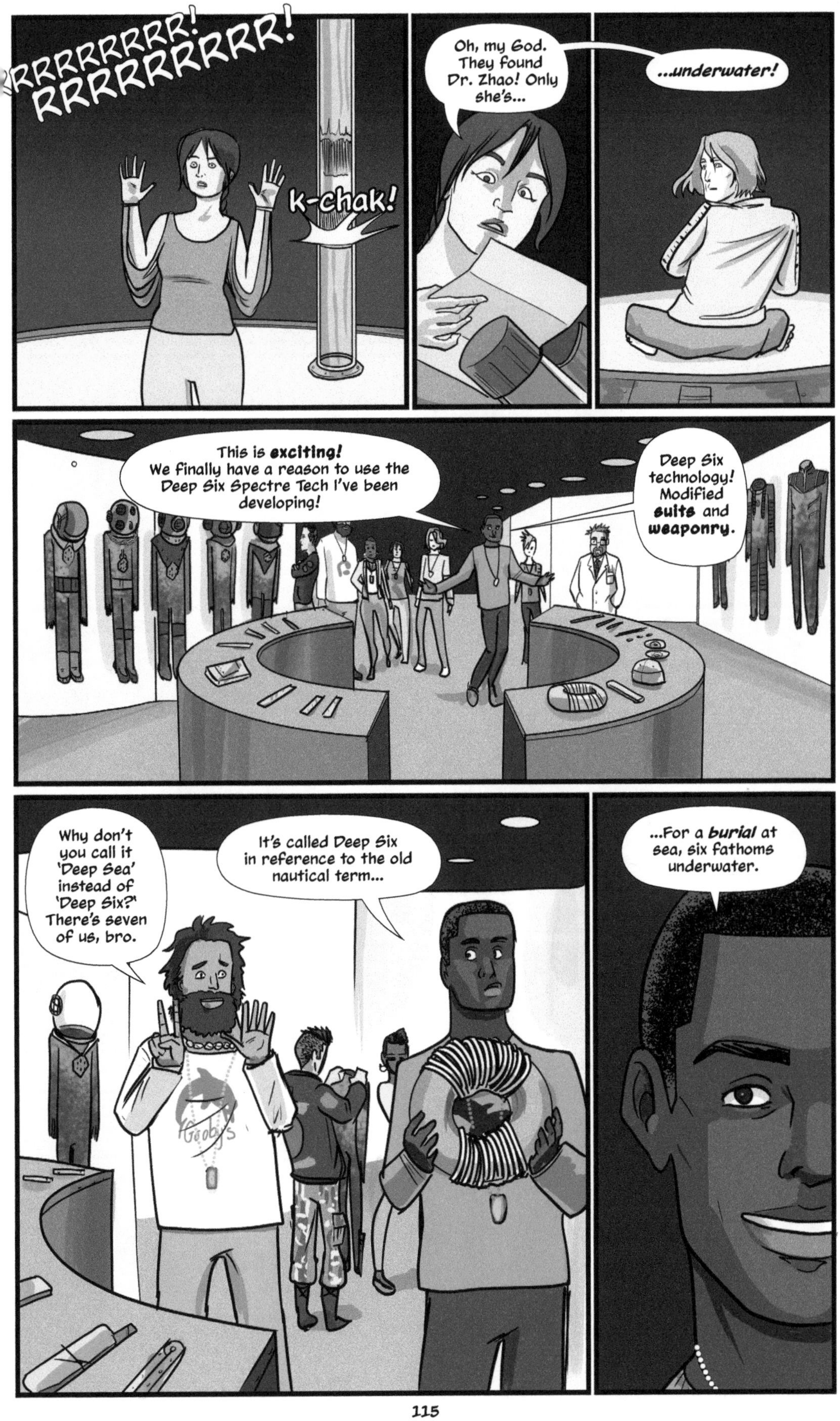
RRRRRRRR!
RRRRRRRRR!
k-chak!
Oh, my God. They found Dr. Zhao! Only she's...
...underwater!
This is **exciting!** We finally have a reason to use the Deep Six Spectre Tech I've been developing!
Deep Six technology! Modified **suits** and **weaponry**.
Why don't you call it 'Deep Sea' instead of 'Deep Six?' There's seven of us, bro.
It's called Deep Six in reference to the old nautical term...
Goby's
...For a *burial* at sea, six fathoms underwater.

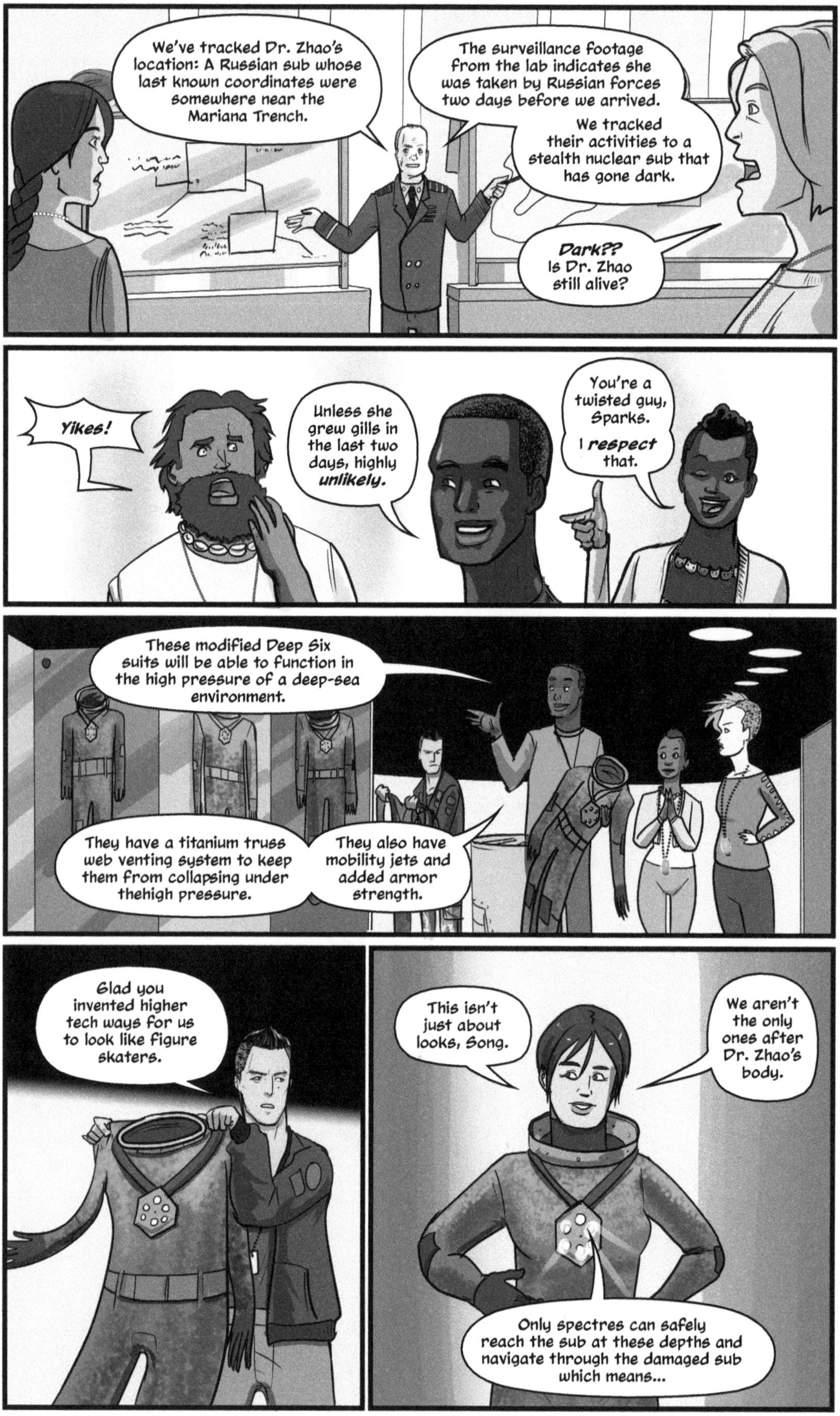
We've tracked Dr. Zhao's location: A Russian sub whose last known coordinates were somewhere near the Mariana Trench.
The surveillance footage from the lab indicates she was taken by Russian forces two days before we arrived.
We tracked their activities to a stealth nuclear sub that has gone dark.
Dark?? Is Dr. Zhao still alive?
Yikes!
Unless she grew gills in the last two days, highly unlikely.
You're a twisted guy, Sparks.
I respect that.
These modified Deep Six suits will be able to function in the high pressure of a deep-sea environment.
They have a titanium truss web venting system to keep them from collapsing under thehigh pressure.
They also have mobility jets and added armor strength.
Glad you invented higher tech ways for us to look like figure skaters.
This isn't just about looks, Song.
We aren't the only ones after Dr. Zhao's body.
Only spectres can safely reach the sub at these depths and navigate through the damaged sub which means...

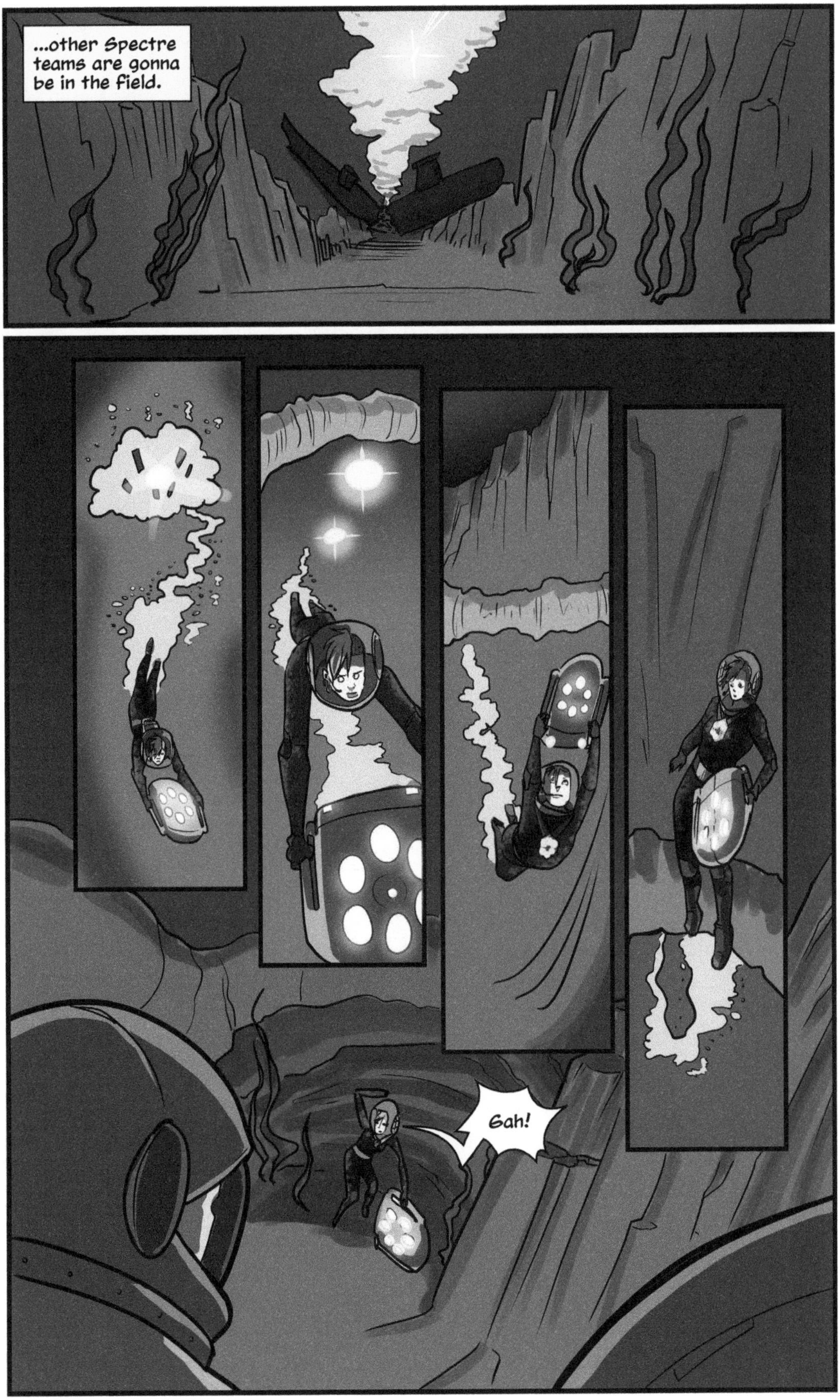
...other Spectre teams are gonna be in the field.
Gah!

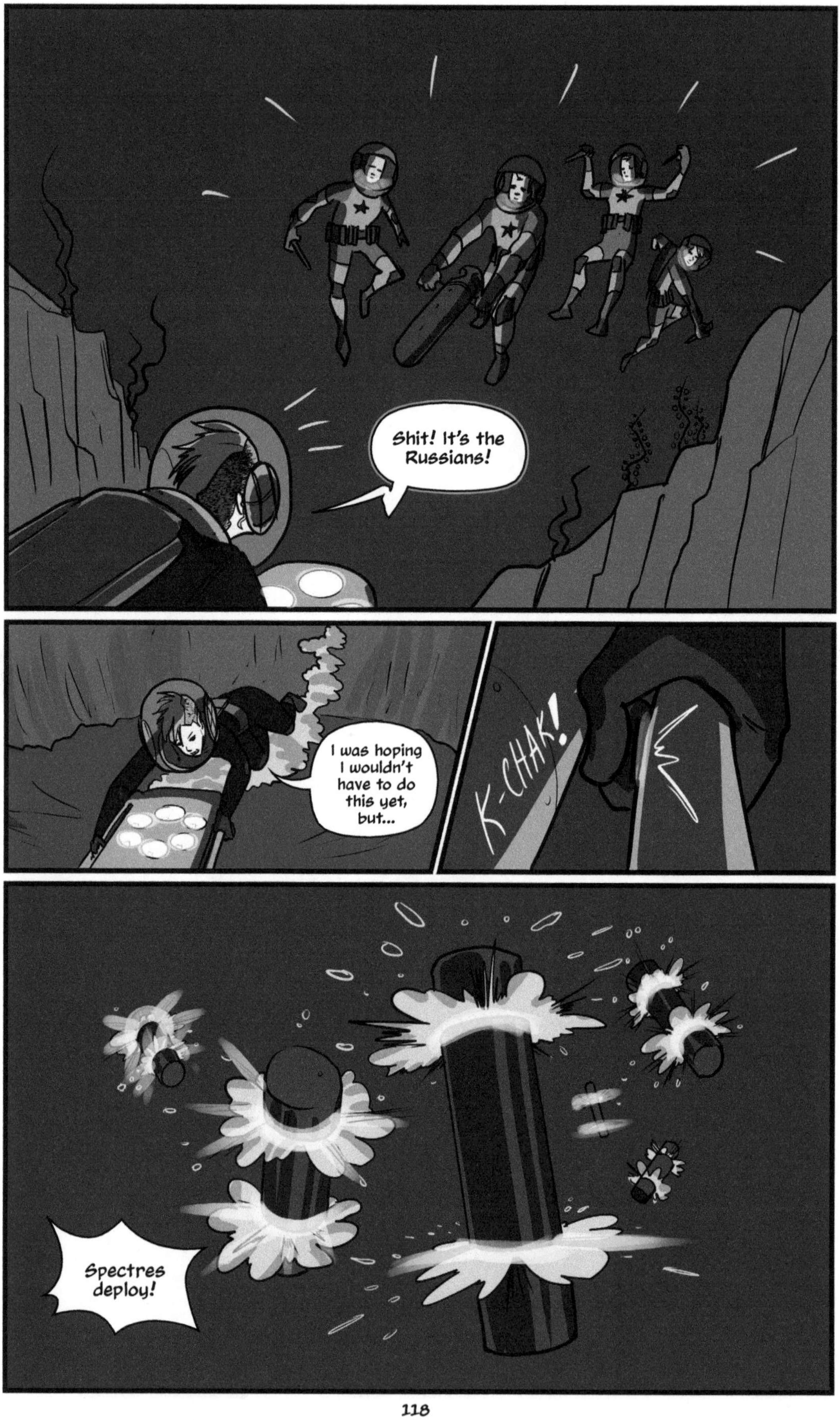
Shit! It's the Russians!
I was hoping I wouldn't have to do this yet, but...
K-CHAK!
Spectres deploy!

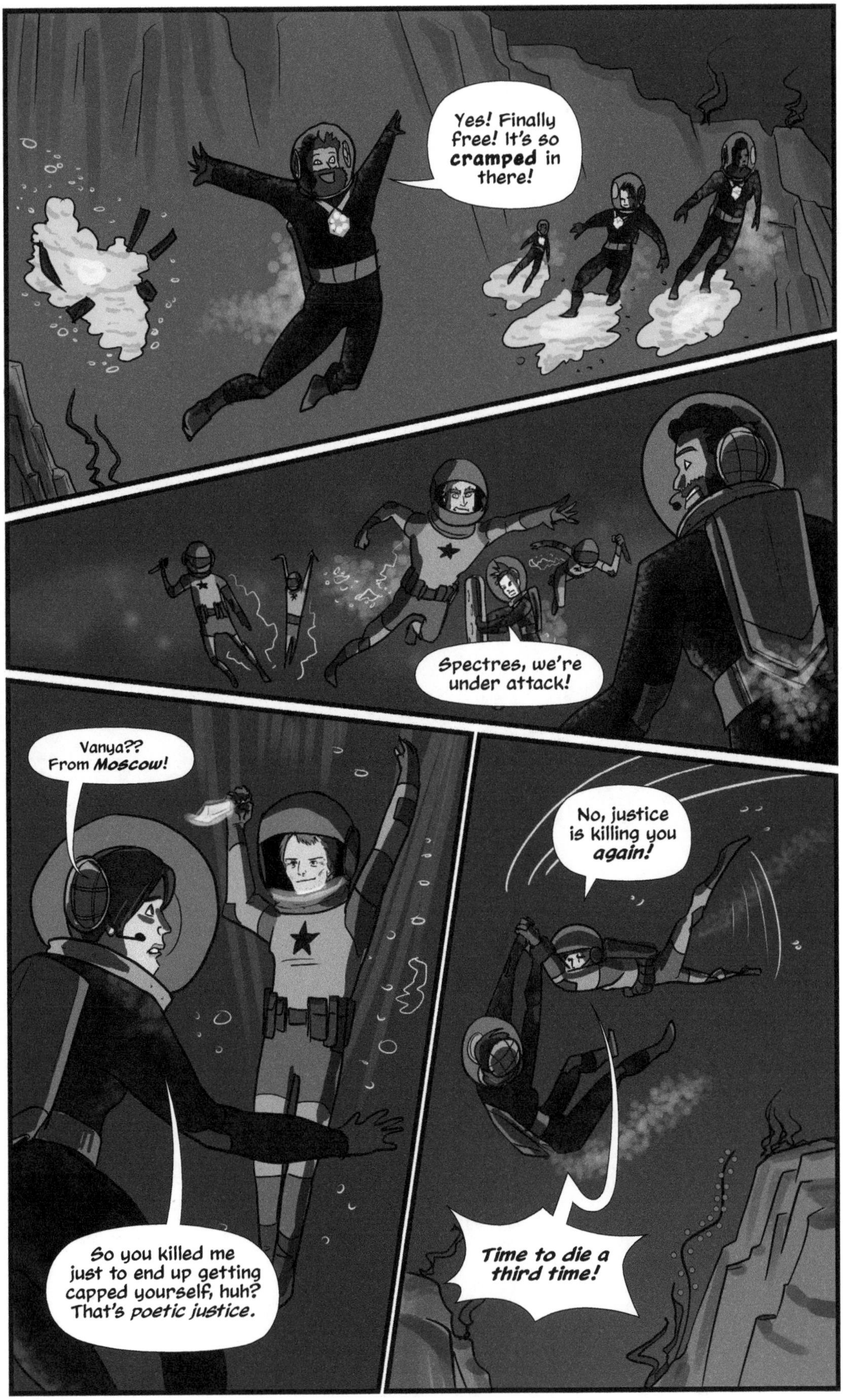
Yes! Finally free! It's so **cramped** in there!
Spectres, we're under attack!
Vanya?? From *Moscow*!
So you killed me just to end up getting capped yourself, huh? That's *poetic justice*.
No, justice is killing you *again!*
Time to die a third time!

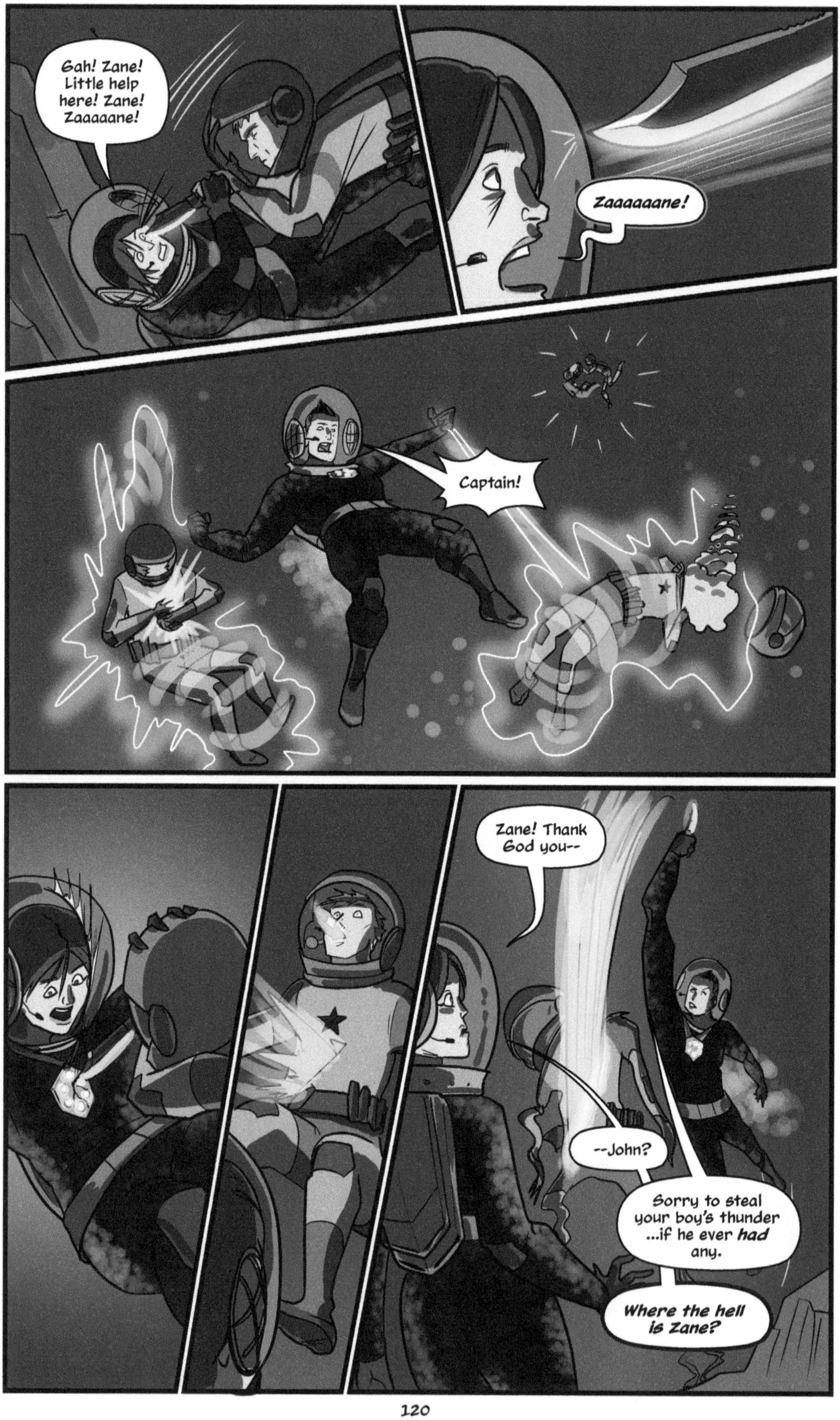
Gah! Zane! Little help here! Zane! Zaaaaane!
Zaaaaaane!
Captain!
Zane! Thank God you--
--John?
Sorry to steal your boy's thunder ...if he ever *had* any.
Where the hell is Zane?

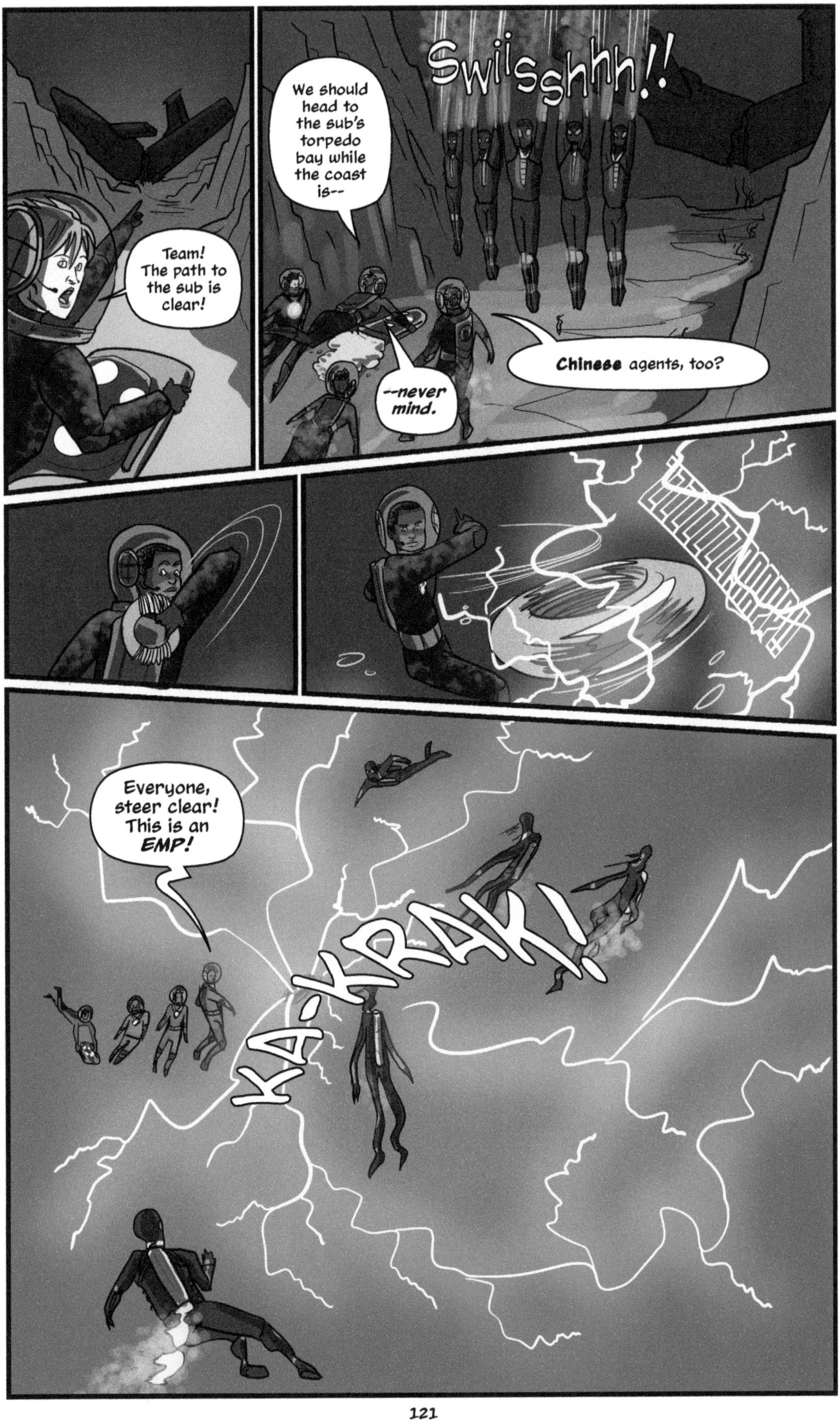
Team! The path to the sub is clear!
We should head to the sub's torpedo bay while the coast is--
Swiisshhh!!
--never mind.
Chinese agents, too?
Everyone, steer clear! This is an ***EMP!***
KA-KRAK!!

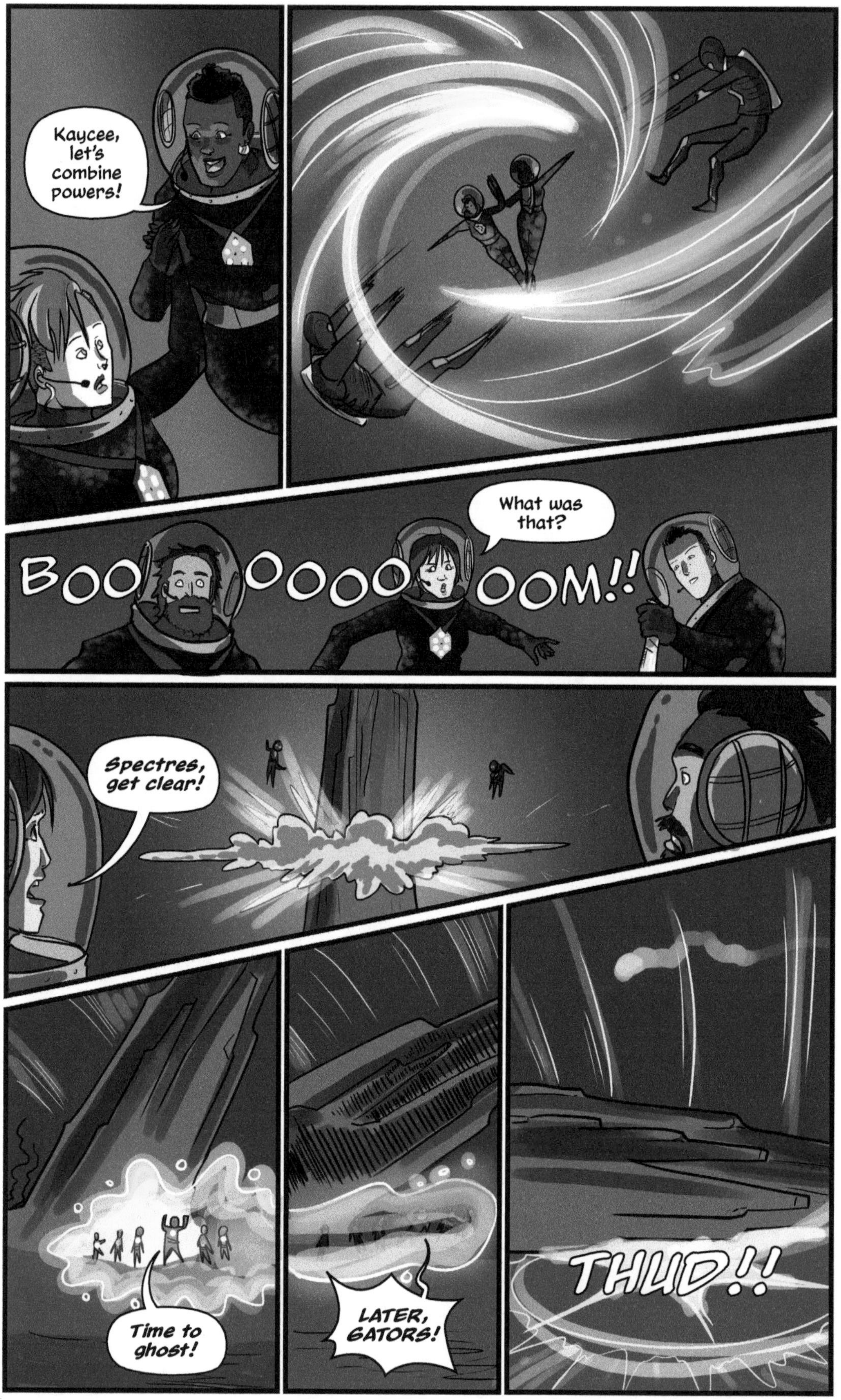
Kaycee, let's combine powers!
BOOOOOOOOOM!!
What was that?
Spectres, get clear!
Time to ghost!
LATER, GATORS!
THUD!!

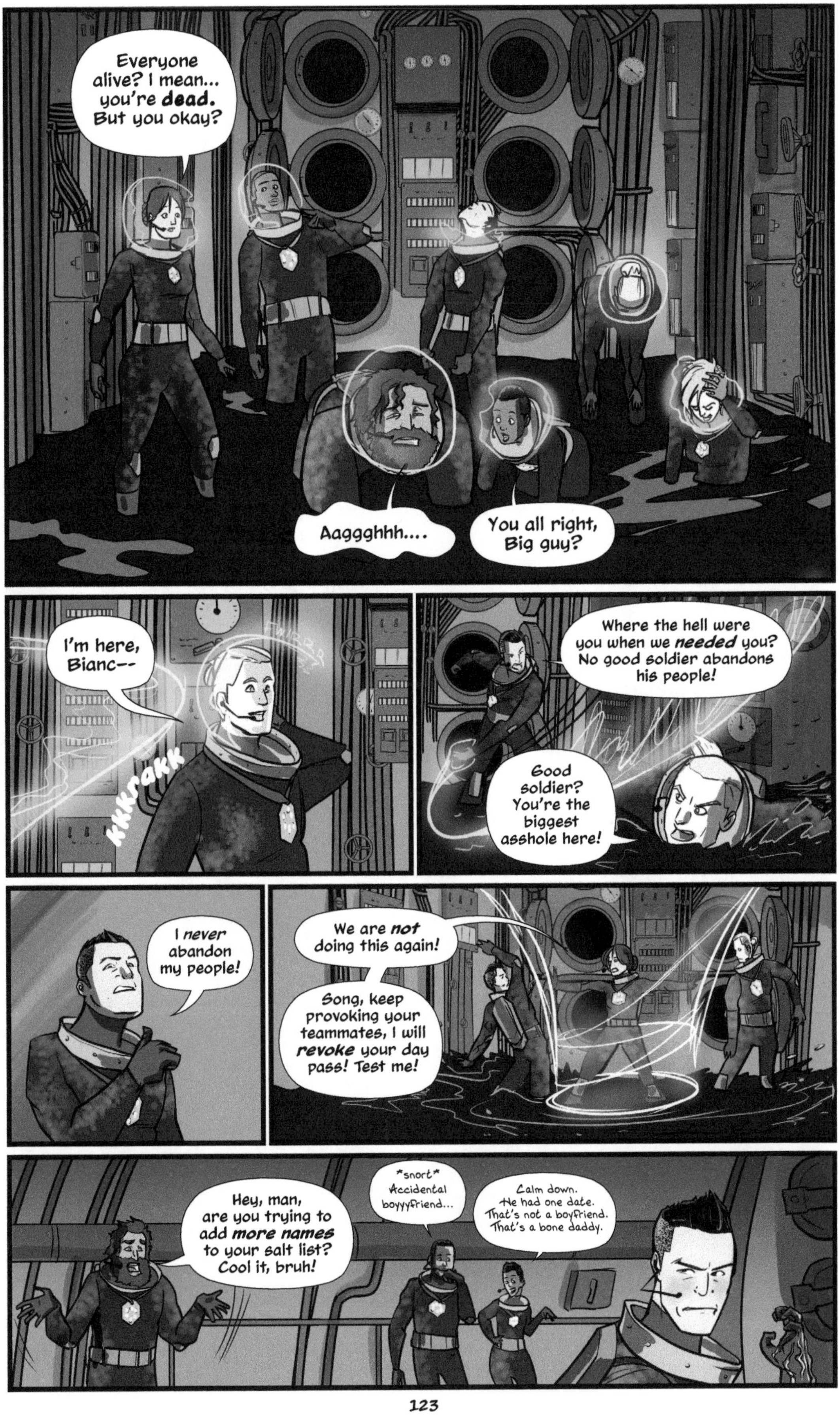
Everyone alive? I mean... you're dead. But you okay?
Aaggghhh....
You all right, Big guy?
I'm here, Bianc--
KKKRAKK
Where the hell were you when we needed you? No good soldier abandons his people!
Good soldier? You're the biggest asshole here!
I never abandon my people!
We are not doing this again!
Song, keep provoking your teammates, I will revoke your day pass! Test me!
Hey, man, are you trying to add more names to your salt list? Cool it, bruh!
snort Accidental boyyyfriend...
Calm down. He had one date. That's not a boyfriend. That's a bone daddy.

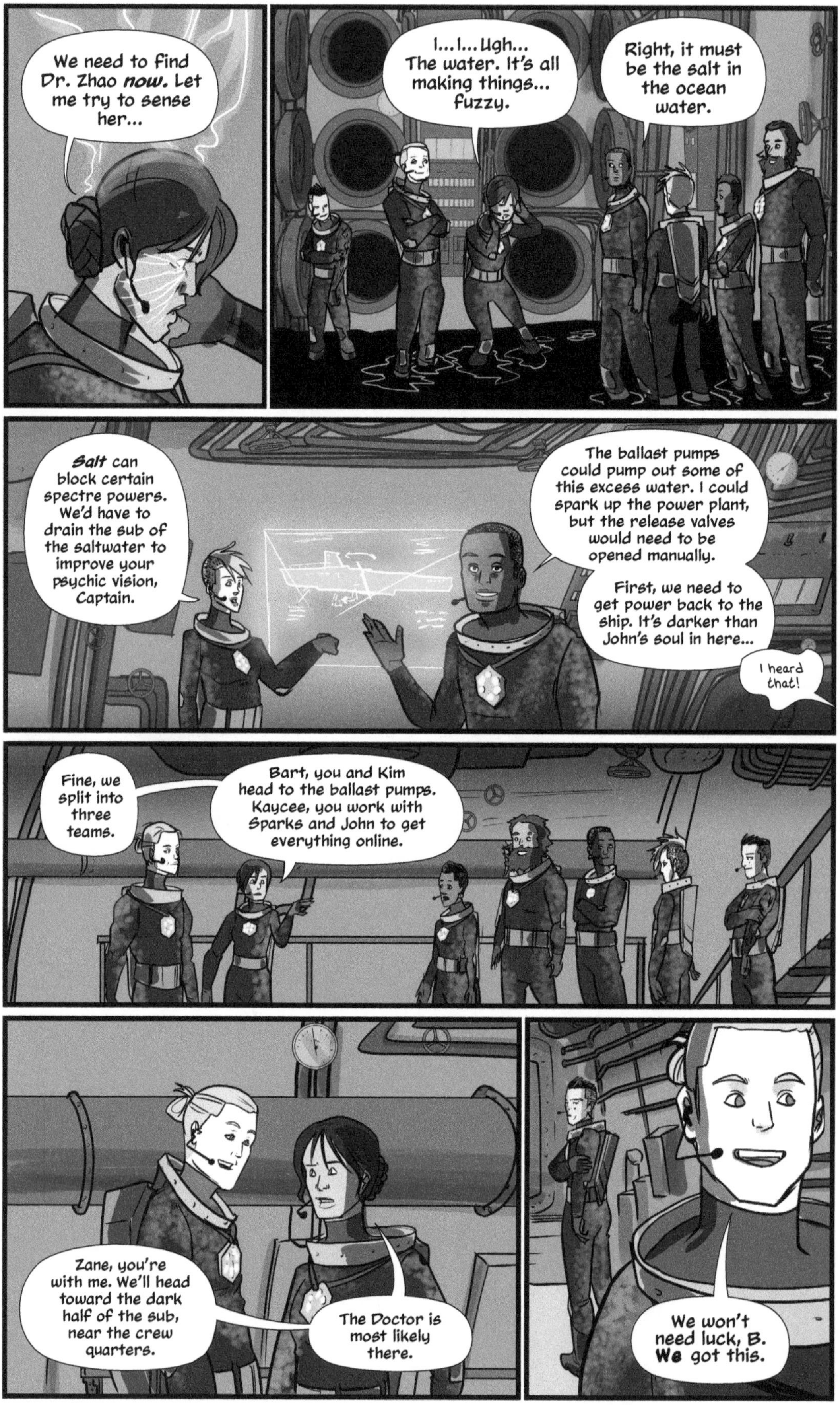
We need to find Dr. Zhao **now.** Let me try to sense her...
I... I... Ugh... The water. It's all making things... fuzzy.
Right, it must be the salt in the ocean water.
Salt can block certain spectre powers. We'd have to drain the sub of the saltwater to improve your psychic vision, Captain.
The ballast pumps could pump out some of this excess water. I could spark up the power plant, but the release valves would need to be opened manually.
First, we need to get power back to the ship. It's darker than John's soul in here...
I heard that!
Fine, we split into three teams.
Bart, you and Kim head to the ballast pumps. Kaycee, you work with Sparks and John to get everything online.
Zane, you're with me. We'll head toward the dark half of the sub, near the crew quarters.
The Doctor is most likely there.
We won't need luck, B. **We** got this.

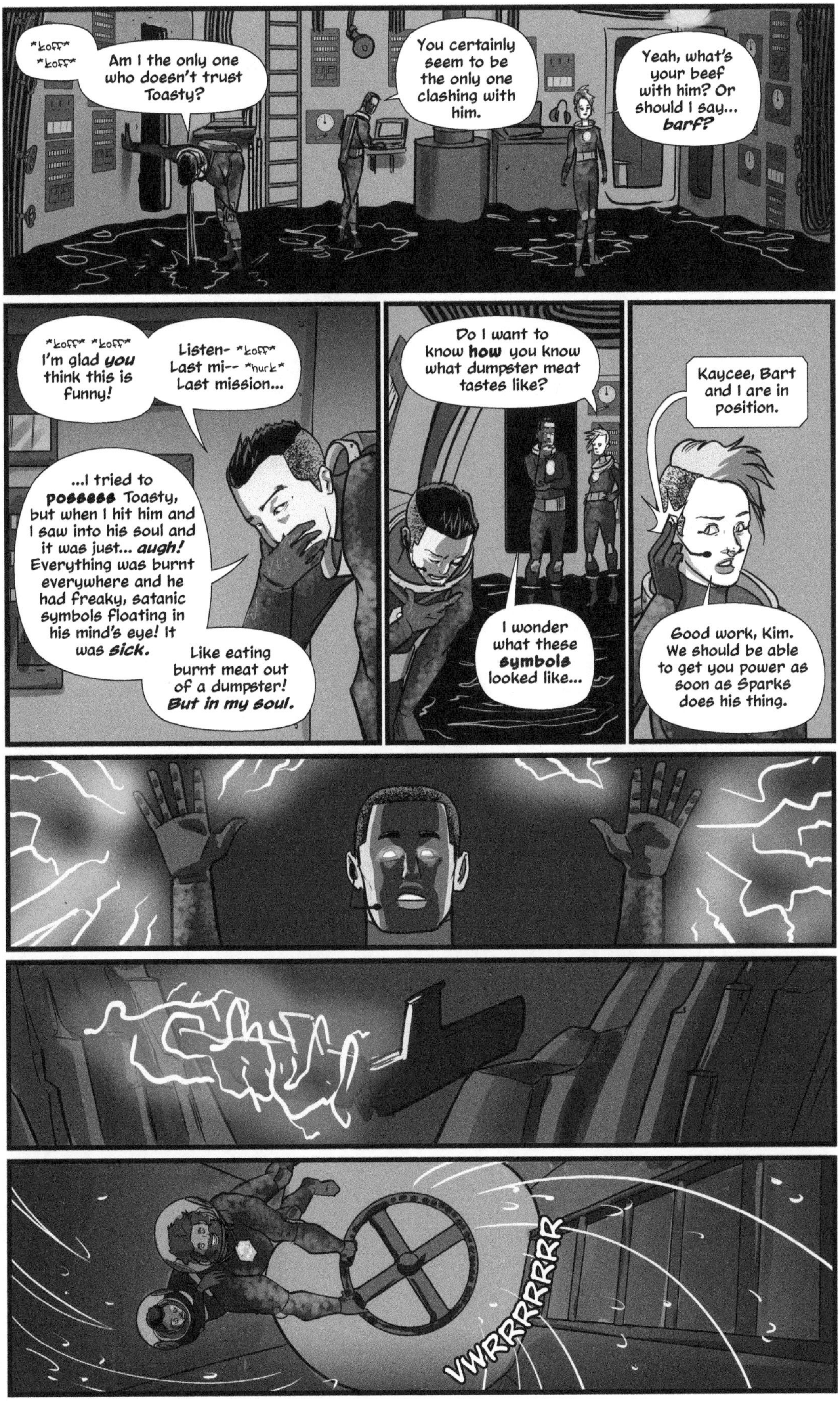
koff *koff*
Am I the only one who doesn't trust Toasty?
You certainly seem to be the only one clashing with him.
Yeah, what's your beef with him? Or should I say... barf?
koff *koff* I'm glad you think this is funny!
Listen- *koff* Last mi-- *hurk* Last mission...
...I tried to possess Toasty, but when I hit him and I saw into his soul and it was just... augh! Everything was burnt everywhere and he had freaky, satanic symbols floating in his mind's eye! It was sick.
Like eating burnt meat out of a dumpster! But in my soul.
Do I want to know how you know what dumpster meat tastes like?
I wonder what these symbols looked like...
Kaycee, Bart and I are in position.
Good work, Kim. We should be able to get you power as soon as Sparks does his thing.
VWRRRRRRR

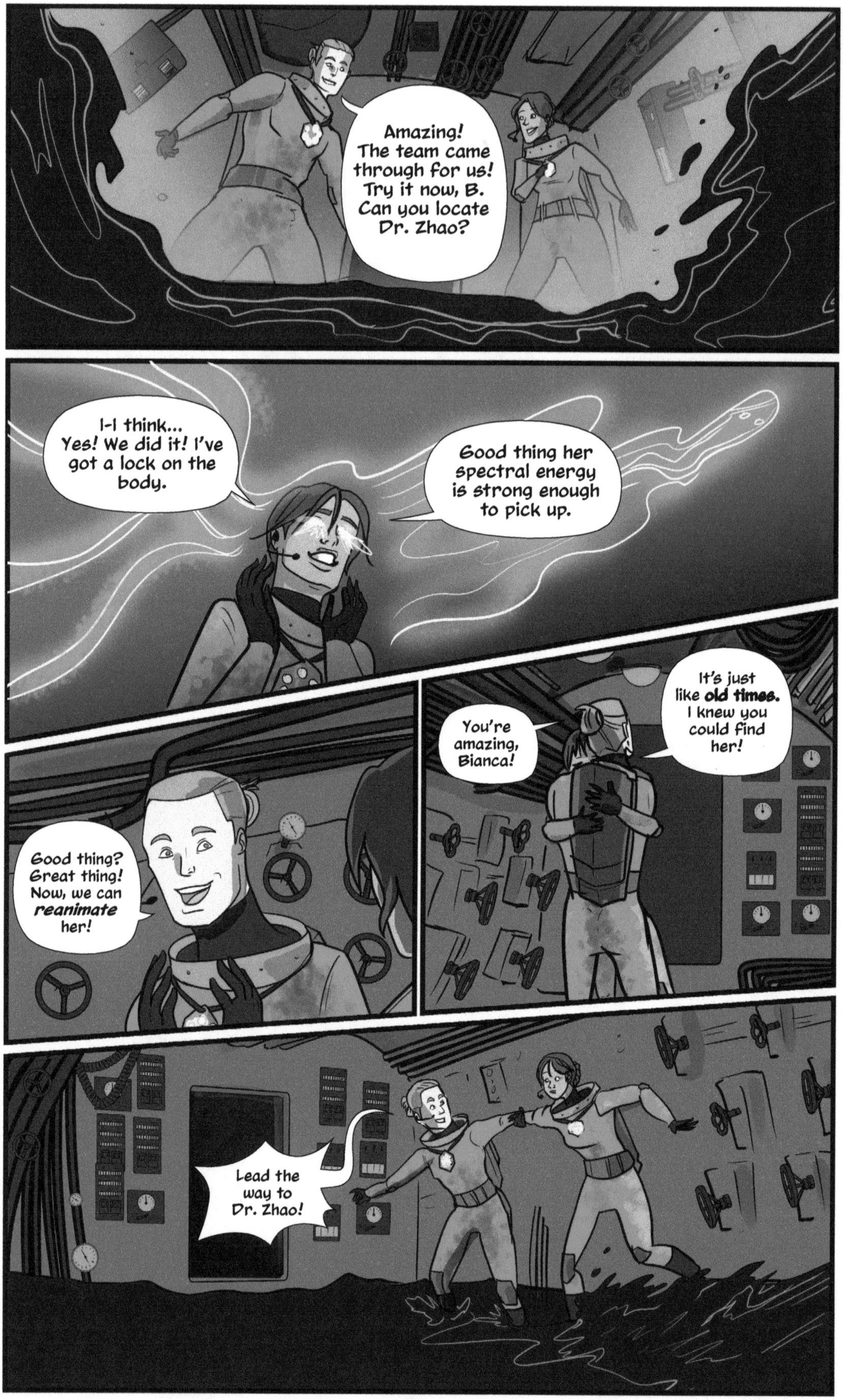
Amazing! The team came through for us! Try it now, B. Can you locate Dr. Zhao?
I-I think... Yes! We did it! I've got a lock on the body.
Good thing her spectral energy is strong enough to pick up.
Good thing? Great thing! Now, we can *reanimate* her!
You're amazing, Bianca!
It's just like **old times.** I knew you could find her!
Lead the way to Dr. Zhao!

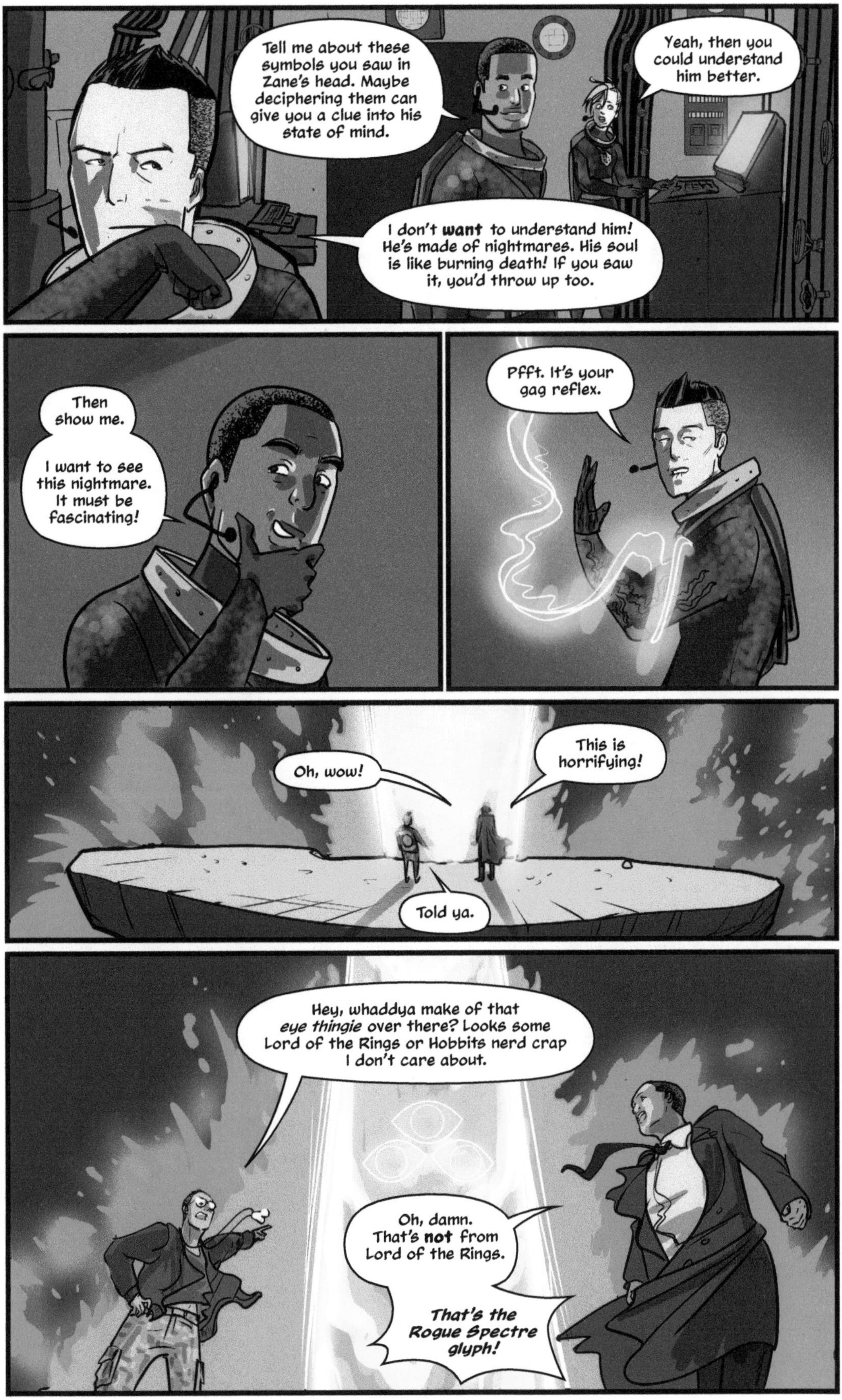

Tell me about these symbols you saw in Zane's head. Maybe deciphering them can give you a clue into his state of mind.
Yeah, then you could understand him better.
I don't **want** to understand him! He's made of nightmares. His soul is like burning death! If you saw it, you'd throw up too.
Then show me.
I want to see this nightmare. It must be fascinating!
Pfft. It's your gag reflex.
Oh, wow!
This is horrifying!
Told ya.
Hey, whaddya make of that *eye thingie* over there? Looks some Lord of the Rings or Hobbits nerd crap I don't care about.
Oh, damn. That's **not** from Lord of the Rings.
That's the Rogue Spectre glyph!

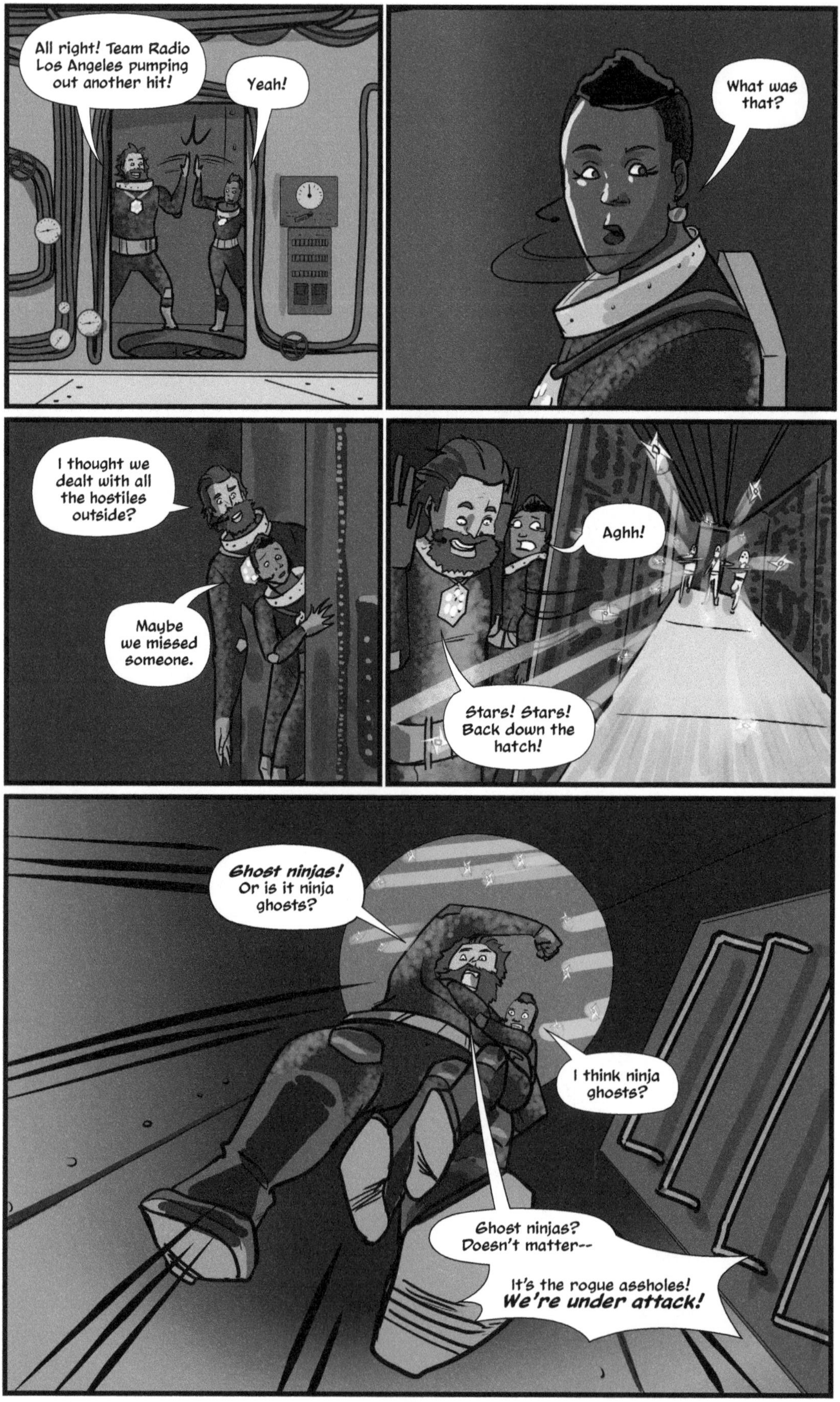
All right! Team Radio Los Angeles pumping out another hit!
Yeah!
What was that?
I thought we dealt with all the hostiles outside?
Maybe we missed someone.
Aghh!
Stars! Stars! Back down the hatch!
Ghost ninjas! Or is it ninja ghosts?
I think ninja ghosts?
Ghost ninjas? Doesn't matter--
It's the rogue assholes! ***We're under attack!***

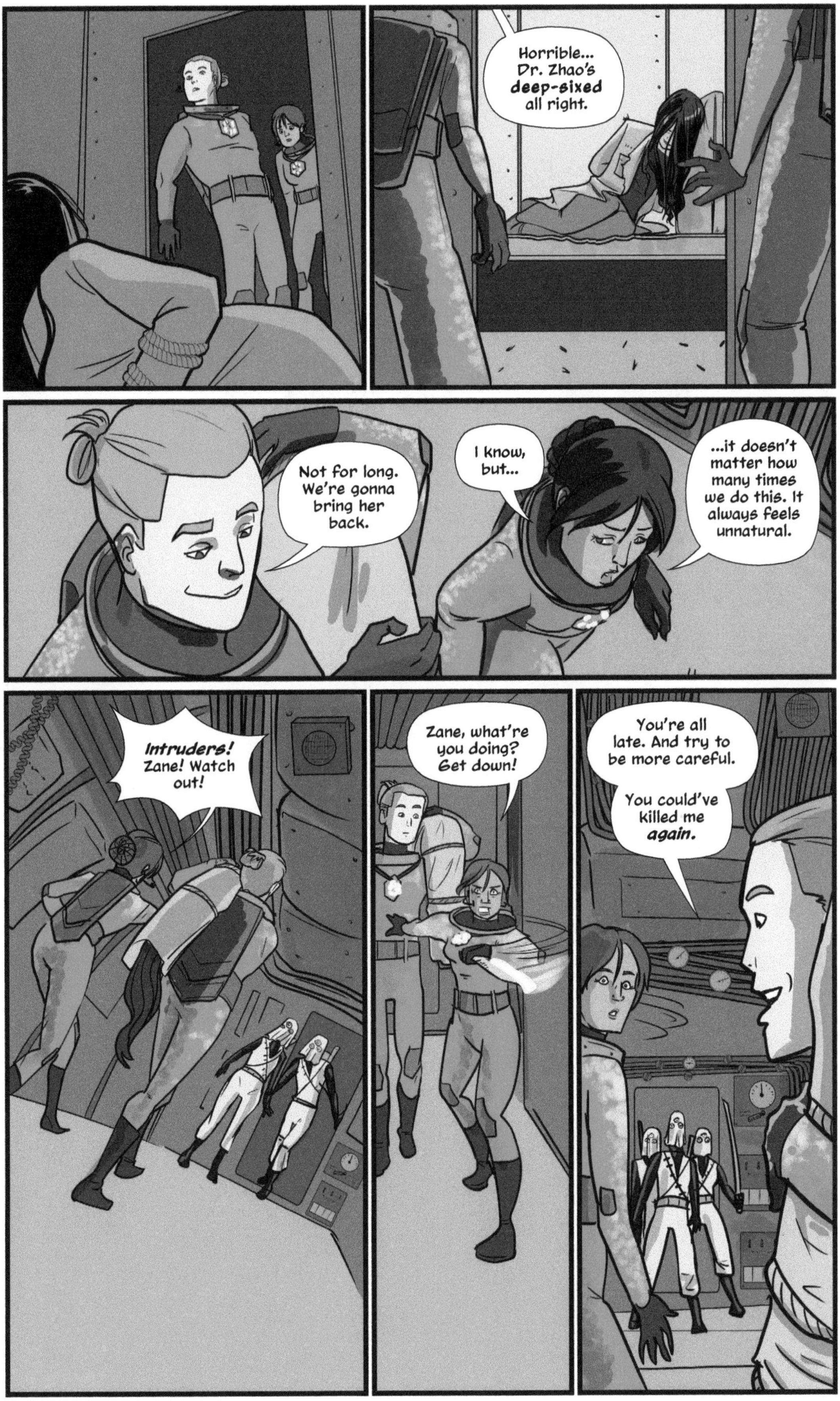

Horrible... Dr. Zhao's **deep-sixed** all right.
Not for long. We're gonna bring her back.
I know, but...
...it doesn't matter how many times we do this. It always feels unnatural.
Intruders! Zane! Watch out!
Zane, what're you doing? Get down!
You're all late. And try to be more careful.
You could've killed me ***again.***

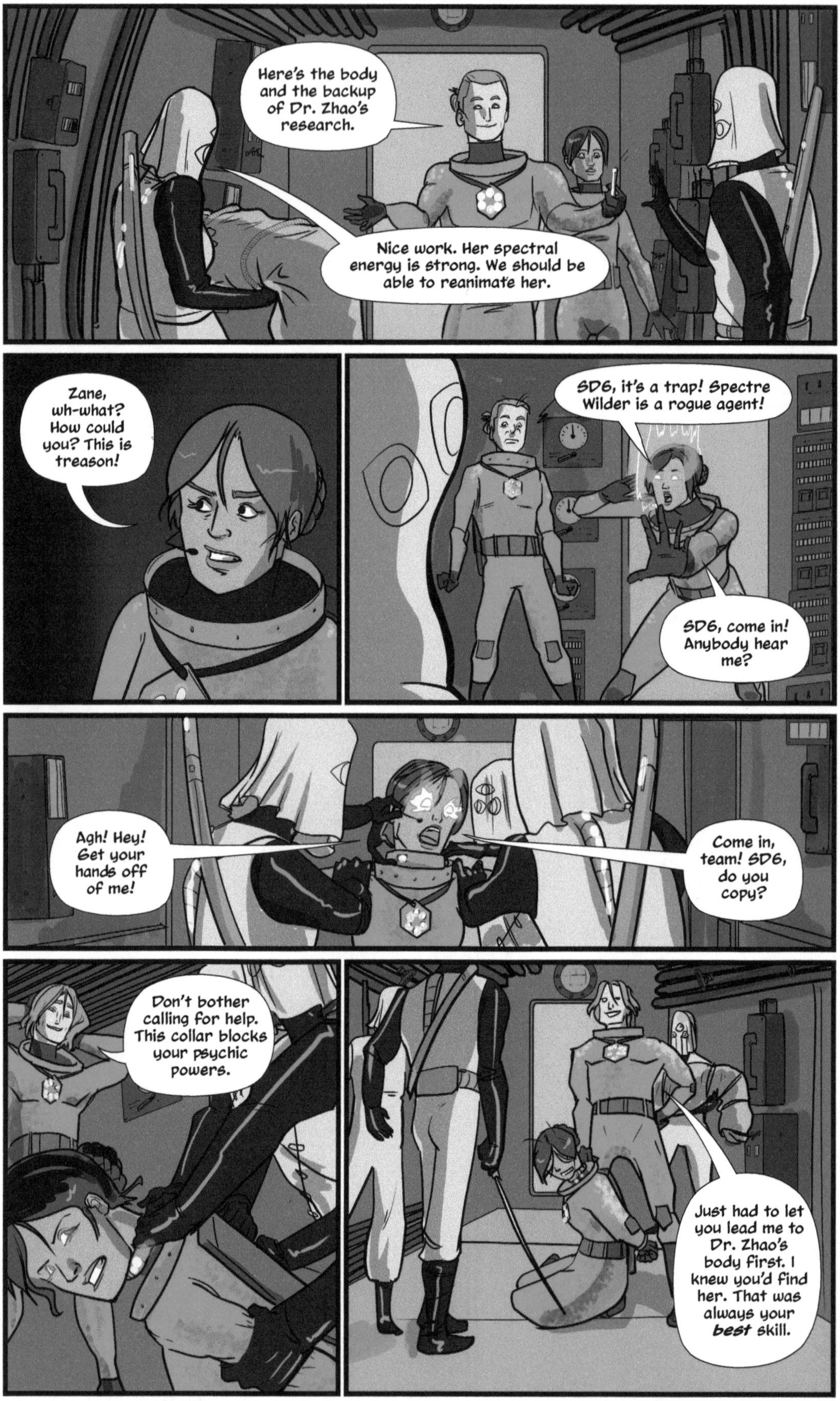
Here's the body and the backup of Dr. Zhao's research.
Nice work. Her spectral energy is strong. We should be able to reanimate her.
Zane, wh-what? How could you? This is treason!
SD6, it's a trap! Spectre Wilder is a rogue agent!
SD6, come in! Anybody hear me?
Agh! Hey! Get your hands off of me!
Come in, team! SD6, do you copy?
Don't bother calling for help. This collar blocks your psychic powers.
Just had to let you lead me to Dr. Zhao's body first. I knew you'd find her. That was always your ***best*** skill.

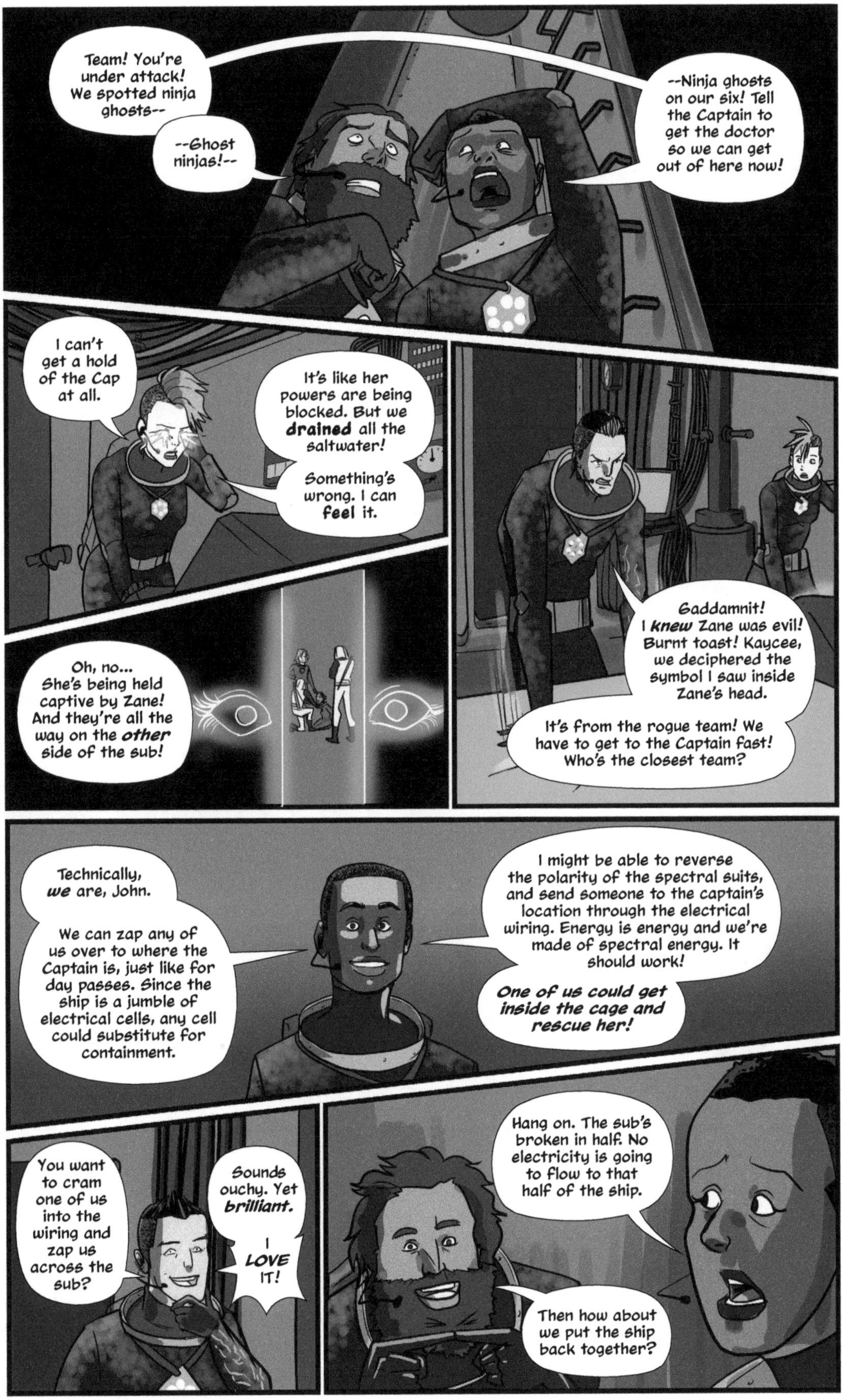
Team! You're under attack! We spotted ninja ghosts--
--Ghost ninjas!--
--Ninja ghosts on our six! Tell the Captain to get the doctor so we can get out of here now!
I can't get a hold of the Cap at all.
It's like her powers are being blocked. But we **drained** all the saltwater!
Something's wrong. I can **feel** it.
Oh, no... She's being held captive by Zane! And they're all the way on the ***other*** side of the sub!
Gaddamnit! I ***knew*** Zane was evil! Burnt toast! Kaycee, we deciphered the symbol I saw inside Zane's head.
It's from the rogue team! We have to get to the Captain fast! Who's the closest team?
Technically, ***we*** are, John.
We can zap any of us over to where the Captain is, just like for day passes. Since the ship is a jumble of electrical cells, any cell could substitute for containment.
I might be able to reverse the polarity of the spectral suits, and send someone to the captain's location through the electrical wiring. Energy is energy and we're made of spectral energy. It should work!
One of us could get inside the cage and rescue her!
You want to cram one of us into the wiring and zap us across the sub?
Sounds ouchy. Yet ***brilliant.***
I ***LOVE*** IT!
Hang on. The sub's broken in half. No electricity is going to flow to that half of the ship.
Then how about we put the ship back together?

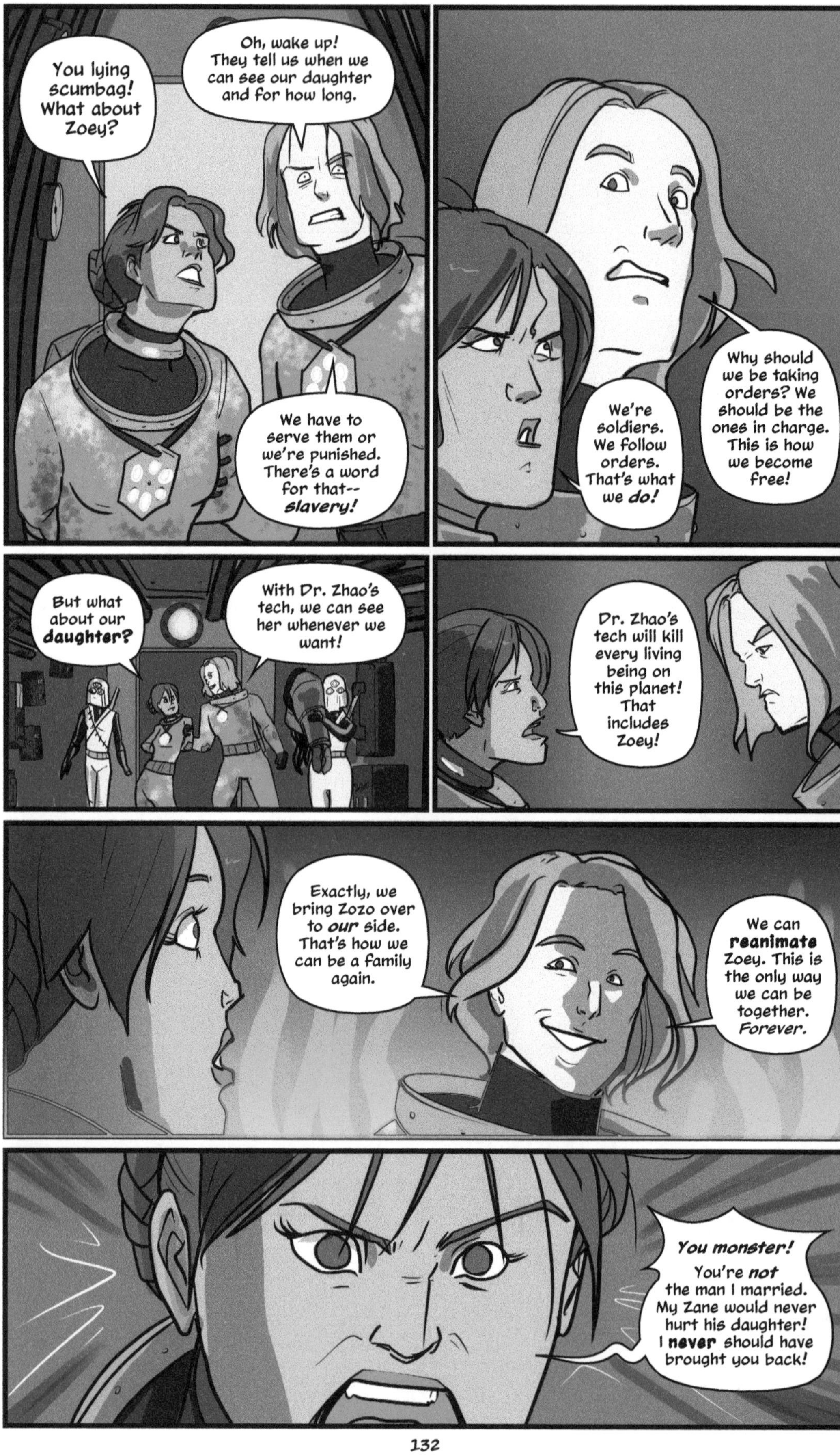
You lying scumbag! What about Zoey?
Oh, wake up! They tell us when we can see our daughter and for how long.
We have to serve them or we're punished. There's a word for that-- *slavery!*
We're soldiers. We follow orders. That's what we *do!*
Why should we be taking orders? We should be the ones in charge. This is how we become free!
But what about our **daughter?**
With Dr. Zhao's tech, we can see her whenever we want!
Dr. Zhao's tech will kill every living being on this planet! That includes Zoey!
Exactly, we bring Zozo over to *our* side. That's how we can be a family again.
We can **reanimate** Zoey. This is the only way we can be together. *Forever.*
You monster!
You're *not* the man I married. My Zane would never hurt his daughter! I **never** should have brought you back!

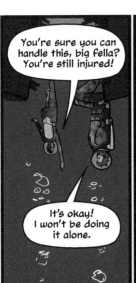

You're sure you can handle this, big fella? You're still injured!

It's okay! I won't be doing it alone.

I've got one of my best buds with me. We'll do this **together!**

Yeah, let's rock this sub back together!

That's it Bart—we're doing it! Keep going!

I'm caspering! Look at me! I'm a happy ghost!

It feels so good to be *myself!*

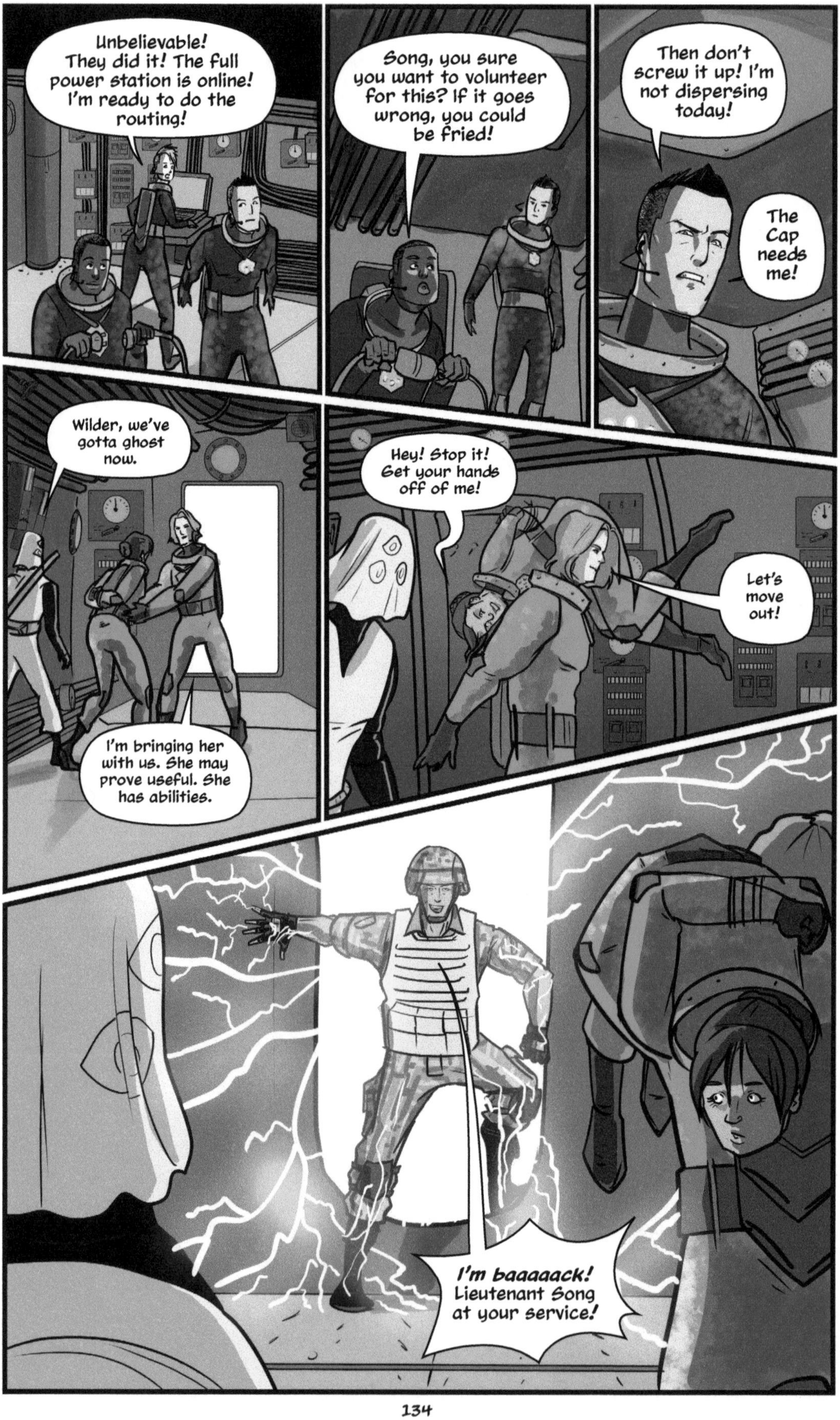
Unbelievable! They did it! The full power station is online! I'm ready to do the routing!
Song, you sure you want to volunteer for this? If it goes wrong, you could be fried!
Then don't screw it up! I'm not dispersing today!
The Cap needs me!
Wilder, we've gotta ghost now.
I'm bringing her with us. She may prove useful. She has abilities.
Hey! Stop it! Get your hands off of me!
Let's move out!
I'm baaaaack! Lieutenant Song at your service!

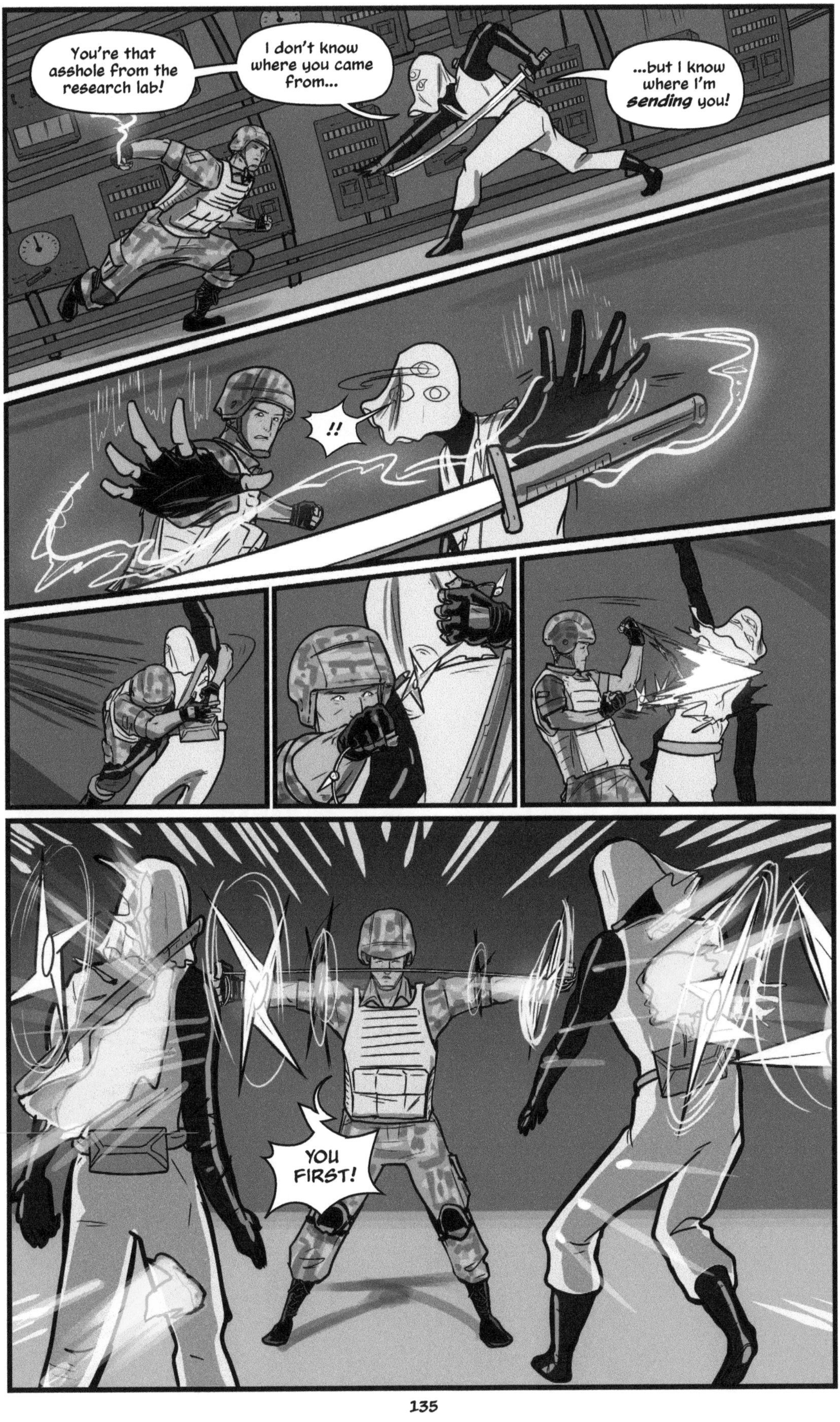
You're that asshole from the research lab!
I don't know where you came from...
...but I know where I'm *sending* you!
!!
YOU FIRST!

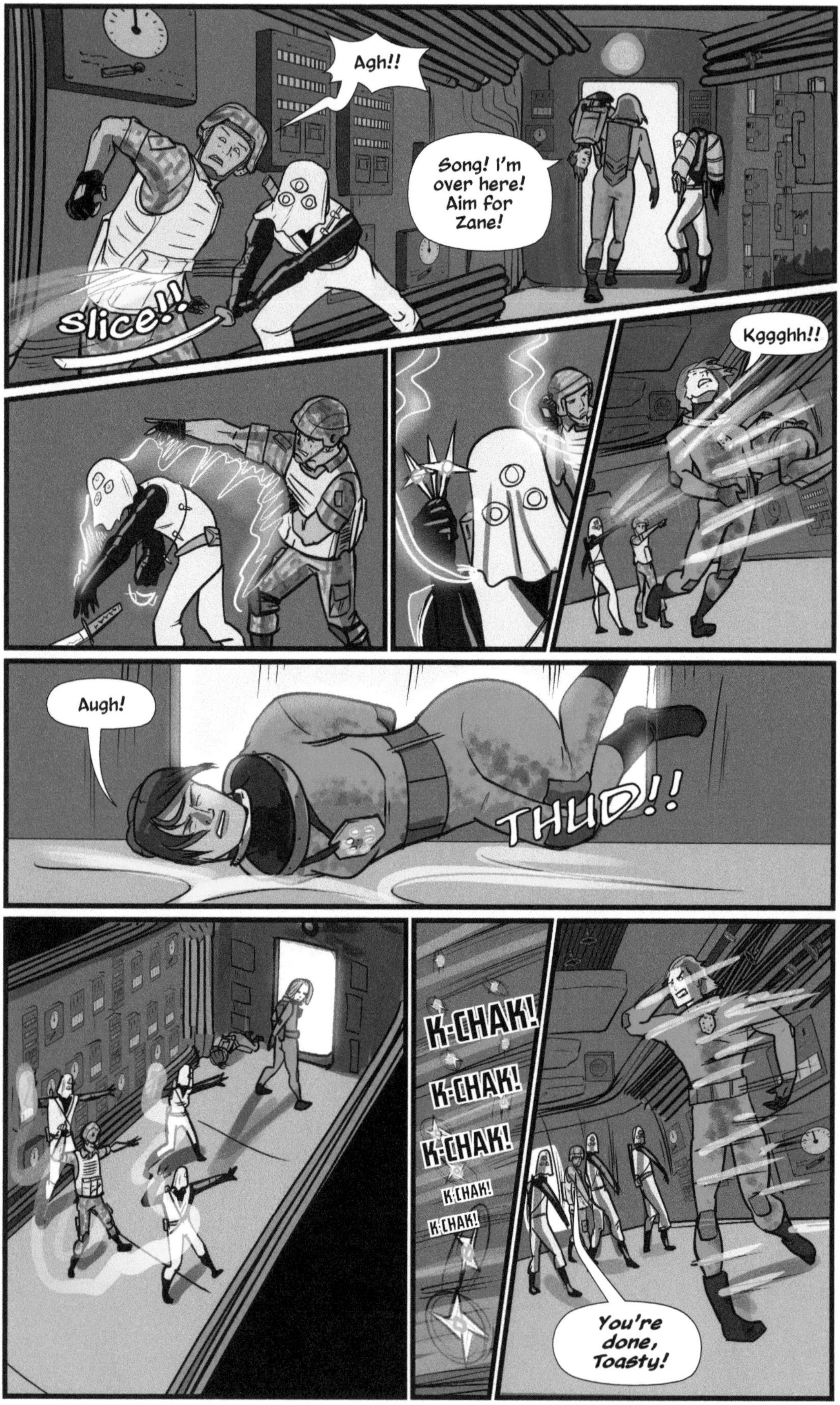
Agh!!
slice!!
Song! I'm over here! Aim for Zane!
Kggghh!!
Augh!
THUD!!
K-CHAK!
K-CHAK!
K-CHAK!
K-CHAK!
K-CHAK!
You're done, Toasty!

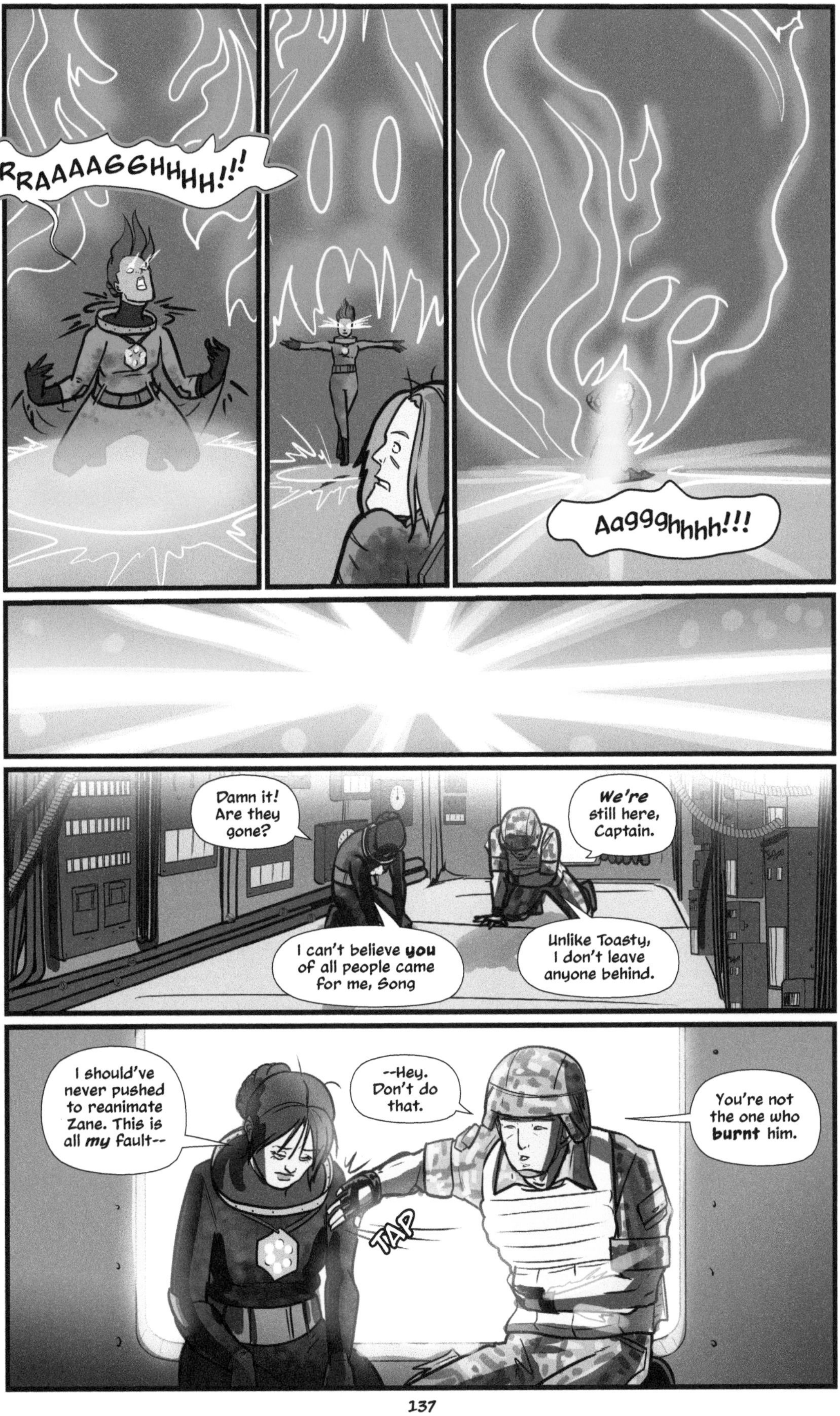
RRAAAAGGHHHHH!!!
Aagggghhhh!!!
Damn it! Are they gone?
We're still here, Captain.
I can't believe you of all people came for me, Song
Unlike Toasty, I don't leave anyone behind.
I should've never pushed to reanimate Zane. This is all my fault--
--Hey. Don't do that.
You're not the one who burnt him.
TAP

EPILOGUE

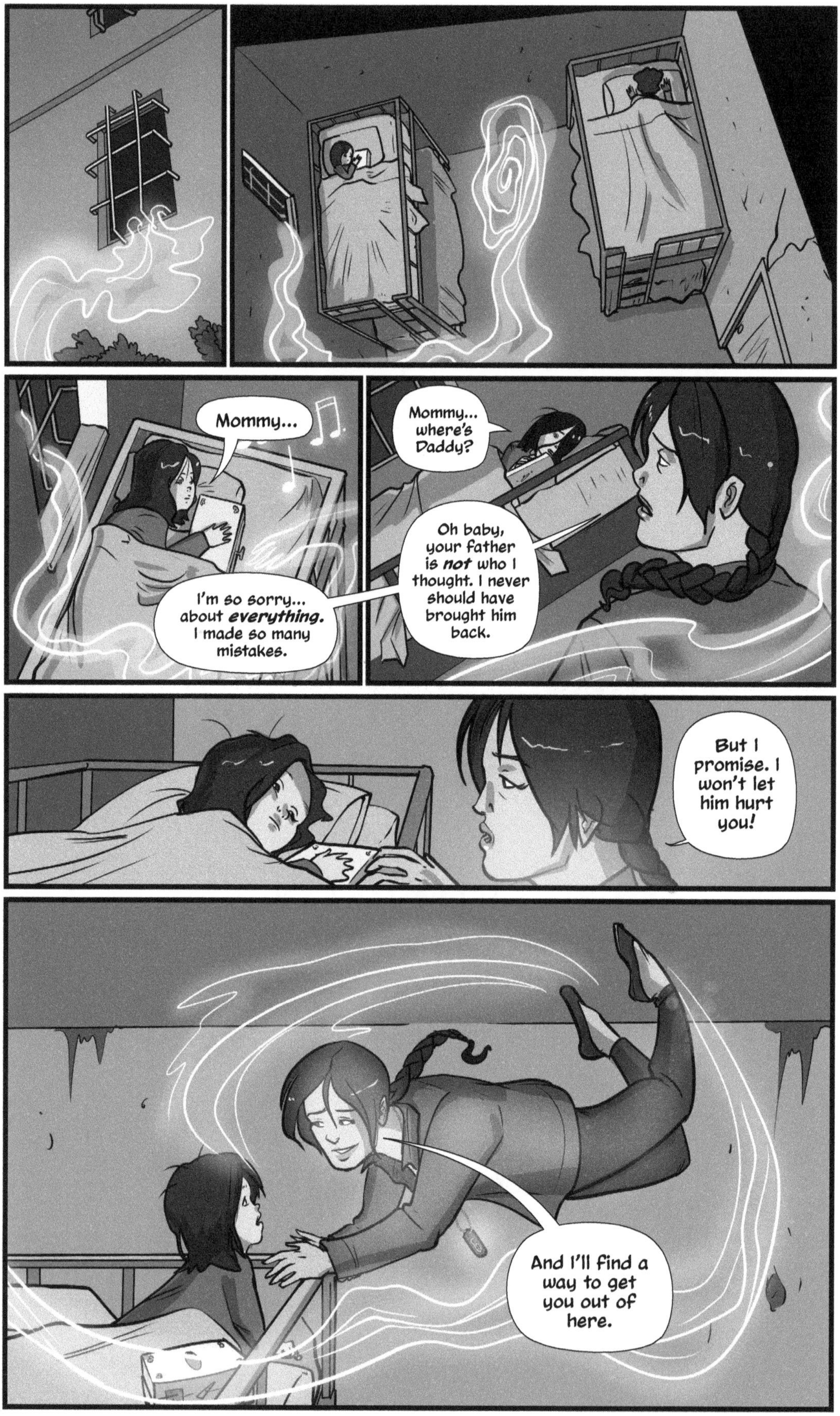

Mommy...
Mommy... where's Daddy?
I'm so sorry... about *everything.* I made so many mistakes.
Oh baby, your father is ***not*** who I thought. I never should have brought him back.
But I promise. I won't let him hurt you!
And I'll find a way to get you out of here.

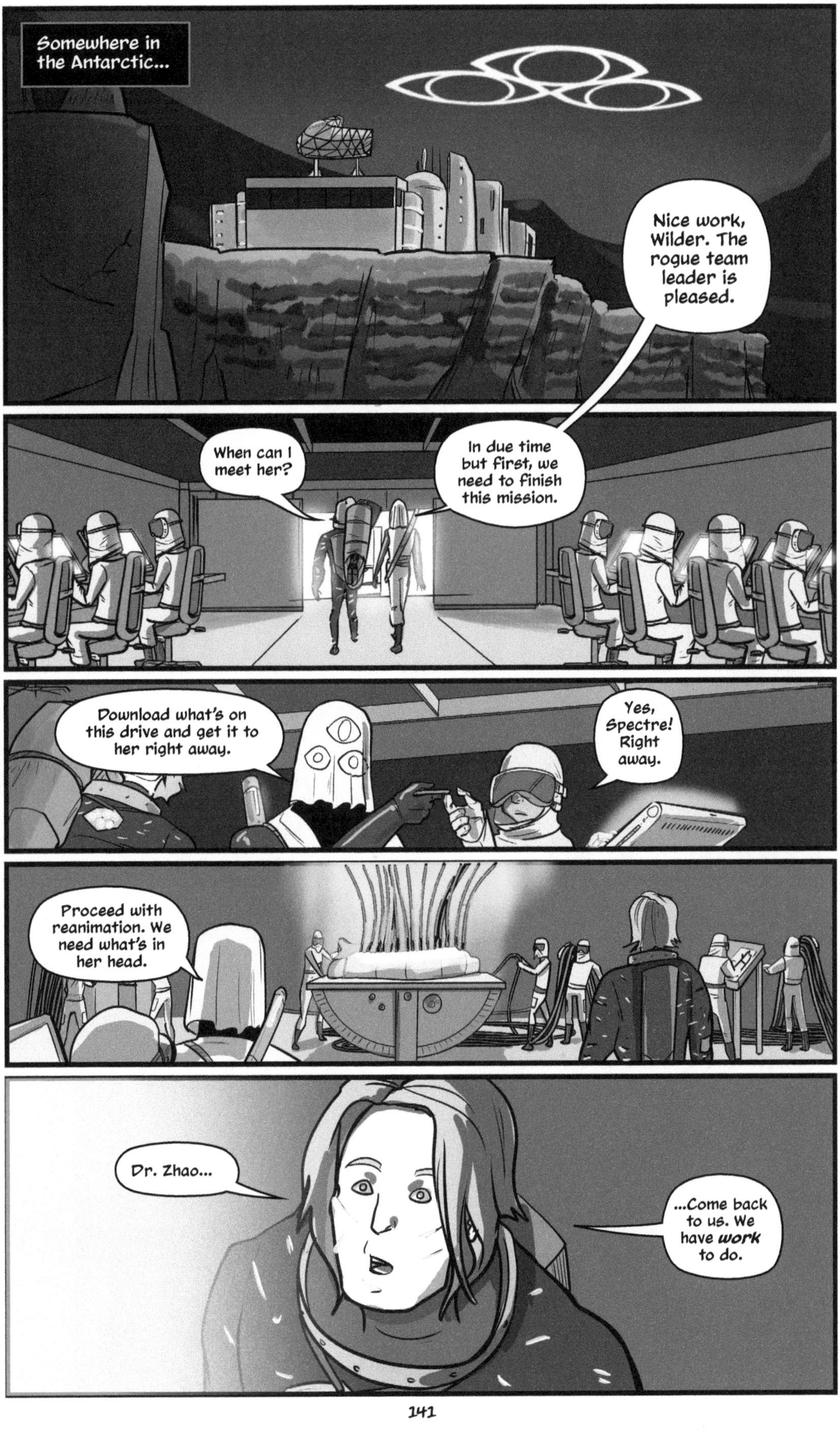
Somewhere in the Antarctic...
Nice work, Wilder. The rogue team leader is pleased.
When can I meet her?
In due time but first, we need to finish this mission.
Download what's on this drive and get it to her right away.
Yes, Spectre! Right away.
Proceed with reanimation. We need what's in her head.
Dr. Zhao...
...Come back to us. We have *work* to do.

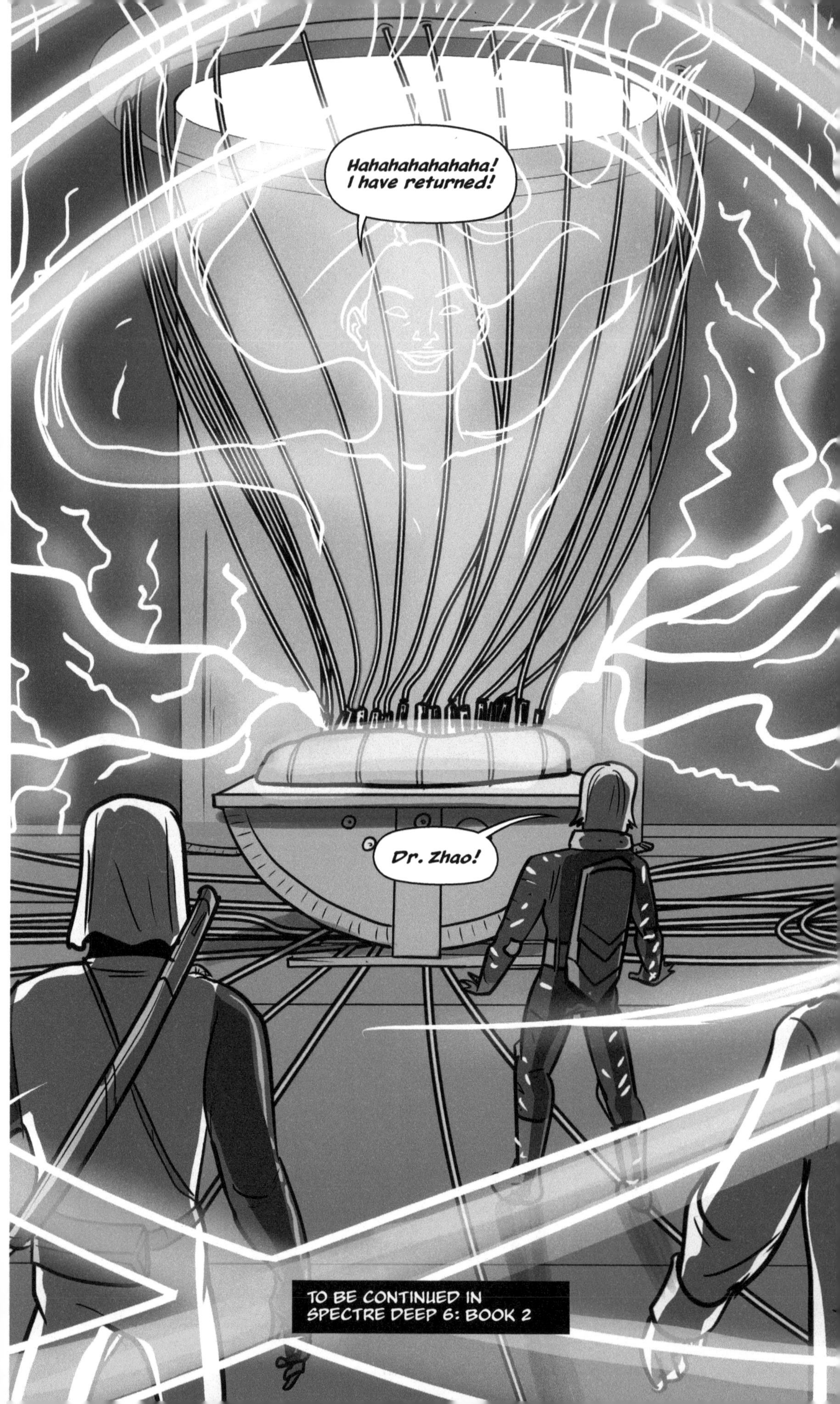
Hahahahahahaha! I have returned!
Dr. Zhao!
TO BE CONTINUED IN SPECTRE DEEP 6: BOOK 2

EXTRAS

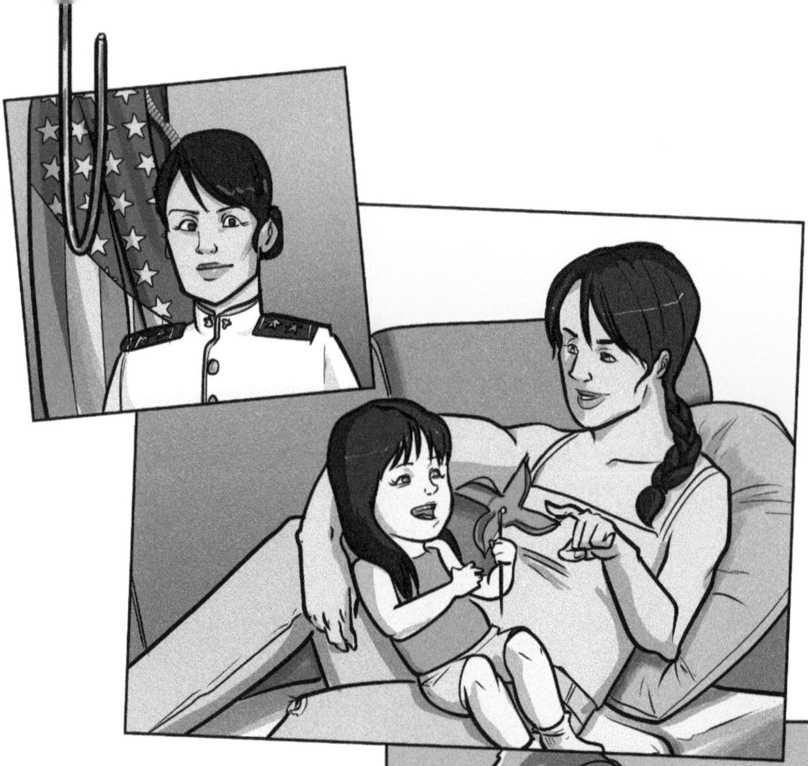

(I don't get it.
He's not that cute...)

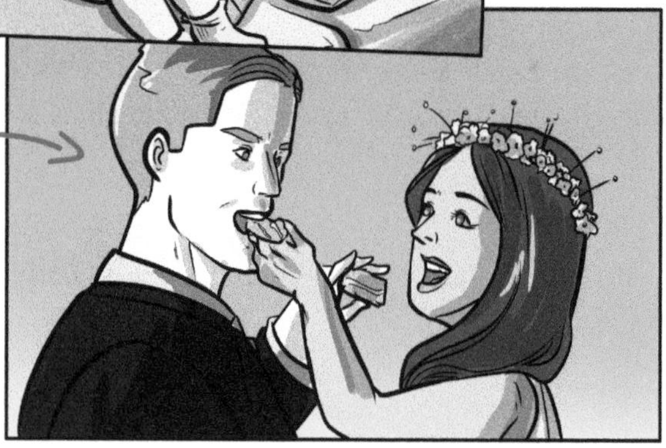

NAME: Spectre Captain Bianca Vasquez

CAUSE OF DEATH: Stab wound to the back

MANNER OF DEATH: Homicide

CONDITION ON ARRIVAL: Fairly good

SPECTRE EXTRACTION: Difficult

ENERGY READING: 125 MJ (Very high)

ABILITY: TELEPATHY, SUBJECT TRACKING

ANALYSIS: Spectre Vasquez demonstrates great leadership abilities and attachment to her teammates. If anything, Spectre Vasquez cares too much, being too willing to sacrifice herself for 'the greater good.' Possible equipment loss risk. Also, demonstrates exaggerated attachment to her surviving family. Recommend close monitoring of her visitation time.

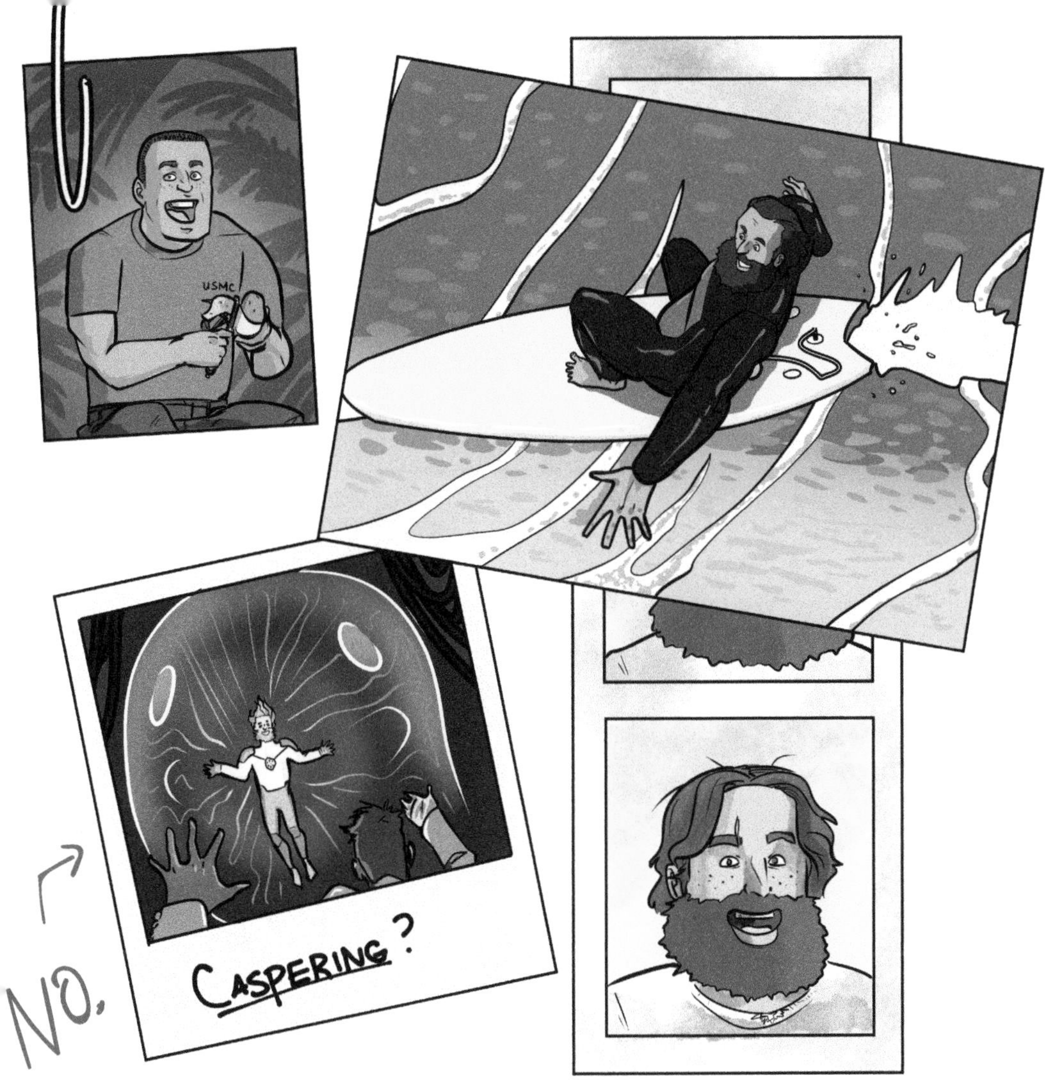
USMC
CASPERING?
NO.

NAME: Spectre Bart Bartholomew

CAUSE OF DEATH: Broken neck

MANNER OF DEATH: Accident

CONDITION ON ARRIVAL: Waterlogged

SPECTRE EXTRACTION: Moderate

ENERGY READING: 150 MJ (Extremely high)

ABILITY: POLTERGEISTING (The friendly ghost thing is not a good look)

ANALYSIS: Spectre Bartholomew demonstrates high energy readings, but non-aggressive tendencies. Positive disposition. Willing to follow orders. Effective in the field, despite some unorthodox image manifestation. The team is working with Spectre to correct this anomaly. Recommend approval of video game console in his containment to encourage aggressive battle tactics.

—CUTE!

NAME: Spectre Kim Masters

CAUSE OF DEATH: Animal Mauling — (A bear hug is <u>not</u> a friendly hug.)

MANNER OF DEATH: Accident

CONDITION ON ARRIVAL: Severe lacerations to the face and chest. Left arm dismembered.

SPECTRE EXTRACTION: Easy

ENERGY READING: 85 MJ (Medium)

ABILITY: HEALING

ANALYSIS: Spectre Masters demonstrates an ability to restore her teammates in the field as well as a sunny disposition. Very cooperative. Overly willing to share photos of her cats. Recommend continued activity as normal, as long as her needs for cat toys are met.

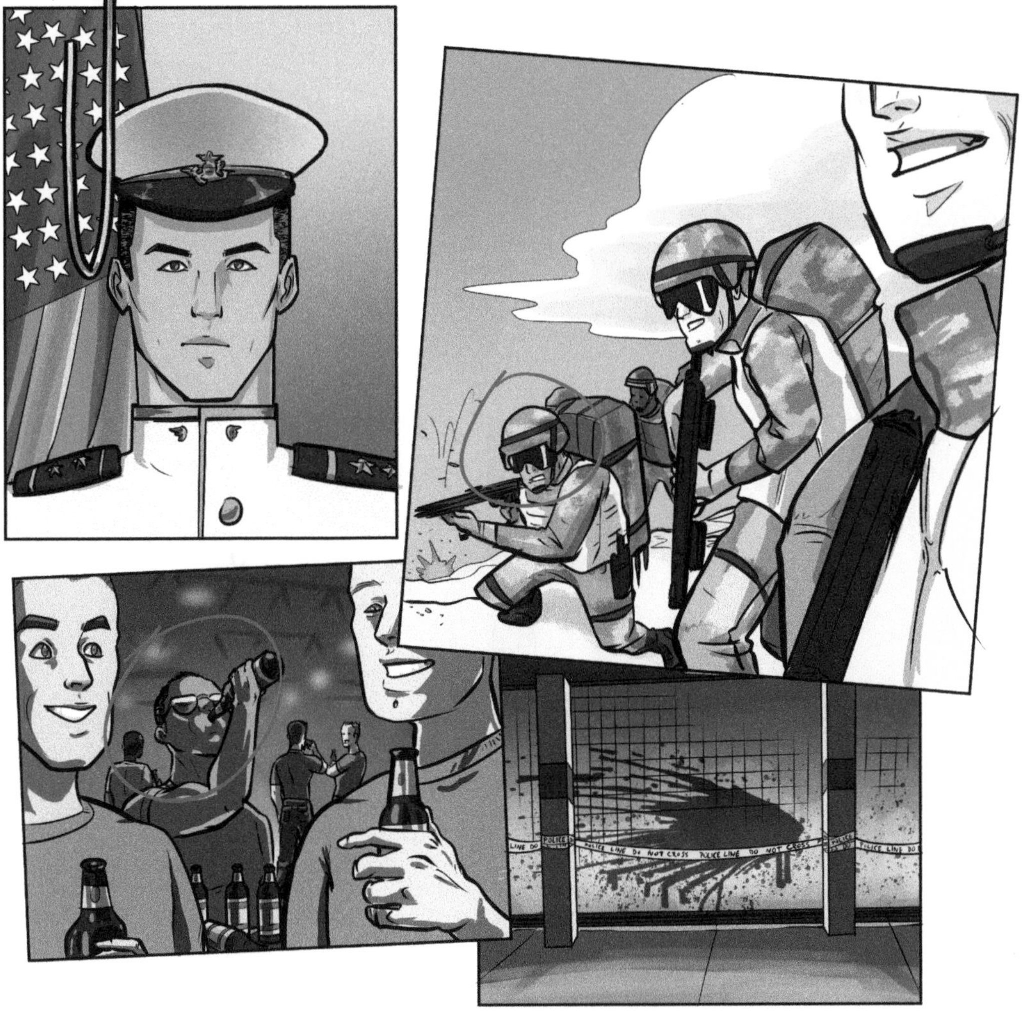
POLICE LINE DO NOT CROSS

NAME: Spectre John Song

CAUSE OF DEATH: Massive trauma due to train collision

MANNER OF DEATH: Suicide

CONDITION ON ARRIVAL: Unidentifiable (He was Hamburger.)

SPECTRE EXTRACTION: Difficult

ENERGY READING: 145 MJ (Extremely high)

ABILITY: POSSESSION

ANALYSIS: Spectre Song demonstrates a keen ability for combat, especially close quarters combat, which, combined with his spectre abilities, makes him extremely effective in the field. Off the field, he is uncooperative and aggressive. Several staff members have filed reports regarding Song's behavior (see attached). Recommend limited interaction with staff outside mission launch and debrief procedures and approval for boxing equipment in his containment.

LET HIM BLOW OFF STEAM!!

SUBJECT 0416 : 07.25.20 15:32

SUBJECT 0416 : 07.25.20 15:38

NAME: Spectre Kaycee Flame

CAUSE OF DEATH: Brain Aneurysm

MANNER OF DEATH: Natural Causes

CONDITION ON ARRIVAL: Good

SPECTRE EXTRACTION: Easy *(but confusing...)*

ENERGY READING: 70 MJ (Low to Medium)

ABILITY: TELEPATHY, TRACKING

ANALYSIS: Spectre contributor body was male but spectre appears to have manifested as female. Team still researching the anomaly. Spectre Flame demonstrates abilities for tracking key items in the field and team coordination. Agreeable disposition. Questionable taste in music. Recommend continued activity as normal upon approval for budget extension for make up and hair products.

High end brands this time!

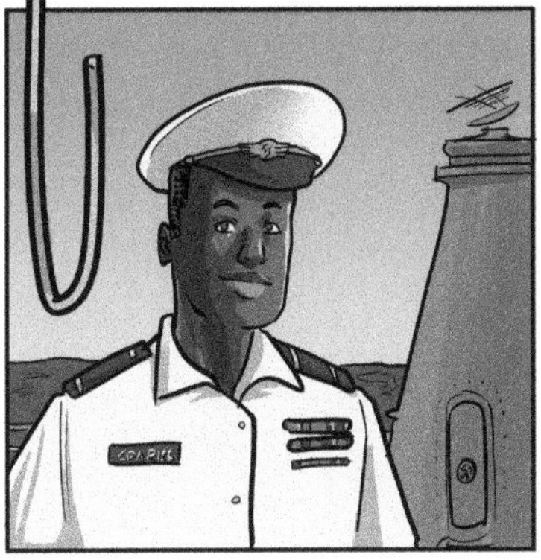

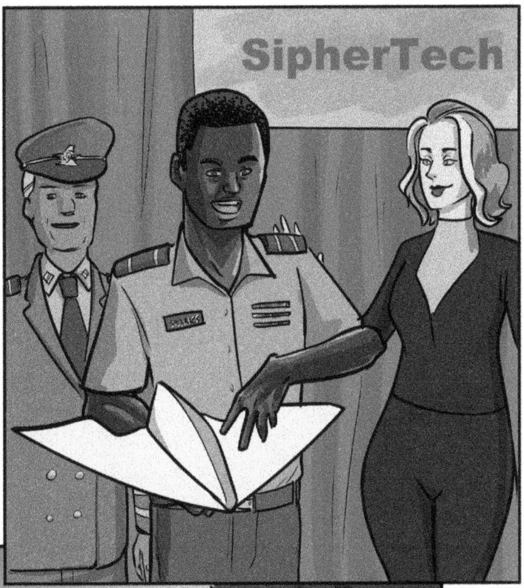
SipherTech

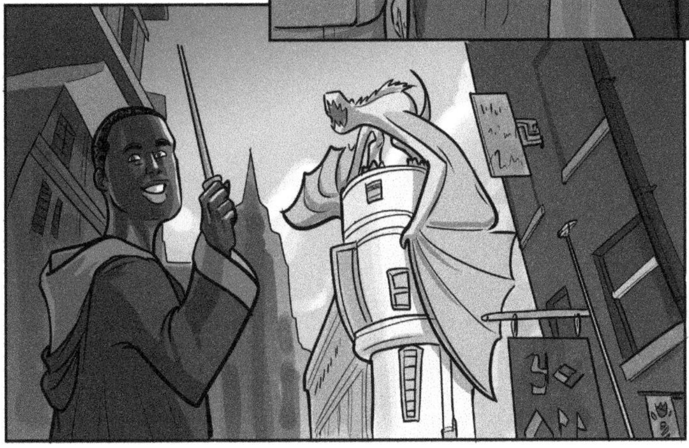

<u>NAME:</u> Spectre James Sparks

<u>CAUSE OF DEATH:</u> Massive trauma due to car collision

<u>MANNER OF DEATH:</u> Accident (Or so the coroner says...)

<u>CONDITION ON ARRIVAL:</u> Crushed skull, several lacerations to face and chest.

<u>SPECTRE EXTRACTION:</u> Moderate

<u>ENERGY READING:</u> 100 MJ (High)

<u>ABILITY:</u> ELECTRICAL DISCHARGE

<u>ANALYSIS:</u> Spectre Sparks demonstrates a brilliance for strategy and technical design. He has also made several positive contributions to the tech development of the Spectre program itself. Some of the staff have reported his behavior as cold or unusual, but suspect this might be a part of the reanimation process. Recommend continued activities as normal but deny request for soldering iron to use in containment. (Containment environments are too flammable)

We can't tell if being a spectre made him creepy or if he was always that way

CREATORS

Jennifer Brody **CREATOR | WRITER**
Jennifer is the award-winning author of *The 13th Continuum* and the *Disney Chills* series, writing as Vera Strange. She's a graduate of Harvard University and a film and television producer and writer. She began her career in Hollywood on many films, including *The Lord of the Rings* and *The Golden Compass*. She lives and writes in downtown LA, where she's hard at work on her next book.

Twitter: @JenniferBrody
Instagram: @JenniferBrodyWriter
Facebook: JenniferBrodyWriter

Jules Rivera **CO-CREATOR | ARTIST**
Jules is an illustrator, colorist, animator, and writer, prompting SyFy Wire to call her "a multi-talented force in indie comics." She contributed to the Eisner Award winning *Puerto Rico Strong* (Lion Forge) and Ringo Award winning *Where We Live, A Benefit for the Survivors in Las Vegas* (Image Comics). Jules is the creator of a weekly autobiographical cartoon strip, *Love, Joolz*, and feminist sci-fi epic, *Valkyrie Squadron*. She also creates sci-fi designs for TV and film and teaches storyboarding at California Lutheran University. She lives and works in LA and goes surfing on the weekends.

Twitter: @julesrivera
Instagram: @julesriveraart
Facebook: Jules.Rivera.Art

ACKNOWLEDGEMENTS

Many thanks to everyone who supported our journey to the other side and back with our ragtag band of *spectres*. First up, many thanks to Turner Publishing and their fantastic team, who not only took a big chance on my Continuum Trilogy, but also on my new foray into graphic novels (not only one—but two ... *200* is coming next). Especially Stephanie Beard, Todd Bottorff, and Heather Howell. Thanks also to my book agent Deborah Schneider, who never blinks when I take a hard left turn and decide to try something new. So lucky to have you in my corner always.

This book is a happy accident born from collaboration. Special thanks to AnaCon and Emily Otis, where Jules and I first connected on a nerdy panel and realized that we had to find a way to combine forces and create something epically rad. We also want to thank our friends and families, who put up with our creative insanity, and Commander Ryker, my adorable monster of a dog and our team mascot, who hung out in my loft while we broke this story wide open. We couldn't be more excited to share this book with you, dear readers. See you on the other side! (to quote Bart)

And don't worry, there are two more installments in the works ... stay tuned!

-Jennifer Brody

I want to thank all my loved ones who helped me stay sane, sheltered and fed in the process of making this book. I especially want to say thank you to everyone who took a chance on me, to create this story. Coming into this project, I had a few scant credits, but otherwise I was an unknown quantity. And then Jen showed up to that crazy panel of ours at AnaCon and saw something valuable in what I was doing. All I had to my name that day were my words and some indie books no one had ever heard of. That was all. I was nothing.

But Jen believed in me. Jen vouched for me and opened up a lot of doors I wouldn't have had opened for me otherwise. I want to thank everyone at Turner, including our editor Stephanie Beard, for also taking that leap of faith. I want to thank our book agent, Deborah Schneider, for also embracing my work and believing in me the way Jen did.

I want to thank everyone who took that chance. Not everyone in this industry gets that chance, but I did and I will always be grateful.

I was nothing and now I am a graphic novelist.

Thank you, Jen.

-Jules Rivera

SPECTRE DEEP 6

VOLUME 2
Resurrection

Coming 2021